MODERN FINANCIAL
MACROECONOMICS

To my loving and supportive family:
Deb, Edie, and Daphne

MODERN
FINANCIAL
MACROECONOMICS
Panics, Crashes, and Crises

Todd A. Knoop

Blackwell Publishing

First published 2008 by Blackwell Publishing Ltd

1   2008

Library of Congress Cataloging-in-Publication Data

Knoop, Todd A.
Modern financial macroeconomics : panics, crashes, and crises / Todd A. Knoop.
p. cm.
Includes bibliographical references and index.
ISBN 978-1-4051-6180-0 (hbk. : alk. paper)—ISBN 978-1-4051-6181-7 (pbk. : alk. paper)
1. Macroeconomics. 2. Finance. 3. Financial crises. I. Title.

HB172.5.K63 2008
332.01—dc22
2007048188

A catalogue record for this title is available from the British Library.

Set in 10/12pt Times
by Newgen Imaging Systems Pvt. Ltd., Chennai
Printed and bound in Singapore
by Fabulous Printers Pte Ltd

The publisher's policy is to use permanent paper from mills that operate a sustainable forestry policy, and which has been manufactured from pulp processed using acid-free and elementary chlorine-free practices. Furthermore, the publisher ensures that the text paper and cover board used have met acceptable environmental accreditation standards.

For further information on
Blackwell Publishing, visit our website at
www.blackwellpublishing.com

Contents

List of Figures

List of Tables

List of Case Studies

Preface

This book examines the role that financial markets and financial institutions play in modern macroeconomics, particularly focusing on the causes of recessions and depressions, both in the U.S. and internationally. It discusses both the empirical and theoretical links between financial systems and economic performance as well as case studies of the role of finance in specific business cycle episodes. In addition to targeting a general readership interested in finance and macroeconomics, this text will appeal to three groups. First, scholars who are interested in a nontechnical review of the recent and important advances in our understanding of the macroeconomic impact of financial systems will find this book attractive. Second, this book is appropriate for use in upper-level undergraduate courses (300–400 level) with a macroeconomic focus such as Financial Macroeconomics or Monetary Economics. Finally, this book will also be useful as an ancillary text in courses on Money and Banking, International Financial Economics, Financial Institutions, Commercial Banking, Business Cycles, and Intermediate Macroeconomics.

There is no existing book that examines the theory, the empirics, and specific case studies of the role of finance in modern macroeconomic thought. The need for this book became obvious to me as I was finishing work on a previous book entitled *Recessions and Depressions: Understanding Business Cycles*. Writing this book convinced me of two things. First, understanding the workings of financial systems is indispensable if you want true insight into modern macroeconomics. Second, no book exists that highlights the crucial role that financial systems play in macroeconomic performance and which fully encompasses much of the new research that has taken place over the last decade on the macroeconomic effects of financial systems. This book presents the interplay between current research in the fields of financial macroeconomics and business cycles in a way that is both interesting and accessible.

The books most directly comparable to this one would be the numerous Money and Banking textbooks that are available. This book differs from these textbooks in two significant ways. First, this book will focus on macroeconomic analysis. While there will be some discussion of institutional issues, the primary aim of this text is to provide the reader with a deeper understanding of the role of finance in macroeconomic performance, particularly the role that financial systems play in economic instability. Unlike existing Money and Banking texts, the goal is not to broadly (but superficially) cover all aspects of finance. Second, while this book is appropriate for use in upper-level courses in economics, it is not written in a style that will limit its use to only that of a textbook. This book is written in nontechnical language and in a style that will avoid technicalities, graphs, and excessive amounts of data whenever possible. In other words, my hope is that its readership will not be limited to that of undergraduate economics students but can be expanded to a more general audience.

I received a great deal of help in putting this book together, for which I am truly appreciative. I want to thank Cornell College for their support, particularly for a grant from the Campbell R. McConnell Fellowship fund that helped to support a sabbatical during which much of the work on this book took place. I also want to thank Micah Pollack for his excellent research assistance during crucial phases of putting this book together. Finally, and most importantly, I want to thank my two darling daughters, Eden and Daphne, and my wife and best friend, Debra DeLaet, for their consistent love and support. I hope my small contributions are something they can be proud of.

Introduction

Objectives and Summary of This Book

During the late 1990s and early 2000s, two topics dominated discussions of economics. The first was the "New Economy," which was a phrase used to describe the belief that productivity and output growth had reached permanently high plateau because of advances in communications and information technology. The second was economic globalization, or the increasing interconnectedness of economies across the globe. Somewhat lost in all of this talk about the New Economy and globalization was the most significant change in modern economics: an unprecedented increase in the size and integration of financial markets and financial institutions across the world. The volume of capital flows both within countries and between countries has grown much faster than trade in goods and services, and it has been this incredible expansion in the trade of financial assets that has largely driven economic globalization.

As a result, when people talk about the New Economy or globalization, what they are often really talking about is the process of "financialization," or the increasing size and integration of capital markets (bonds, equity, foreign exchange, and financial derivatives) and financial intermediaries (banks, investment funds, insurance, and pension companies) within and between countries. Financial development has dramatically expanded the amount of capital available to firms and consumers; at the same time it has significantly reduced the costs of borrowing. It has also greatly increased economic efficiency and growth in those countries that have chosen to pull down barriers and open their markets to capital flows. Asian countries are excellent examples of the benefits of these strategies. Financial integration and development in East Asia and China has dramatically increased standards of living throughout the region by allowing firms to invest more, by allowing savers to receive higher returns on their assets, and by allowing consumers greater access to credit that enables them to better smooth their consumption.

However, financialization has also meant that the well-being of investors, firms, markets, and economies as a whole are increasingly interlinked, for better or for worse. There is a common perception among the public, including many world leaders and politicians, that there has recently been an increase in economic volatility and in the number of economic crises across the globe, and that this increase in economic uncertainty has been the direct result of financial development. It is true that certain types of economic crises have become more frequent over the last two decades and that financial systems have played a prominent role in many of these economic fluctuations. The best example of this was the East Asian crisis between 1997 and 1999, in which currency crises, asset market crashes, and banking collapses precipitated depressions in South Korea, Thailand, Indonesia, and Malaysia. The importance of financial systems in generating economic volatility has also been evident in a number of smaller emerging economies outside of Asia such as Russia, Brazil, and Argentina that have suffered from economic crises. Finally, the dangers of financial volatility have even been evident in developed countries such as Japan, which suffered a 12-year recession and an ongoing banking crisis, and in the U.S., where the recession of 2001 followed an unprecedented boom/bust cycle in the stock market and a steep decline in investment. Like the picture on the front cover of this book, time and time again we see that problems in one link of the economic train, that link being the financial system, has had the unfortunate consequence of derailing the whole thing.

Given this, it is surprisingly difficult to tell just how important finance is to modern macroeconomic performance by reading most current textbooks on macroeconomics. Curiously, the attention that financial systems have received in macroeconomic research has gone through its own boom and bust cycles. The earliest theories of macroeconomic fluctuations focused closely on the role of money and finance. Keynes' *General Theory*, which was the first true macroeconomic model, placed a great deal of emphasis on the role of financial markets and banks in propagating business cycles. Surprisingly, however, in the 30 years following World War II, the role played by financial systems in mainstream macroeconomic theory diminished. Its importance was first downplayed by subsequent "Keynesian" economists and then by a series of Neoclassical theories such as Monetarism, the Rational Expectations model, and Real Business Cycle models.

One of the biggest omissions in the study of macroeconomics today is that these same models that discount the importance of finance are also the ones that are taught to most new students of macroeconomics. The result has been generations of macroeconomics students whose thoughts on finance go no deeper than savings equals investment. This lack of basic financial understanding about how financial systems work and what impact they have on macroeconomic performance has been a huge obstacle that has not only hindered economists' ability to develop better theories that can explain business cycles but also has limited our ability to develop policies to combat macroeconomic instability.

However, this bias toward minimizing the role of finance in macroeconomics has gradually begun to disappear in much of the new macroeconomic research that has been conducted over the last 20 years. Increasingly, economists have turned to microeconomic models of market failure to explain business cycles and other macroeconomic phenomena, particularly focusing on market failures that take place in the financial sector. These "New Institutional theories of finance" are reshaping macroeconomics in general, finance and business cycle theory in particular.

Given both this distant and more recent history, there is a need for a book that takes a comprehensive, but nontechnical, look at the interplay between financial systems and macroeconomic performance, particularly the role that financial systems play in generating macroeconomic volatility. There are three reasons for placing the focus here on macroeconomic fluctuations. First, the cause of recessions and depressions has always been one of the most controversial issues in macroeconomics. The debate on the causes of business cycles has fueled much of the development of modern macroeconomic theory. Second, the macroeconomic benefits of financial development have been much less controversial than its potential costs: namely, increased instability. Examining this question about the role that financial systems play in economic contractions is important if we are to have an informed debate about the costs and benefits of financial development in the future. Third, the most important insights of New Institutional theories of finance relate to the role that financial systems play in magnifying economic volatility. These new advances in financial theory deserve more attention than they have received in other macroeconomics books currently in the market. By largely ignoring them, many of the standard classroom texts leave the mistaken impression that not only do financial systems play little role in business cycles, but that they also play a minor role in macroeconomics in general.

The objective of this book is not to end the debate about the causes of business cycles and the role of financial systems in creating them but to provide a broad and well-organized presentation that frames this debate in clear, readable language. This book reviews both historical and modern macroeconomic theories and the role that finance plays in macroeconomics. This book looks at the empirical links between financial systems and economic performance, as well as examines international case studies of specific financial developments and economic crises. This book also takes a close look at the role that governments do and should play in moderating (or exacerbating, as the case may be) financial volatility and economic fluctuations. Finally, this book identifies questions that must be addressed in future economic research if we are to better manage financial development and allow its full benefits to be enjoyed by all.

Outline of This Book

This book is divided into four parts.

Part I: An introduction to finance and macroeconomics

The primary purpose of this section is to provide a succinct introduction to some basic concepts in financial economics in preparation for a discussion of macroeconomic theory in the next section. Chapter 1 (The Basics of Financial Markets and Financial Institutions) covers fundamental information that would typically be included in a Money and Banking course. Included is a discussion of the reasons why financial intermediation is different from other economic transactions; an examination of the implications of imperfect and symmetric information; a look at the theoretical and empirical support for the claim that financial systems are crucial to growth and development; and a discussion of the advantages and disadvantages of each of the primary financial assets: bonds, stocks, bank loans, and foreign exchange. Case studies are included in this chapter, which examine microfinance, the financial systems of China and India, and the similarities and differences in financial systems across countries.

Chapter 2 (A Brief History of Financial Development) provides a short historical review of financial systems, with its primary emphasis on the development of the U.S. financial system, particularly its banking industry. Included is a review of the debate over and suspicion of banking in U.S. history; a discussion of the Great Depression and its implications for the government regulation of financial systems; and an overview of the significant deregulation and consolidation that has taken place within the financial industry since the 1980s. The development of central banking has been an important component of financial development. The history of central banking, the responsibilities central banks' assume in modern economies, and central banks' role in determining the money supply are briefly discussed here. This chapter also includes a description of the incredible increase in the globalization of financial systems that has occurred since the 1990s. This explosion of international capital flows is put into some historical perspective and the factors behind the most recent expansion of capital flows are discussed in detail. This chapter concludes with two case studies—one on the housing and mortgage markets and one on hedge funds—that illustrate the complexity and ingenuity of the financial development that is taking place today. These case studies also demonstrate the potential power of financial development not only to improve standards of living but also to increase economic insecurity and create business cycles.

Part II: Macroeconomic theory and the role of finance

In this section, macroeconomic theories of finance are reviewed. Chapter 3 (Business Cycles and Early Macroeconomic Theories of Finance) begins this discussion by presenting few of the basic concepts regarding business cycles. A case study is presented that examines three basic facts about business cycles both in the U.S. and internationally; these are facts that economic theories need to explain. In addition, information about the cyclical behavior of key financial variables over the business cycle is presented. This chapter then moves to a review of few early macroeconomic theories of business cycles. This includes the Sunspot theory, early monetary theories, the Classical model, and the Debt-Deflation theory. These early theories are simple and limited in scope, but they identify potentially important factors that play a role in business cycles, such as the importance of expectations, the money supply, the supply and demand for credit, taxes and regulation, debt levels, and financial risk. These early theories lay the foundation for modern theories of macroeconomics.

Chapter 4 (Keynesian, Monetarist, and Neoclassical Theories) discusses the role of finance in modern macroeconomic theories developed before the 1980s. It includes an examination of Keynes' General Theory, the Keynesian model, the Financial Instability Hypothesis, the Monetarist model, and Neoclassical models such as the Rational Expectations model and Real Business Cycle models. Financial systems play a primary role in Keynes' General Theory. Many of the financial aspects of Keynes' General Theory are modified and amplified in Minsky's Financial Instability Hypothesis, which places financial instability at the heart of economic volatility. However, financial systems were subsequently marginalized in the more mainstream heir to Keynes—the Keynesian IS–LM model—because of its emphasis on equilibrium analysis and on the importance of consumption volatility as opposed to investment volatility in sparking business cycles. This trend toward minimizing financial systems in macroeconomics was continued in the Monetarist model and the Rational Expectations model, where changes in the money supply drive temporary changes in economic activity, with financial systems only reacting passively to these changes. The pinnacle of this trend is Real Business Cycle models, where all markets are perfectly competitive and financial systems always efficiently distribute resources to those projects with the highest returns, meaning financial issues can be effectively ignored as a source of economic disturbances. One driving factor behind this lack of attention paid to financial systems in macroeconomic theory prior to the 1980s was a lack of understanding regarding the microeconomic foundations of finance and how market failure in financial systems can create macroeconomic instability.

Chapters 5 and 6 cover what is known as New Institutional theories of finance. While a wide variety of different models fall under this moniker, these models have four things in common. First, each of these models focuses on explaining the microeconomic fundamentals behind the operations of financial markets and institutions, particularly the implications of heterogeneity and imperfect competition. Like earlier theories, such as the Debt-Deflation theory and the Financial Instability Hypothesis, the financial fundamentals of firms play a key role in explaining how microeconomic behavior can have macroeconomic impacts. Second, each recognizes that the money supply is an imperfect measure of the level of credit and financial intermediation within an economy. Third, each model incorporates the effects of asymmetric information, or the fact that borrowers know more about their credit worthiness than lenders. Asymmetric information plays an integral role in explaining why financial markets fail to operate efficiently because it increases default risk through two important avenues: moral hazard and adverse selection. Fourth, each of these models explains how market failure can lead banks and financial markets to restrict credit, creating persistent disequilibrium in financial markets that amplifies macroeconomic instability.

Chapter 5 (New Institutional Theories of Finance: Models of Risk and the Costs of Credit Intermediation) focuses on risk and the role of risk in determining the costs of financial intermediation. The primary model examined here is Bernanke and Gertler's (1989) Financial Accelerator model. In this model, lenders do not have perfect information about the credit worthiness of entrepreneurs and as a result charge borrowers a lending premium, referred to as the cost of credit intermediation, based on the borrowers' perceived default risk. The costs of credit intermediation rise as the net worth and other measures of the financial soundness of both borrowers and lenders deteriorate. Under these conditions, small external shocks to borrowers' and lenders' balance sheets, such as those that occur during the early stages of a recession, are magnified into large changes in lending and economic activity, especially if the overall financial position of firms and lenders in the economy is weak. This in turn magnifies the size of business cycles. In order to evaluate this Financial Accelerator model, this chapter examines the empirical evidence in support of this model and the hypothesis that changes in financial fundamentals and the cost of credit intermediation magnify the size of business cycles. This chapter ends with a case study that reviews Ben Bernanke's (1995) cross-country analysis of banking systems during the Great Depression and its empirical support for New Institutional theories of finance.

Chapter 6 (New Institutional Theories of Finance: Models of Credit Rationing) focuses on models of credit (or quantity) rationing based on Stiglitz and Weiss' (1981) Nobel Prize-winning research. In models of credit rationing, lenders are reluctant to adjust interest rates to the supply and demand for credit because of the impact of changes in interest rates on the overall credit risk of their loan portfolios. By setting interest rates at a level above that which will clear the market, lenders can be more choosy about whom they lend to, allowing them to reduce the levels of default risk associated with their borrowers. Of course, this comes at the expense of restricting the quantity of credit, and these restrictions in the level of credit become particularly acute during economic downturns when the financial position of borrowers and lenders deteriorate. As a result, credit rationing can create credit cycles that magnify business cycles. The considerable empirical support that exists for credit rationing is evaluated in this chapter. This chapter also includes a case study of "credit crunch" episodes in the U.S. and the role that financial regulation, such as capital adequacy requirements, plays in restricting lending during recessions. Credit rationing models also have important implications for our understanding of the role of finance in economic development, particularly among poorer and emerging economies, which is discussed in a case study at the end of this chapter.

Part III: Financial volatility and economic [in]stability

This section examines additional avenues by which financial systems serve to magnify or diminish macroeconomic volatility. Chapter 7 (The Role of Financial Systems in Monetary and Stabilization Policy) examines the effectiveness of macroeconomic stabilization policy in eliminating or dampening business cycles. This chapter begins by sketching the traditional arguments regarding the monetary transmission mechanism, or the channels through which monetary policy influences output. Next, the theoretical arguments for rethinking the monetary transmission mechanism are analyzed based on insights from New Institutional theories of finance. For example, if the costs of credit intermediation remain high or borrowers are up against credit limits, changes in monetary policy that only influence interest rates may have no impact on the overall level of credit and little impact on the economy. As a result, the monetary transition mechanism needs to be reevaluated and the goals of monetary policy have to be rethought in the presence of financial market failure.

This chapter also includes a look at the empirical evidence on the effectiveness of monetary policy in the face of rapid financial development. A case study of the 2001 recession in the U.S., which illustrates both the limits and the power of modern monetary policy, is investigated. New theories of the monetary transmission mechanism have also led economists to rethink the ways that monetary policy should be used in the future. Traditional debates over the effectiveness of stabilization policy and new debates over this issue are also examined here. Finally, a case study is presented which analyzes the role that financial development and monetary policy have played in the reduced frequency of recessions in the U.S. during the postwar period, particularly over the last 20 years.

Chapter 8 (Banking Crises and Asset Bubbles) examines on the role of domestic financial crises in the form of banking crises and asset bubbles in generating macroeconomic instability. This chapter begins with a discussion of the causes and consequences of banking crises, particularly whether such crises are driven by expectations (belief-based) or real shocks (fundamentals-based). The role that government policies such as bank bailouts, lending regulations, and deposit insurance play in preventing (or exacerbating) banking crises is investigated. Extensive empirical work has been conducted investigating the causes and costs of banking crises, and this is reviewed along with a case study of the Savings and Loan crisis in the U.S. in the early 1990s. Asset bubbles in stock and real estate markets are often associated with banking crises. A discussion of the causes and costs of asset bubbles, as well as their relationship to banking crises, is also included here. Finally, five case studies on asset bubbles are examined: one on monetary policy and its role in responding to asset bubbles, one on the international real estate boom, one on the subprime mortgage crisis of 2007, one on the Northern Rock bank run, and one on the banking crisis and long recession in Japan in the 1990s.

Part IV: International finance and financial crises

Finance has become increasingly internationalized, to the benefit of many developed and particularly less developed countries. Economic crises have also increasingly taken an international character and financial systems have played a prominent role in many recent crises. The primary aim of this section is to explain why the rising influence of finance, which has led to a remarkable increase in the rates of economic development across the globe, has often been associated with increased economic instability.

Chapter 9 (Capital Flight and the Causes of International Financial Crises) begins with a brief examination of currency crises, in which overvalued exchange rates lead to capital flight and large devaluations. Two questions associated with currency crises are investigated. First, are currency crises driven by changes in expectations (belief-based) or by real shocks (fundamentals-based)? Second, are currency crises contagious, meaning that a crisis in one country increases the probability of a crisis in another country? These two questions are analyzed from both a theoretical and an empirical perspective, including a case study of the Russian/Long Term Capital Management Contagion episode in 1999. The discussion then moves to an examination of the twin crisis phenomena, in which currency crises and banking crises occur simultaneously. During a twin crisis, the large devaluations that result from a currency crisis lead to a complete collapse of fragile banking systems, resulting in a large reduction in financial intermediation and economic activity. This process is described in detail. Many international crises fit the basic pattern of a twin crisis, including the Great Depression. The best recent example of a twin crisis is the East Asian crisis, which is examined in a comprehensive case study in this chapter. Particular attention is given to the reasons why East Asian financial systems were so weak at the same time that their economies were relatively strong. It is clear that deregulation in these countries led to a pattern of inattention to the problem of moral hazard and credit risk, each of which played a crucial role in weakening financial fundamentals and increasing the susceptibility of these economies to a financial collapse. Thus, the East Asian crisis is consistent with New Institutional theories of economic contractions.

One of the most important reasons that many East Asian and many other emerging economies have been able to grow so fast during the postwar era has been the increased globalization of finance, which has dramatically expanded the flow of capital across countries. Unfortunately, this remarkable growth in international lending has also increased the fragility of financial systems in many developing and emerging economies. In Chapter 10 (International Financial Crises: Policies and Prevention), the role that international capital flows have played in economic growth and in economic crises is examined. Included is a look at both the benefits and the costs of the international trend toward financial deregulation. On the basis of recent cross-country experiences with financial liberalization, this chapter specifies five broad guidelines that, if followed, would allow governments to enjoy more of the benefits and less of the instability associated with foreign capital flows. Of course, any form of government regulation serves to restrict the flow of capital across boarders, and the benefits and costs of some specific capital control regulations are also examined here. This includes a look at international regulations such as the Basel agreement, which have been adopted in an attempt to increase the stability of international financial systems.

The International Monetary Fund (IMF), as the referee of the international financial system, has come under intense criticism in many circles for their role in many of the international financial crises that have taken place in recent years, particularly the East Asian crisis. A brief discussion of the IMF's role in mitigating crises (or magnifying crises by pushing for reckless financial liberalization) is presented in Chapter 10, including a discussion of the many critiques of the IMF—complaints that range from the IMF being either too soft or too hard in dealing with countries suffering through a crisis. A case study of the IMF's involvement in the East Asian crisis and in Argentina concludes, which illustrates many of the important themes of this chapter.

Part V: Conclusions

Chapter 11 (What We Have Learned, What We Still Need to Learn about Financial Macroeconomics) concludes the book with a brief review of our current understanding of the interaction between finance and macroeconomics and the crucial role that financial systems play in both initiating and propagating recessions and depressions. This book's primary conclusion is that understanding economic growth and economic instability is impossible without considerable knowledge of financial systems, particularly their failures and inefficiencies. One of the most important advances in macroeconomics over the last two decades has been a deepening of our understanding of how market failure in financial markets affects the availability of financial intermediation and credit, which in turn affects investment, consumption, and output. This chapter highlights the most important things that economists have learned in their continued research in financial macroeconomics.

The intermediate goal of future research should be to continue this progress on the theoretical front so that we can develop a unified model of macroeconomics that incorporates important aspects of modern financial systems. The long-term goal is to figure out how we can use this model to develop policies that allow countries to improve the efficiency of their financial systems and at the same time reduce the volatility of financial intermediation and economic performance. This book concludes with a discussion of the major questions that still need to be addressed before countries can reach these goals and enjoy the full benefits of globalization and financial development.

PART I
AN INTRODUCTION TO FINANCE AND MACROECONOMICS

CHAPTER 1

The Basics of Financial Markets and Financial Institutions

Introduction

A financial system is somewhat like a car's carburetor: we know that it is important if things are to operate properly, but we are less sure about how it works and why it is so important. If pressed to explain why financial systems are vital to an economy, many of us could piece together a response including the words "investment" and "savings," but this answer is sure to be somewhat vague and most likely unconvincing.

The purpose of this chapter is to fill in some fundamental gaps in our financial knowledge. Here, we discuss some of the basic concepts of financial economics. Our discussion is not intended to be comprehensive; for that, there are a number of excellent Money and Banking textbooks available that discuss the operations of financial systems in exhaustive detail. Instead, we focus on the most basic concepts in modern finance, beginning with an exploration of the reasons why financial institutions and financial markets are different from other economic organizations and markets. Also examined are the theoretical reasons why financial intermediation is important to economic development and the empirical evidence on whether financial development does in fact stimulate economic growth. In addition, this chapter presents some of the basic facts regarding the four principal forms of financial intermediation: bond markets, stock markets, financial intermediaries (banks), and foreign exchange markets. The advantages and disadvantages of each of these financial arrangements are discussed. This chapter also includes three brief case studies of international financial systems that examine microfinance, the financial systems in China and India, and the differences in financial intermediation across countries.

What is Financial Intermediation and Why is It Different from Other Economic Transactions?

Any discussion of finance has to begin with a discussion of money. In everyday usage, the word "money" is used interchangeably with words such as "wealth," "income," "currency," and so on. Economists, on the other hand, have a very specific meaning in mind when they use the term money. *Money* refers to any asset that is generally accepted in payment for goods, services, or in the repayment of debts. As a result, money could be almost any object of value, from *commodity money*, or money with intrinsic value such as gold, silver, or cigarettes, to *fiat money*, or paper money that has value only because people accept it in exchange.

Money is important to the efficient workings of economic systems because it simultaneously serves three crucial functions. First, it is a *medium of exchange*, or a way to make trade easier. In an economy without money, all goods would have to be bartered for, making trade tedious and time consuming because it would always have to involve a double coincidence of wants. Money, on the other hand, allows individuals to break transactions into separate parts. Someone who would like to trade their goat for a sweater does not have to find someone who wants their goat and who also has a sweater. Instead, such a person can sell the goat for money, then take the money to the mall and buy a sweater.

Money is also a *store of value*, or an asset that can be easily turned into goods and services. Money provides individuals an easy and safe way to save, or postpone purchases of goods or services until a later date. This is an important service because economic theory tells us that households prefer to spread their consumption evenly over time and not see it fluctuate with income. Saving through holding money is an easy way for households to achieve this goal.

Finally, money is a *unit of account*, or a way to measure the relative value of things. Money is essentially the language of economics—it is a tool that can be used to succinctly communicate a large amount of information. If someone tells you that their car is worth four goats, that probably will not mean much to you. If someone tells you their car is worth $1,000, it quickly and clearly communicates something important to you: that they have an old, beat-up car.

Because money is so important in conducting economic transactions, money is itself the object of many economic transactions. *Financial intermediation* refers to the trading of money across time, or the trading of money today for money tomorrow, and the conditions that are attached to such transactions. Usually, financial intermediation is accompanied by a *financial instrument*, or a legal contract that specifies the responsibilities of the person who is giving up money now for money later (the lender) and the person who is giving up money later for money now (the borrower).

Financial intermediation is very different from other economic transactions such as purchasing a goat or a computer. The biggest difference is that financial intermediation involves the element of time. An exchange is not made for something now, but for the promise of something in the future. This involves significant uncertainty and risk for lenders. There is uncertainty on the lender's part about their borrowers' ability or willingness to repay in the future. This risk comes from a lack of perfect knowledge of the future, or what economists call *imperfect information*. Lenders are also subject to the additional risk that the borrower has better information about their likelihood to pay in the future than the lender. Borrowers know better about exactly how committed they are to making future payments, about whether they intend to engage in activities that might reduce their likelihood of future payment, and whether their uses for the borrowed funds are likely to be profitable. Economists refer to the fact that borrowers know more about the true risk associated with any loan than a lender as *asymmetric information*.

Since Adam Smith (1776), it has been widely recognized that the existence of imperfect and asymmetric information means that financial markets are not perfectly competitive. Instead, information-based market failure can lead to inefficient outcomes, such as less lending or more volatile lending than is socially optimal. This means that Pareto improvements can be made through government intervention in financial systems aimed at alleviating these information problems and increasing the incentives for lenders to provide financial intermediation to borrowers. It is for this reason that financial systems are among the most widely regulated sectors of modern economies.

To combat these information problems, proper government regulation focuses on achieving three goals. The first is to improve the quality of financial information that is available to financial institutions and the purchasers of bonds and stocks. This is important in order to reduce fraud and also to ensure that the kind of information needed for making efficient financial decisions is available to the public. To improve the quality of financial information, governments impose financial reporting requirements on publicly held firms. In the U.S., the monitoring and enforcement of financial information requirements are primarily handled by the Securities and Exchange Commission.

The second goal of government regulation is to stabilize the financial system by limiting the risk exposure of banks and other financial institutions. This is in part accomplished by requiring financial institutions to publicly disclose relevant financial information. Also, governments provide deposit insurance aimed at both protecting depositors and at preventing banking panics and deposit withdrawals. Finally, banks are subject to extensive restrictions on who can operate a bank, the kinds of activities banks can and cannot engage in, and the amount of capital that banks must hold. In the U.S., the monitoring of banks is conducted by multiple agencies including the Federal Reserve, the Federal Deposit Insurance Corporation, the Comptroller of the Currency, and numerous state regulatory agencies.

The third role of government in financial systems is to serve as an arbiter of the legal arrangements associated with financial intermediation. In a world of imperfect and asymmetric information, some borrowers will not meet the conditions of their loans. Governments play a significant role in reducing lending risk when they act to protect the rights of creditors by enforcing the legal clauses associated with financial instruments. On the other hand, governments also play an important role in legally protecting borrowers that are in financial difficulties by allowing them to declare bankruptcy and restructure their payments.

What is Money?

In modern economies, there is no clear distinction between assets which are money and assets which are not money, primarily because in our working definition of money the phrase "generally accepted" is ambiguous. Clearly, currency is generally accepted in trade, but are checks written on money market accounts? Treasury bills and treasury bonds are often exchanged in many large financial transactions. Are they money? What about credit cards?

In the U.S., the Federal Reserve has created multiple definitions of money; the two primary definitions are cleverly referred to as M1 and M2. M1 refers to assets that are clearly money and includes currency, coins, and checkable deposit accounts. M2 includes everything in M1 plus bank assets that can easily be turned into M1, with minor restrictions. This includes assets with check-writing features, such as money market deposit accounts issued by banks and money market shares issued by mutual funds, and deposits at banks that can easily be withdrawn, such as small certificates of deposit and savings accounts. In economic parlance, we say that an asset is more *liquid* the more quickly and easily it can be converted into currency. Thus, the assets in M2 are less liquid than the assets in M1.

Notice that credit cards are not included in any of these definitions of money because credit cards are only a means of postponing payment, not actually making payment. Of course, credit cards have had a significant impact on many of the components of the money supply. For example, currency and checking deposit holdings are less important today than they have been in the past because of the growing use of credit cards to make purchases.

Table 1.1 presents U.S. data on M1 and M2. Note that the total money supply is fairly large relative to GDP—M1 is 11 percent of nominal U.S. GDP (which was more than $13 trillion in 2006), while M2 is 52 percent of U.S. GDP. The sheer size of these numbers, however, highlights some of the difficulties in measuring the money supply. For example, there is over $700 billion in currency held by the public, or roughly $2,400 a person, and two-thirds of this in $100 bills. Clearly, there are very few families of four that are holding $10,000 in currency. Where is it all? The U.S. Treasury estimates that at least two-thirds of total currency is held

Table 1.1 Measures of the Money Supply in the U.S.

	Value[a] ($ Billions)	Percentage of GDP[b]
M1 = Currency	742.5	
+ Traveler's check	6.9	
+ Demand deposits	328	
+ Other checkable deposits	316.6	
Total M1	1394	11
M2 = M1		
+ Savings deposits and money market deposit accounts	3619	
+ Small-denomination time deposits	1049.3	
+ Retail money funds	734.2	
Total M2	6796.5	52

[a] Value as of May 2006, seasonally adjusted.
[b] GDP data from first quarter 2006.

Source: Federal Reserve Statisitical Release H.6, June 16, 2005 at http://www.federalreserve.gov/releases/h6/, Federal Reserve FREDII database at http://research.stlouisfed.org/fred2/.

outside the country, primarily because holding dollars is a liquid and relatively safe means for foreigners to save and because dollars are the standard currency for a wide range of international transactions. Some of these dollars are held in support of *Eurodollar accounts*, which are dollar-denominated accounts that are held in banks and other financial institutions outside U.S. borders. Also, quite a large amount of this money circulates in the underground and illegal economies. These facts raise questions about how much measures such as M1 and M2 can really tell us about the actual amount of money circulating in the U.S. economy. These problems also explain in part why measures of the money supply may not always be closely correlated with the actual amount of financial intermediation that is taking place within an economy.

The Importance of Financial Systems in Stimulating Long-Run Growth

A system that promotes efficient financial intermediation is crucial to developing well-functioning economies. Economic agents often find themselves in positions in which they would like to purchase goods now instead of later but do not have the available resources to do so; for example, a firm that would like to invest in new capital to expand its production or a household that would like to purchase a house. Likewise, many agents find themselves in situations in which they would like to purchase goods later and not now (particularly if they are compensated for it); for example, a household that is trying to save for retirement or a firm that has high revenues but lacks new business opportunities in which to invest. In fact, most firms and households are both savers and borrowers at the same time. For example, many people have a home mortgage loan and a 401K account to save for retirement. The more quickly and cheaply financial systems can transfer money between borrowers and lenders and turn savings into consumption and investment, the higher and more stable consumption, investment, production, and aggregate output will be.

Modern macroeconomic theory has highlighted six primary avenues through which financial development stimulates long-run growth:

Financial development helps borrowers and lenders hedge, pool, and diversify risk
Risk is an integral part of financial transactions because of imperfect and asymmetric information. One of the fundamental functions of financial systems is to transfer risk from people who prefer more certainty to those who are willing to tolerate more risk if they are compensated for it. Financial systems do this through *hedging risk* (creating financial instruments in which one party transfers part of the risk associated with a financial transaction to another party), *pooling risk* (aggregating small amounts of savings so that everyone shares the risk of the assets purchased with this pool of savings), and *diversifying risk* (purchasing large portfolios of assets so that the risk associated with a single asset alone is spread over the entire pool of savings). The more efficiently risk can be transferred from those who want to avoid it to those who are willing to accept it, the more economic activity will take place.

Financial development reduces risk by increasing liquidity
More developed financial systems increase the volume of trade in financial instruments. More trades make it easier and cheaper to sell a wide variety of assets and turn them into money. This is particularly important for long-term assets, which are firms' preferred method of financing long-term investment projects. The problem is that long-term assets are not as attractive to savers because long-term assets tie up funds for extended periods of time. However, when savers see that they can more easily sell these long-term assets in secondary (resale) markets, they are more likely to purchase them. This encourages investment, production, and long-run growth.

Financial development increases the amount of aggregate savings in an economy
This in turn increases investment and aggregate production. Better financial systems not only reduce the risks associated with savings, but they also increase the returns to saving by creating the conditions under which these funds can be used more productively. Lower risk and higher returns increase the incentives to save, increasing the amount of loanable funds that are available to firms and other borrowers that would like to engage in productive investment. Walter Bagehot

(1873), one of the first and most insightful observers of modern financial systems, argued that the industrial revolution was not initiated by new technologies, as is often argued in high school history books. In fact, most of the technologies that we associate with the industrial revolution, such as the steam engine, actually existed before the industrial revolution took place. Instead, Bagehot argues that the industrial revolution was fueled by the development of financial systems, which attracted and pooled large levels of savings that could then be used to finance the enormous amounts of investment that were needed to fully take advantage of existing technologies (this same argument has been more recently echoed by other economic historians, such as John Hicks [1969]).

Financial development allows financial systems to more efficiently allocate resources

As we have discussed, information is one of the key inputs into the provision of financial services. Information is costly to obtain. However, as financial systems get larger, they are able to take advantages of economies of scale in the gathering of information. For example, banks are able to gather much better information about a wider range of customers because of the information technologies they have invested in, the information databases they have created, and the monitoring and screening processes that they have developed over time. Better information eliminates some of the market failure associated with imperfect and asymmetric information and leads to more and more stable financial intermediation, facilitating growth.

In addition, better information helps financial systems make better decisions about whom not to provide finance to, resulting in more efficient allocation of resources. Joseph Schumpeter (1911) argued that the most crucial way that banking systems facilitate growth is through accumulating information about entrepreneurs and identifying exactly which entrepreneurs are likely to use investment funds most productively, thus playing a crucial role in the development of new technologies that fuel long-run growth.

Financial development facilitates trade

Without financial intermediation, many economic transactions could not take place. Many firms would not be able to sustain production without the provision of trade credit that allows them to acquire inputs now but pay for them later. Also, many consumption purchases, particularly durable goods such as appliances and cars, could not take place without consumer financing. And of course, many investment projects could not take place without financial intermediation, particularly in the case of small firms that cannot rely on internal funds.

Financial systems also encourage firms and individuals to specialize by providing the financial arrangements that allow them to more easily rely on trade partners, freeing them to outsource services they would otherwise be forced to perform themselves. As Adam Smith first noted, specialization is the cornerstone of productivity growth. By facilitating trade and specialization, financial development stimulates productivity, aggregate demand, aggregate supply, and improves standards of living.

Financial development allows for better monitoring of managers of firms and corporations
Information is important not just in making financial decisions; it is also important to the operation of firms, particularly in publicly held corporations where it is difficult for shareholders to monitor and evaluate the actions of those who are running the corporation on a day-to-day basis. However, more developed financial systems more widely distribute the financial instruments issued by corporations, increasing the demand for information about these corporations. As a result, larger financial systems provide services such as instantaneous stock pricing, current financial information, financial information agencies, credit rating agencies, and so on. Each of these important sources of information helps stockholders monitor the behavior of managers.

In reality, the six avenues through which financial development increases growth are not mutually exclusive but instead interact in ways that may completely halt financial intermediation even if one avenue breaks down. Ross Levine (1997) presents what he calls an economic parable about the ways that financial systems facilitate production. Consider a man named Fred who has an idea for a new type of heavy machinery that improves upon existing mining equipment. To produce this machine, Fred will need specialized inputs such as equipment and human capital as well as specialized production processes. The financial system plays a role in every step of acquiring these inputs. One of the most basic services financial systems provide is to create the money that Fred will need to purchase inputs; imagine how difficult it would be to hire specialized workers or purchase capital if it had to be bartered for. Financial intermediation also plays a role in creating the labor and capital that Fred will need; for example, many specialized labor skills are not acquired through working but through time spent on education, which often has to be funded through borrowing. Likewise, most technical production processes are based on the assembly line concept, which necessitates a large number of specialized transactions that take place between producers and outsiders that provide certain inputs into production. Such specialization would be difficult without financial systems to help facilitate payments between the parties.

Where will Fred get the resources to purchase these inputs? Even if Fred has enough savings to purchase them himself, it is unlikely that he would want to do so because then his savings would become illiquid and undiversified, increasing his risk. However, if Fred can borrow the money to finance his operations, either through a bank or through issuing stocks or bonds, Fred can maintain the diversity and liquidity of his savings while reducing his individual risk. Of course, to borrow these funds, they must first be available. Financial systems help increase

the amounts of loanable funds that can be lent to entrepreneurs by providing
with higher returns and less risk than they would get by hoarding their m
nonfinancial assets, then pooling the savings of a large number of indi
together to make large loans. In addition, the financial system acquires these funds
more cheaply and quickly than Fred could himself because of the information
networks it has established and because of the existence of economies of scale in
the process of financial intermediation.

One hurdle still remains for Fred. Fred will not be able to obtain financing
unless institutional decision makers determine that Fred and his project represent
an acceptable level of default risk. Without some process of reliably determining
the default risk of borrowers and the projects they engage in, financial intermediation will not take place. Financial systems reduce the cost of acquiring
information by regularizing the transfer of information about Fred, such as his
credit record. In addition, financial systems have developed expertise in screening investment projects in order to determine whether they are economically
and technically viable. Finally, financial systems have developed processes to
monitor Fred and his business after lending takes place in order to make sure
that Fred continues to act responsibly and to ensure that Fred incurs costs if he
does not.

This story only focuses on the ways that financial systems facilitate the production of new products; it ignores the ways that financial systems facilitate the
demand for existing goods and services or the ways that they encourage the production of new technologies. However, this story does illustrate many of the numerous
avenues through which financial development spurs economic growth.

The Empirical Evidence on Financial Development and Growth

An extensive body of empirical research on the growth benefits of financial development has reached three clear conclusions. First, higher levels of financial
development stimulate long-run growth. Second, financial development enhances
growth because of scale effects (increasing the number of financial transactions
and the level of aggregate savings). Finally, financial development also enhances
growth by improving economic efficiency (improving the quality of financial decisions, improving the efficiency of resource allocation, and reducing the costs of
financial intermediation).

A few individual empirical studies are worth noting. The seminal study on this
issue was conducted by King and Levine (1993), who found a strong correlation
across 77 countries between various indicators of bank development and both
contemporary and future economic growth. In fact, King and Levine find that past
levels of bank development are a significant predictor of investment, productivity,

and growth 10–30 years into the future. Levine, Loayza, and Beck (2000) update King and Levine's study using new methodologies and data and obtain the same results. In addition, they find that three factors appear to play a significant role in determining which countries have more developed banking systems: better laws that favor creditor protection in the case of default, better contract enforcement mechanisms, and better financial information disclosure requirements. In other words, governments that focus on the three goals of financial regulation discussed previously are more likely to have large and efficient financial systems and, as a result, growing economies.

Aghion, Howitt, and Mayer-Foulkes (2005) look at the impact of financial development on *convergence*, or the tendency of a poor country to grow faster than the richest country such that their per-capita levels of income approach each other over time. They find that higher levels of financial development increase the likelihood of convergence among poor countries, while countries with a lack of financial development fail to converge.

Other studies have examined the role of stock markets in economic growth. Levine and Zervos (1998) find that increases in both the size and the liquidity of stock markets along with increases in the quantity of bank lending increase long-run growth in investment, productivity, and output. Demirgüç-Kunt and Maksimovic (1996) also find that stock market development increases growth, but only in countries with legal systems that promote contract enforcement and creditor protection.

Taking a more microeconomic perspective, Rajan and Zingales (1998) examine industry-level data across countries and find that those industries that rely more heavily on financial markets or banks grow faster in countries with more developed financial systems. These finance-dependent industries are most likely to be populated with newer and smaller firms, and, as a result, Rajan and Zingales' results suggest that financial underdevelopment is most likely to harm startup firms and favor older, established firms. Because startup firms are those that are most likely to be engaged in creating new products and new technologies, this bias likely reduces long-run productivity and output growth. Beck *et al.* (2004) also look at cross-industry data and find that higher levels of financial development increase growth in industries with a higher fraction of small firms, which are most likely to rely on finance and not retained earnings.

Another channel by which financial development can impact growth is by limiting the impact of macroeconomic volatility on growth. Many studies have found that higher levels of output variability reduce long-run average growth rates (Ramey and Ramey [1995]). As discussed before, financial development allows households and firms to better smooth their consumption and investment, limiting the impact of business cycles on growth. Using cross-country data, Aghion *et al.* (2005) find that output volatility had a smaller impact on growth in countries with more developed financial systems.

While financial development appears to stimulate economic growth, it is also true that economic growth stimulates financial development, if only because as standards of living rise people are able to save a larger fraction of their income. The studies discussed above controlled for this reverse causation, but did not take a systematic look at the effects of growth on levels of financial development. Demirgüç-Kunt and Levine (1996) correct for this omission and find that as countries get richer, the size of both their stock markets and banking systems increase relative to GDP. While there is a great deal of variability across countries, typically growth in bank credit and in nonbank financial transactions (insurance companies, pension funds, and investment banks) are greater than the growth in stock market transactions. They also find that larger financial systems tend to be less volatile, more liquid, less dominated by the assets of a small number of firms, and exist in countries with legal systems that better protect creditors and enforce contracts. Their indicators of financial development, such as the ratio of financial transactions relative to GDP, point to the U.S., Japan, and the U.K. as having the most highly developed financial systems. Surprisingly, many emerging economies, particularly those in East Asia (such as Korea), have more developed financial systems than many rich countries, particularly France and Germany.

CASE STUDY: Microfinance in Poor Countries

A bias has long existed among many policy makers with regard to the importance of financial systems among the poor nations of the world. Traditionally, it was thought that the poor did not need financial services because they could not save, had few viable investment opportunities, and were bad credit risks. Today, financial development is now becoming a focal point of reforms aimed at increasing economic development. In part, this is because of the strong empirical evidence that has come to light regarding the importance of finance to economic growth. This new focus on finance also reflects a gradual recognition that the assumption that the poor do not need financial services is extremely naive. The poor do save— but usually not in banks. For instance, hoarding money or buying assets, such as livestock, are the traditional ways that the poor save, either because bank accounts are not available or because the poor are mistrustful of them. The problem with savings through these traditional means is that they leave wealth vulnerable to loss (theft, drought) and that they do not encourage investment by placing resources in the financial system. In addition, the poor need other financial services in addition to bank accounts: mortgage loans, insurance policies, and payment services such as transferring remittances between family members who work in richer countries and their family members back at home. Without efficient financial systems, the poor are left to deal with money lenders or pawnbrokers to obtain these services, who often provide low quality for exorbitant fees.

Once we recognize that the poor need financial services and that these services increase not only the quality of life of the poor but also the economic growth, the question becomes how to develop financial systems that can provide these services. There are a number of reasons why poor countries have weak financial systems. Their financial systems are often highly regulated, limiting the profitability of institutions and the services they can provide to the poor in order to protect the political and economic interests of the elite. In many Muslim countries, *usury laws* exist that prohibit the charging of interest on loans, greatly inhibiting lending. Corruption also tends to be a big problem in many poor countries. One survey reported that in some Indian states, 8–42 percent of any loan is skimmed-off in theft. In addition, many poor countries do not have the basic infrastructure—reliable power, efficient payment systems, communication technologies—that are necessary for modern financial intermediation to take place. Finally, while the poor do not necessarily have higher rates of default than other borrowers, it is usually much more difficult for the lender to recoup any funds in the case of default because of a lack of collateral. Most poor lack collateral not only because they are poor but also because they lack access to legal systems that can provide them formal title and property rights to the capital they do possess.

In order to overcome these problems, many countries have adopted policies to encourage the provision of *microfinance*. Microfinance is a generic term used to refer to programs that help provide small, uncollateralized loans, and savings services to the poor. Traditionally, the capital to provide these loans comes from governments or philanthropic organizations. Today, however, microfinance organizations are raising their own funds through providing saving services to the poor. Microfinance organizations have become incredibly popular—by one count, there are more than 60,000 microfinance organizations in Indonesia alone. The most successful of these organizations is the Grameen Bank in Bangladesh. Grameen was founded in 1976 by Dr. Muhammad Yunus to provide loans to the poorest Bangladeshis who wanted to engage in business opportunities but who did not qualify for formal loans. Grameen has distributed over \$6 billion in loans to those without access to reasonable credit. The average loan size is less than \$200. Because of the success of Grameen's microlending program, Dr. Yunus was awarded a Nobel Peace Prize in 2006 for implementing what the Nobel committee said "had appeared to be an impossible idea."

Microfinance keeps lending costs low through two methods. First, they take advantage of economies of scale in the provision of small loans. Second, microlending organizations encourage repayment by asking members of the borrower's community, who are often also borrowers themselves, to evaluate and monitor the progress of each loan. Occasionally, microlenders will provide loans to entire groups to distribute among themselves, making the entire group jointly liable for making payments. By involving more than one borrower, microlending creates strong social incentives for repayment and also encourages investment in projects that are most likely to have the largest aggregate benefits for the community. Microloans typically require frequent payments, once again in an effort to monitor borrowers' behavior. These loans are typically offered at rates of less than 20 percent a year, which makes them profitable for the bank but also significantly cheaper than loans provided through informal financial markets such as pawnbrokers or loan sharks.

Microlenders also emphasize providing savings services to the poor and, in fact, are now attracting more savings in microsavings accounts than they are making in loans. Such microsavings accounts not only allow the poor to save more safely and with a higher return, but they also allow the poor to establish credit records and accumulate wealth, which makes them more attractive potential borrowers.

Because of the success of microfinance, a number of private capital institutions, including many multinational banks, are opening subsidiaries aimed at making a profit from microlending. While still in its infancy, the entry of private corporations into the microfinance market has the potential to greatly increase both the efficiency and the amount of loanable funds available to the poor. In fact, you can personally become a microlender. Microfinance institutions such as Kiva.org provide individuals the ability to lend their own resources to small business people across the globe via the Internet.

While these microfinance organizations report numerous success stories, to this point there has not been any systematic empirical evaluation of their impact on economic growth. However, one piece of persuasive evidence as to their success is the fact that microfinance institutions report nonperforming loans of only 1–3 percent of their total lending, which is only slightly higher than that experienced by large banks in rich countries (and significantly below what credit card companies experience). This seems to indicate that the projects being funded by these loans are profitable enough to allow repayment.

The Four Primary Forms of Financial Intermediation

Different borrowers and lenders have different preferences and needs, which create a demand and supply for a wide variety of financial arrangements. While not an exhaustive list of financial instruments, there are four primary forms of financial intermediation.

Bond markets

Bonds are financial instruments with three characteristics: (1) the amount borrowed (the *principal*) is repaid at a fixed point in time (its *maturity date*); (2) interest payments are made regularly at fixed points in time; and (3) the interest rate is fixed throughout the life of the bond. Because the interest rates paid on bonds are fixed, rising market interest rates reduce the attractiveness of existing bonds, leading to a fall in the prices of bonds in secondary markets. Thus, bonds are not riskless. Not only are the bonds subject to some level of default risk, but they are also sensitive to changes in market interest rates, exposing bond holders to significant risk if they want to sell their bond before the maturity date (this is referred to as *interest rate risk*).

Bonds offer certain advantages and disadvantages to both borrowers and lenders. From the point of view of a borrower, or the bond issuer, bonds are attractive because they offer flexibility. Bonds are often long-lived; in fact, many corporate bond issues are for 30 years. This is important, especially if the firm is engaging in long-term investment in which profits may not be immediately realized. In addition, bonds offer the advantage to borrowers that after a bond has been issued, bond holders cannot place additional conditions on issuers as long as their interest rate payments are made. Of course, the disadvantage to borrowers is that bonds require fixed service payments; if the bond issuer fails to make these payments, bond holders have the right to claim default, file suit, and place severe restrictions on the issuer's future activities and finances.

From the perspective of lenders, or the purchasers of bonds, bonds offer higher returns than traditional savings accounts issued by banks. In addition, the fact that bonds make fixed payments makes them attractive to many savers with clear savings objectives, such as those saving for retirement. The disadvantage to lenders is that holding bonds exposes their savings to both default risk and interest rate risk. Default risk can vary considerably across bonds depending upon the details of an individual bond instrument. Many bonds have clauses in which they legally receive higher priority in the case of default, while other bonds are *subordinated*, meaning they receive lower priority in the case of default. *Treasury bonds* (U.S. federal government bonds, often referred to as T-bonds) and *treasury bills* (U.S. federal government bonds with maturity of a year or less, often referred to as T-bills) have essentially zero default risk because the federal government owns the printing presses and can create currency to pay their bills if necessary. *Municipal bonds* (state and local government bonds, which are federal tax exempt), corporate bonds, and *commercial paper* (corporate bonds with maturities of a year or less) vary in default risk depending upon the financial conditions of the issuer.

Stock markets

A *stock* (or *equity*) is a financial instrument that grants the holder a share of limited ownership of a corporation. Stockholders' power is limited by the fact that shareholders get to vote for the board of directors and other top executives of the corporation, but do not have the right to play a direct role in the firm's day-to-day operations. In the case of default, stockholders cannot lose more than the price of the stock that they purchased. Stockholders have a right to share in the net income of the corporation, either through periodic payments made by the firm to stockholders, referred to as *dividends*, or through the appreciation of the value of the stock as the net worth of the firm increases.

The advantage to borrowers, or the issuers of stock, is that stock does not require fixed payments. This lowers the default risk that issuers face and provides them with increased financial flexibility. The disadvantage to issuers is that they have to give up partial ownership, which includes losing a share of the profits as well as losing some control over the corporation's operations. In addition, by continually issuing new shares, firms might be sending the signal to markets that their existing shares are overvalued, which may limit their ability to obtain additional financing in the future.

From the perspective of lenders, or the holders of stock, equity offers the potential of exceptional returns if the firm becomes highly profitable. Of course, with potential returns comes high default risk. If a company does default, stockholders only receive payment if there are assets remaining after all creditors and bond holders have been paid-off, which is unlikely. In addition, even if the firm does not default, estimates of future profits are highly subjective and therefore highly volatile. Disagreement on what the proper price of most stocks should be fuels speculative behavior in stock markets and adds to their unpredictability and risk. John Maynard Keynes compared a stock market to a beauty contest based not on the judges' own opinion of who is most beautiful but on their opinion of who they think the other judges will think is most beautiful; such subjectivity creates potentially large market movements in response to even the smallest piece of new information.

Financial intermediaries

Financial intermediaries are institutions that facilitate the transfer of money from small savers to borrowers. Financial intermediaries take many forms. *Insurance companies* collect premiums from contract holders and use these premiums to purchases large asset portfolios, making payouts to contract holders when specific events occur. *Mutual funds* issue shares and use the proceeds to purchase large asset portfolios, changes in the value of which are reflected in the prices of the mutual fund's shares. *Finance companies* are institutions often tied to consumer product corporations that provide financing to the purchasers of these products by raising funds, primarily through bond issues. Finally, *depository institutions* are banks that issue deposit accounts and certificates of deposit, then use these funds to make commercial loans, consumer loans, and to purchase bonds.

Mutual funds and insurance companies play important roles in modern financial systems. However, in this book, it is banks, particularly commercial banks as opposed to *savings and loans* (banks that specialize in mortgage lending) and *credit unions* (banks organized to serve particular groups and which specialize in consumer lending), which will be our primary focus. There are three reasons for the primacy of commercial banks in our discussions. First, they are the largest type of financial intermediaries, with over 75 percent of all assets of depository institutions (more than $8 trillion in U.S. deposits in 2005). Second, they are the most interesting because they provide a wide array of financial services that are crucial to well-functioning financial systems. Finally, commercial banks specialize in providing these services to households and small firms, which are the most dependent on external finance. As a result, commercial banks play a vital role in not only the fastest growing but also the most volatile sectors of economies.

Banks provide a number of advantages to savers. First, they reduce risk by pooling and diversifying savings. Banks do this by accumulating the savings of a large number of individuals and investing these funds across a wide variety of borrowers and financial assets. Second, banks specialize in dealing with small borrowers in which asymmetric and imperfect information is a particular problem. By taking advantage of economies of scale and developing expertise in information gathering, banks are able to obtain better information on potential borrowers in order to more effectively screen and monitor those whom they lend to. The end result is higher returns with lower default risk. In addition, by taking advantage of economies of scale, banks are also able to offer savers a wide variety of services, such as checking accounts, that would otherwise be too expensive to be provided.

While banks minimize risk, they are still risky institutions because they generally borrow short term by issuing deposits and lend long term through mortgages and commercial loans. Even the best-run banks are exposed to a great deal of interest rate risk. In addition, because they specialize in dealing with small borrowers, their customer base and assets tend to have higher levels of default risk. As a result, the risk associated with saving in bank deposits is high. In fact, the perception of this risk is often acute enough to lead to deposit flight, or *bank runs*, in which depositors remove their funds en masse. To alleviate this risk to savers as well as to stabilize banking systems, most governments offer some form of deposit insurance that promises to repay depositors in the case of a default by their bank.

Banks provide significant advantages to borrowers as well. There are large transaction costs associated with attaining funds directly through financial markets, such as the fees charged by *investment banks*, or financial institutions that specialize in issuing stocks and bonds. In addition, most small borrowers lack the financial history or other information that could convince large investors with no ties to the borrower to hold their bonds or stocks. As a result, small borrowers are effectively shut out of financial markets, and it is a crucial function of banks to serve this clientele that would otherwise be unable to obtain financing.

Bank lending does have a number of disadvantages to borrowers, however. Bank lending is more expensive; interest rates on bank loans exceed the interest rates on most bonds. Unlike stocks, bank lending involves fixed interest payments, increasing default risk. Also, commercial loans to firms tend to be short term, which is risky for firms that want to invest in long-term projects. Finally, because of the higher default risk of the clients that banks typically serve, bank loans are usually accompanied by much more intrusive monitoring conditions than bond debt. The time and effort spent in accumulating information as well as the restrictions imposed in lending can be very costly to borrowers.

The foreign exchange market
Foreign exchange is the trading of one currency for another currency, either at current (spot) prices or at fixed future prices. The foreign exchange market, like bond markets and some stock markets, has no physical location but is simply a network of currency traders representing major financial institutions, primarily international banks.

The foreign exchange (FX) market is by far the largest financial market in the world. In 2004, each day on average over $2 trillion (one-sixth of U.S. GDP) in trades are made in the FX market. In fact, many individual FX traders have yearly trade volumes that by themselves surpass the level of U.S. GDP. The total volume of FX trades dwarfs the actual amount of trade in goods in services made worldwide. Only between 2 and 5 percent of FX trades are directly linked to the international trade of goods and services. The rest of these trades represent currency exchanges needed to facilitate international capital movements, such as the buying and selling of international financial instruments, and transactions made by traders that are speculating on future movements in exchange rates and other assets.

CASE STUDY: Which Forms of Financial Intermediation are Most Important and Why? An International Comparison

There are no strict empirical regularities across countries regarding the relative size and importance of financial intermediaries, stock markets, and bond markets. However, some general observations about international financial systems can be made. Let us begin by making a few observations about the financial system in the U.S. and then compare the U.S. financial system to those in other countries.

In the U.S., bonds are the largest source of financial intermediation, followed by banks, and then equity. The bond market is the largest domestic financial market in the U.S., with the value of U.S. bonds totaling approximately $25 trillion (or nearly twice U.S. GDP) in 2006, compared to the total value of equity of roughly $15 trillion. Not only are existing bond issues large, but new bond issues are more than ten times the value of new stock issues in the U.S. during an average year.

From the perspective of firms, however, bank lending remains the most important source of financial intermediation. Figure 1.1 presents the sources of financing for nonfinancial firms in the U.S. Bank loans comprise the largest share of commercial financial intermediation, followed closely by bonds, then nonbank lending (such as lending from finance companies), and finally stocks.

When the U.S. is compared to other countries, however, we see that the U.S. is something of an anomaly, particularly in regard to its exceptionally large bond

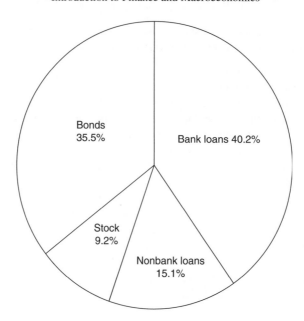

Figure 1.1
Sources of Finance for Nonfinancial Firms in the U.S.
Source: Schmidt, 2001.

market. In contrast to the U.S., banks tend to be far and away the largest source of financial intermediation for firms internationally, followed distantly by bonds and stocks. Figure 1.2 presents the size of bank loans, nonbank loans, bonds, and stock for the U.S., Germany, and Japan from 1970 to 1996. We see that bank lending accounts for between 80 and 90 percent of total financing to nonfinancial firms in Germany and Japan, which is typical of many economies in Europe, Asia, and throughout the world. In the U.S., banks are much less important, accounting for only 40 percent of financial intermediation. Stocks and bonds, on the other hand, together account for only about 15 percent of total financing to nonfinancial firms in Germany and France, but more than 45 percent of total financial intermediation in the U.S.

Another way to illustrate these differences between countries is to look at the size of their financial markets and financial intermediaries relative to GDP. Table 1.2 presents data on the size of bond markets, stock markets, and bank and other lending institutions relative to GDP from 1980 to 1995 for a sample of industrialized and emerging countries (note that the numbers in columns 1–4 do not have to sum to 100 percent because financial transactions are not included in GDP). Note once again that the U.S. bond market is much larger than in other countries, even when expressed as a fraction of its much larger GDP. The fact that the U.S. has large stock

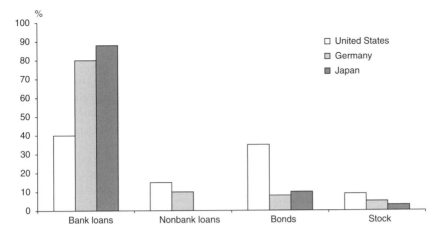

Figure 1.2
Sources of Finance for Nonfinancial Firms in the U.S., Germany, and Japan, 1970–1996.
Source: Schmidt, 2001.

Table 1.2 Size of Financial Intermediaries and Markets Relative to GDP (Averages for 1980–1995)

Country	Stock Market Capitalization as a Percentage of GDP (A)	Outstanding Bond Issues as a Percentage of GDP (B)	Credit Extended by Banks and Other Financial Institutions as Percentage of GDP (C)	Ratio of Intermediate Finance to Financial Markets Finance $C/(A+B)$ (D)
Industrialized countries				
France	19.8	41.2	90.9	1.5
Germany	18.6	37.4	92.3	1.6
Greece	8.1	4.3	40.2	3.2
Italy	11.9	28.1	50.5	1.3
Japan	73.0	30.0	169.3	1.6
United Kingdom	76.3	14.4	74.4	0.8
United States	58.2	52.6	130.7	1.2
Emerging market countries				
Argentina	4.8	5.9	15.0	1.4
Brazil	11.9	4.0	24.7	1.6
India	13.2	5.7	26.8	1.4

Source: Cecchetti (2006).

markets, bond markets, and financial intermediaries at the same time also makes it distinctive. In other countries, different segments of their financial systems are more or less highly developed. For example, some countries have more highly developed financial intermediaries and less developed stock markets (France and Germany), some have more developed stock markets and financial intermediaries but less developed bond markets (Japan and the U.K.), and some have a relative lack of all three (Greece and Italy). In summary, while it is generally true that the most common form of financial intermediation is through banks followed by bonds and then stocks, this is not universally the case.

Along these same lines, one final observation from Table 1.2 is that as measured by the ratio of total intermediary lending relative to the total size of finance conducted directly through financial markets (column D), financial intermediaries constantly play a more important role than bonds and stocks together. Except for the U.K., this ratio is above one across all of the countries in this table and commonly at or above 1.5.

When examining the financial systems of emerging markets and less developed countries, the importance of bank finance relative to direct finance through stocks or bonds becomes even more pronounced. In many poorer countries, holding stocks or bonds is an exceptionally risky proposition because profits are variable, there is a lack of liquidity, and there are few large firms. Another problem for bond and stockholders in many poorer countries is the lack of creditor protection and contract enforcement. In addition, many poorer countries are primarily populated by small firms in which the problems of asymmetric and imperfect information are particularly acute. Banks in these countries, particularly microfinance institutions, are better able to deal with these information problems as well as have the kinds of local contacts that can encourage repayment (the same can be said about informal loan syndicates, which provide many of the functions of banks in areas that are so underdeveloped that no formal banking system exists). The result is that banks dominate the financial systems of most less developed countries, emerging market economies, and even some of the poorer industrialized economies (e.g., Greece). For many emerging economies, higher recent growth rates have not changed the basic nature of their bank-centered financial systems. One key for these economies in the future is to figure out how to better nurture financial market development, which would make long-term financing available to more borrowers and encourage more long-term investment that is needed to sustain growth.

CASE STUDY: Financial Systems in India and China

India and China are populous poor countries that have enjoyed high rates of growth over the last 25 years. India has sustained 4 percent real per-capita growth while China has experienced a remarkable rate of 8 percent real per-capita growth since

1980. Even after this strong growth, however, GDP per person is currently only $4,000 in China a person and $2,900 in India. In fact, the combined GDP of China and India is still less than that of the U.S. even though more than 2.2 billion people live in these two countries as compared to 300 million in the U.S.

Despite their strong recent growth, observers agree that the weakness of their financial sectors is one very important aspect of both of these economies that is limiting growth. India has the more efficient but smaller financial sector. The ratio of financial assets to GDP is only 1.6 in India as compared to China where it is 2.2. This lack of financial development reflects the lack of capital in the Indian banking system, which in turn reflects the high level of government involvement in their financial system. In India, state-owned banks control 75 percent of all banking assets and are generally unprofitable. In addition, all banks are required to hold 25 percent of their assets in government debt, while 36 percent of their lending has to go to "priority sectors" prescribed by the government (often for politically driven as opposed to profit-driven reasons). A McKinsey Global Institute study estimated that if these and other regulations and inefficiencies could be eliminated, over $48 billion in capital would be freed in the Indian banking system and GDP growth would increase by 2.5 percent.

China, on the other hand, has a much larger financial system that is even more inefficient than the Indian financial system. In China, over 60 percent of banks are owned or partially owned by the government. While lending has been growing at 14 percent a year, bad debts and nonperforming loans have been growing as well. Another study by the McKinsey Global Institute suggests that reforms of the Chinese banking system, such as increasing the efficiency of payment systems and reducing lending and borrowing regulations, would increase China's current GDP by 16 percent as compared to where it is today (an increase of roughly $320 billion). Studies such as these suggest that while countries such as China and India are growing at extraordinary rates, they could be growing even faster if they reformed their inefficient and underdeveloped financial systems. Empirical evidence on the role of financial systems in growth supports the view that financial development should be a primary focus of future policy makers in these and other countries that are still depressingly poor.

Conclusions

Financial systems provide so many services to modern economies that they are akin to clean air—something that is easy to take for granted and forget about until it is not there. Financial intermediaries and financial markets facilitate trade in numerous ways. Financial systems create and distribute money, which reduces the transaction costs associated with trade and encourages specialization. Financial systems pool, transfer, and diversify risk. Financial systems create incentives to save, which in turn increases the amount of loanable funds that are available for investment. Finally, financial systems expand the quantity, quality, and distribution of information that helps to overcome the market failures associated with imperfect and asymmetric information and improves the efficiency of resource allocation. This short list is in no way exhaustive, but serves to illustrate just how pervasive finance is to the practice of economics and how crucial well-functioning financial systems are to sustained economic growth.

Financial systems differ significantly across countries. Some of these differences reflect differences in preferences and other economic fundamentals. However, a considerable portion of these cross-country differences reflects differences in government involvement in financial systems. Governments have an important, but limited, role to play in regulating financial systems in order to overcome the market failures associated with imperfect and asymmetric information. Specifically, governments can increase financial intermediation by encouraging the dissemination of financial information, by regulating the behavior of financial institutions and providing deposit insurance in order to reduce risk and increase stability, and by developing legal systems that protect creditor and debtor rights and enforce contracts. Government can also limit growth by excessively regulating financial systems and playing favorites among institutions, lenders, and borrowers. The role of governments in shaping the structure and efficiency of financial systems is examined in more detail in the next chapter, which discusses the history and development of financial systems in the U.S. and in other countries.

CHAPTER 2

A Brief History of Financial Development

Introduction

Financial intermediation has long been an integral part of human and economic history. The oldest surviving written law is the Babylonian code of Hammurabi, which is engraved onto a stone obelisk and dates back to 1800 B.C. Among the many laws codified on this stone are regulations on the provision of credit, including a maximum interest rate on grain borrowing (33 1/3 percent) and on silver borrowing (20 percent). The fact that regulations on financial intermediation are included among our first written history illustrates two important facts: first, finance has always played a crucial role in facilitating trade and determining standards of living; second, governments have consistently played a role in shaping financial systems, influencing both their size and their efficiency.

The purpose of this chapter is to look at financial systems from a big-picture perspective and talk about the ways that they have changed and grown over time. Once again, the objective here is not to be comprehensive, but to highlight some of the important themes and trends in financial development. The historical evolution of banking systems and financial markets is briefly reviewed, with particular attention paid to the U.S. because of its unusual history (and suspicion) of finance. Also, an overview of central banking is provided, including the historical development of central banking, an examination of the responsibilities that modern central banks (such as the Federal Reserve and the European Central Bank [ECB]) assume in modern economies, and a brief discussion of the role that central banks play in managing the money supply.

Financial systems have not developed in isolation; instead, they have become interlinked across countries to the point that financial systems today are truly multinational. *Globalization* is a term often used to refer to the increasing cultural and economic integration among individuals, markets, and nations. After a brief look at the history of international financial flows, this chapter examines some of the new developments in financial systems over the last 25 years, most of which are heavily dependent on two factors: increased globalization and advances in information technology. This chapter concludes with two case studies—one on securitization and the changing nature of the housing market, the other on hedge funds—that illustrate the important ways in which globalization and information technology have changed the nature of finance, modern economics, and the day-to-day lives of most of us.

A Brief History of Banking, Financial Markets, and Central Banking

As mentioned before, financial intermediation has always been an important component of trade, but prior to the 1600s finance tended to be informal and took place between individuals, or groups of individuals, who had previously established economic or family ties with one another. The first institution that somewhat resembles what we would today consider to be a modern financial institution dates back to the renaissance and the Medici family financial empire in Italy.

The first true financial market was the Amsterdam Stock Exchange, established in 1611. In 1634, the world's first boom and bust asset cycle took place in Amsterdam in the market for Tulips. During "tulipmania," the prices of certain tulips rose by nearly 6,000 percent (to more than £20,000 for one kind of tulip), only to fall by 93 percent from this peak in 1637.

While modern finance was started by the Dutch, it first came to full fruition in England in the 1700s. At the time, this small nation ruled over 25 percent of the world's surface and its population. In the opinion of Walter Bagehot (1873), the disproportionate political and economic influence exerted by England had much to do with its highly developed financial system, which allowed the English the unmatched ability to engage in risky and far-reaching trade, finance wars, sustain government bureaucracies, invest in new technologies, and acquire capital. The Bank of England, which was founded in 1694, played an extremely important role in strengthening England's financial system. The Bank of England was both a private and public institution that played many of the roles of modern central banks, including providing the English financial system with a degree of stability and financial concentration unmatched in other countries.

Financial dominance began to move to the U.S. in the early 1900s. The history of the U.S. financial system is interesting because it highlights many of the contradictory feelings that are still felt about finance to this day. In the opinion of Alexander Hamilton (1781): "banks were the happiest engines that ever were invented" for creating growth. On the other hand, many of the other American founding fathers were skeptical of "big finance." Their skepticism was influenced by what they saw as the exploitive behavior of financial institutions in England, particularly the Bank of England, which they viewed as a tool of large industrial interests that worked against the needs of the common man, particularly small farmers. Representing this view, John Adams (1819) claimed that banks damage the "morality, tranquility, and even wealth" of countries. Likewise, Thomas Jefferson (1861) wrote that "I have ever been the enemy of banks . . . (and of) the tribe of bank-mongers, who were seeking to filch from the public their swindling, and barren gains."

This conflict is reflected throughout the history of banking in the U.S. Nationwide Commercial banking began in the U.S. in 1782 with the Bank of North America. Until 1863, all banks in the U.S. were chartered by states and prohibited from expanding across state lines, the primary rationale being to keep banks small and local, not large and impersonal. One result of this was that the U.S. had no national currency, just banknotes issued by various banks in each state. Another result was that the U.S. had a larger number of smaller banks than in other countries. In 1863, the National Banking Act was passed which allowed the federal government to charter banks (which were to be regulated by the Comptroller of the Currency) and establish a national currency, but restrictions on interstate banking remained, insuring banks stayed relatively small and numerous.

The widespread suspicion of big banking significantly influenced the debate over the creation of a central bank in the U.S. In 1791, the Bank of the United States was chartered by the federal government. This was a private bank that also served as the central bank of the U.S. The Bank of the United States was also the only bank that could operate across state lines, quickly making it the country's largest financial institution. Fueled by suspicion that it manipulated interest rates and its lending activities in favor of large industrial borrowers at the expense of small borrowers, its charter was revoked in 1811. However, after the U.S. government had difficulties financing the War of 1812, a general realization took place that the federal government had to take a stronger hand in the financial system. The Second Bank of the United States was chartered in 1816, only to expire again in 1836 at a time when it held one-third of all bank deposits. The deciding factor in its expiration was a veto by Andrew Jackson, who ran for president as a populist on a platform hostile to large economic interests.

The period of time between 1836 and 1863 is often referred to as the "free banking" era in the U.S., largely because the only supervision of the banking industry was conducted by weak and often politically motivated state regulatory agencies. This meant that banks in many states were effectively unregulated. Even after the National Banking Act of 1863, state banks remained weakly regulated, but at least now more individuals had the option of doing business with more highly regulated and safer national banks.

State banks, and to a lesser extent national banks, were prone to failure throughout the mid-to-late 1800s to the early 1900s. This was partly due to the weak regulation of banking, particularly state banks, which often led to fraud or, at the least, risky lending activities. Another factor was the lack of interstate banking, which created small, undercapitalized, and undiversified banks. In addition, many banks in smaller states were effectively monopolies, and this lack of competition allowed them to remain inefficient. As a result, banking crises periodically interrupted financial intermediation and destabilized economic activity over this entire period. Friedman and Schwartz (1963) indicate that every recession but one in the U.S. between 1867 and 1950 was associated with a banking crisis.

In an effort to provide the financial system with an institution that could serve as a lender of last resort in time of crisis and help improve financial stability, the Federal Reserve Act was passed in 1913, which created the Federal Reserve System. The Fed was purposefully structured to remain weak by decentralizing its power among 12 loosely connected regional central banks, once again reflecting the nation's suspicion of big banking. This lack of leadership was a major reason behind why the Fed behaved so ineptly during, and even contributed to, the Great Depression.

The Great Depression, the worst of which occurred between 1929 and 1933, fundamentally changed the nature of financial systems in the U.S. and across Europe. One reason for this is that much of the banking system disappeared: nearly 9,000 banks failed in the U.S., or roughly one-third of all banks, and nearly 3 percent of total deposits (an amount equivalent to nearly $300 billion in today's dollars) were lost by depositors. The Great Depression also ended the antiregulation, or *laissez-faire*, attitude that had existed toward banking in the U.S. and elsewhere, and governments increasingly became focused on acting to reduce the risk and instability associated with financial intermediaries and financial markets. In regards to financial markets, the Securities and Exchange Commission was created in the U.S. in 1933 to enforce accounting and information disclosure standards on firms as well as to enforce restrictions on *insider trading*, or trading based on information that is not publicly available (often by the executives of firms). In regard to the U.S. banking system, the Great Depression led to the creation of federal deposit insurance and stricter banking regulations along with it. In addition, the investment banking, stock, and bond securities industries were legally separated from the banking industry by the Glass–Stegal Act in 1933, based on the belief that stock market speculation by banks played a large role in the stock market crash of 1929. Finally, the Federal Reserve was strengthened and power centralized within a newly created Federal Reserve Board of Governors.

Today, the structure of U.S. banking system continues to reflect many aspects of its unusual history. For example, today roughly two-thirds of U.S. commercial banks are state chartered banks, with the remaining one-third being federally chartered banks. Coupled with the fact that different regulatory agencies have been added as new government programs have been developed over time, the result is a convoluted system of bank regulation in the U.S. that is much tighter and more complex than in most industrialized countries. Every U.S. bank is monitored by multiple regulatory agencies. The agencies that a specific bank is supervised by depends upon whether they are state or locally chartered, the kinds of lending they are engaged in (e.g., whether they conduct investment banking activities), whether they are commercial banks as opposed to savings and loans or credit unions, and whether they are members of the Federal Reserve system. While these complex arrangements appear to be confusing and inefficient, some have argued that it has actually encouraged bank innovation by giving banks some choice over whom they will be regulated by. This creates competition among regulators that discourages overbearing and unnecessary regulation.

Although it remains distinctive in many other ways, the U.S. banking system is slowly becoming more concentrated with a large majority of banking activity taking place within a small number of banks. Over the last 20 years there has been a wave of consolidations and mergers within the U.S. banking industry. Since 1984, the total number of banks has fallen from more than 14,000 (a level that had been roughly constant since the mid-1930s) to less than 8,000 today. However, this is still many more banks than that which exist in other countries; for example, less than 100 banks exist in Japan and no other nation has more than 1,000 banks. Even given this large number of banks, an increasingly small number of banks dominate the U.S. banking industry; the ten largest banks in the U.S. now hold 60 percent of all commercial bank assets. In this respect, U.S. banking has become more like that in Europe and particularly in Asia, in which banking is also highly concentrated within a small number of very large banks.

Much of the consolidation in the U.S. banking industry has been driven by the wave of financial deregulation that has occurred since 1980. Mergers and acquisitions were initially driven by the avoidance and finally the elimination of restrictions on interstate banking, immediately leading to bank mergers across state lines. Consolidation was also fueled by the elimination of restrictions on interest rates and on newly developed methods of acquiring and lending funds, creating economies of scale in banking that could be taken advantage of by larger banks. Finally, consolidation and concentration was driven more recently by the ending of the legal separation of commercial banking from investment banking, which took place in 1999 with the passage of the Gramm–Leach–Bliley Act (although many banks had been finding loopholes in this legal partition for years). Since the repeal of the Glass–Stegal Act, many banks have merged with investment banks and other nonbank financial institutions in order to offer one-stop shopping, or *universal banking*, similar to what exists in Europe and Asia. Under universal banking, banks can hold stocks, bonds, stakes in investment funds, and even seats on the board of directors of nonfinancial firms. Thus, universal banking broadly expands the role banks can play in all sectors of the economy. One example of a universal bank is Citigroup Inc., which was created in 1999 and merged the second largest commercial bank (Citicorp) with the third largest investment bank

(Salomon Smith Barney), along with an insurance company (Travelers Insurance), pension funds, brokerages, mutual funds, and finance companies. Citigroup now forms the largest financial conglomerate in the world with more than $1.5 trillion in assets, surpassing other large banking conglomerates in countries such as Japan that have had universal banking for years.

Modern Central Banking

One important aspect of modern finance that separates it from past eras is the pervasiveness and power of central banks. Central banks play vital roles in ensuring the stability and efficiency of banking systems as well as influencing interest rates, bank lending, asset prices, inflation, output, unemployment, and other crucial aspects of macroeconomic performance. As a result, no other financial institutions (or possibly even government institutions) are as closely scrutinized as central banks.

As discussed previously, central banking has an interesting history in the U.S. After the Great Depression, the Federal Reserve was strengthened and power within it was centralized in order to allow it to more effectively serve as a lender of last resort and better manage the money supply. This was done by weakening the power of the regional Federal Reserve banks and centralizing the majority of the decision-making power, particularly regarding monetary policy, within an executive committee referred to as the Board of Governors. These governors are appointed to 14-year terms, making them fairly independent and insulating them from many (but not all) of the short-term political ramifications of their decisions.

The other most influential central bank is the ECB. The ECB serves as the central bank for the 11 countries that are a part of the European Monetary Union (Austria, Belgium, Finland, France, Germany, Italy, Ireland, Luxembourg, the Netherlands, Portugal, and Spain). Not surprisingly, the ECB is set up along similar lines as the Federal Reserve System given that the ECB also has to serve a geographically diverse constituency that is somewhat skeptical of centralized power (similar to the situation that exists in the U.S.). Regional banks in each member country play a role in decision making, but the majority of the power rests with an independent executive board. In fact, the independence of the ECB is even greater than that of the Fed since the governments of every country in the European Monetary Union would have to agree to change the ECB's structure, while the Federal Reserve could be changed by a single act of congress.

Across a wide range of countries, the current trend is toward granting central banks more policy-making independence. The central banks of England, Japan, New Zealand, and Sweden have recently been granted more independent authority in their decision making. Early results suggest that such changes have been beneficial: Alesina and Summers (1993) find evidence that greater central bank independence leads to lower inflation without any negative effect on output growth.

Central banks serve four important functions in modern financial systems. First, central banks help facilitate financial transactions by issuing new currency, clearing checks and other payments, providing short-term and seasonal loans to banks, and monitoring payment systems. Second, central banks play a role in regulating the banking system, enforcing information disclosure requirements, setting loan and deposit creation standards, approving bank mergers and acquisitions, and monitoring bank activities. Third, central banks serve as a lender of last resort in order to enhance the stability of the banking system. By standing ready to provide loans to banks with short-term liquidity problems, central banks can prevent bank runs before they happen, usually without even providing a single loan. As the power of central banks have grown in the postwar era, bank runs have become much less frequent, to the point that they are now almost nonexistent in industrialized countries. For example, the last bank run and banking crisis in the U.S. was during the Great Depression, before the reform and strengthening of the Federal Reserve and the creation of deposit insurance. Note, however, that the central bank's role as lender of last resort does not extend to poorly run banks; if a bank becomes *insolvent*, or its liabilities exceed its assets, then a central bank has the responsibility to let this bank fail. At that point, the appropriate government agencies that provide deposit insurance will bailout depositors and sell the bank's assets (for U.S. commercial banks, this is the Federal Deposit Insurance Corporation).

The fourth and highest profile function of central banks is to set monetary policy and regulate the money supply. Thinking back to the definitions of M1 and M2 in Chapter 1, it is clear that central banks do not completely control the money supply. For example, central banks do not directly control the level of checking account deposits in M1 or any of the other banking and financial market assets in M2. It is the public's demand for these assets and banks' willingness to issue these assets that determines the money supply.

Central banks, however, play a crucial role in shaping the banking system's ability to issue assets that are part of the money supply. Central banks control two things: currency and total reserves held by banks. Together, the sum of currency plus total reserves is referred to as the *monetary base*. By changing the monetary base, either by changing the level of currency (through issuing more of it) or by changing the level of total reserves (either through extending more loans to banks or purchasing the illiquid assets of banks in return for reserves), a central bank can change the monetary base. As banks hold more currency and reserves, they are able to extend more loans. Some of these loans will be held in bank deposits that allow banks to create even more loans, generating a deposit expansion process that inflates the level of banking assets and the money supply.

While it is a fact that an increase in the monetary base increases the money supply, central banks do not have complete control over how large this increase in the money supply will be. The ratio of the change in the money supply to the change in the monetary base is referred to as the *money multiplier*. For the M1 definition of the money supply, the money multiplier is determined by three things, only one of which central banks directly control. The determinant of the money multiplier that central banks control is the *required reserve ratio*, or the percentage of deposits that must be held in an account at the central bank. When a central bank reduces the required reserve ratio, it allows banks to lend out a greater fraction of any deposits they receive, expanding the deposit expansion process and increasing the money multiplier.

The other two determinants of the money multiplier are not controlled by the central bank. The first is the currency-to-deposit ratio, or the fraction of deposits that the public or banks choose to hold as currency. As this ratio increases, less money is deposited in banks and the deposit expansion process is weakened, reducing the money multiplier. The other determinant is the excess reserves-to-deposit ratio, or the fraction of deposits that banks choose not to lend out but to hold. Once again, as the excess reserve-to-deposit ratio increases, a smaller fraction of deposits is lent out and the deposit expansion process is weakened, reducing the money multiplier.

There is a common misperception that central banks have complete control over the money supply. In reality, they have complete discretion in setting one component of the money supply, the monetary base, but they have limited control over how changes in the monetary base translate into changes in the total money supply. One way to think about how central banks influence the money supply is the following analogy: think about the money supply as a poorly trained dog on a walk, the dog's leash as the tools that the central bank controls (the monetary base and the required reserve ratio), and the central bank as the person who is holding the leash. As the money supply begins to veer off route, the central bank has the power to yank the money supply back on course. However, the dog's path will not proceed in a straight line, and if the leash is long or the dog is strong, the path might be quite unpredictable at times. Likewise, a central bank's control over the money supply is good over the long term, but over the short term it can be quite loose.

A Brief History of International Capital Flows

Finance does not just take place nationally; international capital flows have been an important component of financial intermediation since the late 1800s. However, while the pace of domestic financial development in industrialized countries has been consistently positive, international financial flows have ebbed and flowed over time to a much greater extent.

Barry Eichengreen (2003a) identifies four international lending booms since the industrial revolution. The first era of financial globalization took place between

1880 and the beginning of World War I in 1913. This era's lending boom was driven by three factors that have also driven subsequent international lending booms: an expansion in world GDP and in international trade, financial innovation, and pro-trade government policies. The financial innovations that took place during this era were improvements in communications (such as telephones), transportation (railroads and shipping), and the development of bond markets and investment trusts (a precursor to modern mutual funds). In regard to the political environment, Europe was relatively peaceful and outward looking after the end of the Napoleonic wars. Finally, world economic growth and international trade were strong over this period. In many ways, this period was the height of international finance: capital flows as a percent of world GDP reached 3.5 percent, which is a level that has not been reached since, despite all of the recent talk of a new era of globalization (today, capital flows as a percentage of world GDP are roughly 2.5 percent). However, almost all of this international finance was between developed economies.

Pro-trade government policies disappeared during the World War I and were only reestablished during the early 1920s, sparking the second international capital boom. This boom was heavily influenced by expanding world GDP and ended with the onset of the Great Depression.

The Great Depression, which was followed by the World War II, marked the beginning of a protracted period of restricted international capital flows that lasted until the 1970s. Much of this was the result of the Bretton Woods agreement, which was a system of fixed exchange rates established in 1945. Under the Bretton Woods agreement, the U.S. maintained the dollar on the gold standard, and every other country maintained a fixed exchange rate to the dollar. While the stated purpose of Bretton Woods was to encourage capital and trade flows, in reality it opened up many avenues for governments to manipulate exchange rates and create trade barriers to protect their domestic industries. It also provided governments with a rationale for clamping down on domestic financial systems in an effort to discourage speculation and other activities that could undermine their exchange rate target. Together, these factors served to depress the international movement of capital. Skepticism regarding international capital movements during this era was prevalent even in the economics profession. The preeminent economist of the time and one of the architects of the Bretton Woods agreement, John Maynard Keynes (1936), stated: "Ideas, knowledge, science, hospitality, travel—these are the things which should of their nature be international. But let goods be homespun whenever it is reasonable and conveniently possible, and above all else let finance be primarily national."

During the mid-1960s, however, international capital flows began to gradually expand. In fact, expanding capital flows eventually led to the collapse of the Bretton Woods system as countries found it increasingly difficult to maintain overvalued exchange rates in a world where capital could so easily and so quickly flow into and out of countries. (The Bretton Woods system, its collapse, and the role of the International Monetary Fund are discussed in more detail in Chapter 10.) The lending boom of the 1970s was driven by the same factors that drove previous international lending booms. World trade increased by 9 percent a year over this decade. A number of new financial developments took place, including larger financial markets, Eurodollar accounts, the growth of large institutional investors, and improved communication and computer technologies. The 1970s also began an extended period of financial deregulation and liberalization in which the barriers to financial flows at both a national and international level were gradually reduced. Finally, a large portion of the capital flows during the 1970s were driven by a spike in oil prices, which encouraged many countries with oil reserves, especially those that were poorer, to borrow heavily against these reserves. This was a unique development in the history of international capital flows because prior to the 1970s most capital flowed from rich countries to other rich countries, with less developed nations receiving a relatively small fraction of foreign lending.

Unfortunately, the debt boom of the 1970s was not sustainable after oil prices plummeted in the early 1980s. In fact, it took most of the 1980s for banks and debtor nations to clean up the foreign debt crisis that resulted. The governments of many industrialized nations, particularly in Europe and the U.S., played active roles in restructuring debt payments and negotiating debt relief in an attempt to prevent massive defaults and renew the flow of foreign capital to poorer economies.

Globalization and Financial Development in the 1990s

Over the last 20 years, a fourth international lending boom has taken place across the globe. Many economies, both rich and poor, have enjoyed incredible amounts of financial development in the size of financial markets, the size of financial intermediaries, in the types of financial services, and in the types of financial assets that they offer. To get some idea of the size of this expansion, the U.S. serves as an interesting example. Table 2.1 presents the levels of selected financial assets at the end of 2003 and the growth rates of these assets over the previous 24 years. The sustained growth rates of all of these assets, many of which barely existed 20 years ago, have been remarkable. To get a feel of how large this asset explosion has been, nominal GDP growth over this same period was 6.1 percent a year, meaning that the growth rates of all of these instruments have outpaced nominal income growth. Similar growth, though generally to a somewhat lesser extent than in the U.S., has taken place in other industrialized and many emerging economies.

This remarkable growth has also been stimulated by the creation of different types of financial intermediaries that are able to offer new and unique services to savers. The best example of this is the amazing growth of the mutual fund industry, which has seen its assets grow by 20 percent a year since 1980. In 1990, mutual

Table 2.1 Growth of Financial Assets in the U.S.

Type of Instrument	Amount Outstanding as of December 31, 2003 ($ Billions)	Average Annual Growth Rate (Percent) 1980–2003
Commercial paper	1,289	12.1
U.S. T-bills	929	6.7
Eurodollars	212	6.7
Negotiable CDs	1,233	6.2
Residential mortgages	7,685	8.9
Corporate bonds	3,582	9.8
U.S. T-bonds	2,646	8.3
State and local government bonds	1,899	8.5
Commercial and farm mortgages	1,588	6.9
Corporate equities	15,473	12.4
Mutual funds	4,665	20.7

Sources: Federal Reserve System, Flow of Funds Accounts, release Z.1 at http://www.federalreserve.gov/releases/Z1, U.S. Treasury Bulletin, and Economic Report of the President.

funds had roughly one-third of the assets of commercial banks and held 12 percent of household wealth. Today, they hold more assets than commercial banks (more than $6.4 trillion in assets in 2006) and hold more than 22 percent of household wealth.

Three factors have driven this fourth international boom in capital flows. First, the 1990s were a good time for the world economy, not just in the industrialized countries such as the U.S. and Europe, but in emerging market economies in Asia, China, parts of Latin America, and India. In addition, the development strategies of many of these emerging economies were pro-trade and placed a heavy emphasis on expanding export markets. Many of these countries were following the export promotion strategies followed so successfully in Japan and East Asia.

The second factor in the recent lending boom is government policy. Government policies became increasingly pro-trade and pro-capital flows beginning in the mid-to-late 1980s. Many factors drove this economic liberalization: the end of the Cold War, the success of export-dominated development policies in East Asia, increasing economic integration in Europe and in North America (with the formation of the European Economic Union [EU] and the North American Free Trade Agreement [NAFTA]), the development of international trade agreements that liberalized trade across the globe (with the expansion of the Generalized Agreement on Tariffs and Trade [GATT]), and increasing financial liberalization at the national level.

The third factor driving today's globalization boom is the rapid advancement in information and communications technology. As we have talked about before, finance is fueled by information. With the development of cellular and wireless communications, the Internet, and computer infrastructure systems, the amount of information available is larger and the costs of obtaining this information are lower now than it has ever been before. Information is particularly important in international finance, where the availability and costs of information in many countries prior to new communication technologies made finance prohibitively risky and expensive. Information technology has also encouraged international finance by reducing transactions costs and risk in many other ways. By eliminating the use of middlemen in many financial market transactions, information technology has increased the number of transactions, making markets more efficient and liquid. Information technology has reduced the monitoring and screening costs associated with financial intermediation. Finally, information technology has also led to the creation of new financial assets that were unavailable until reductions in information and computational costs made them possible; these new assets allow for better hedging of risk, better diversification, and more collateral, each of which facilitates lending.

The globalization of finance has also had a big impact on financial intermediaries, particularly commercial banks. Banking is increasingly becoming an international business. Overall, U.S. banks earn 15 percent of their income from foreign operations, but the five largest U.S. banks earn 45 percent. Likewise, foreign banks operating in the U.S. own 10 percent of domestic banking assets and provide 19 percent of the lending in the U.S. Figure 2.1 presents the level of cross-country bank lending worldwide, illustrating that nearly twice the level of international bank lending is taking place today as 10 years ago. Because foreign banks are required to abide by the same rules and regulations as the domestic banks in the countries in which they operate, it is increasingly the case that the country of origin of international banks means very little to its customers. For example, the largest U.S. bank, Citigroup, earned 60 percent of its income outside of the U.S. in 2006, raising questions about whether such a corporation can still be classified as American.

Globalization has also had a big impact on financial markets. Figure 2.2 presents cross-country trades in bonds, illustrating the incredible extent to which bond markets have become internationalized over the last 20 years.

Another important way that finance has been internationalized is through the development of new markets and new instruments that meet the specific needs of foreign investors. One such new source of international finance has come from the growth of Eurodollar accounts and *Eurobonds* (bonds issued in one market but denominated in a foreign currency, usually in dollars). The use here of "Euro" is a misnomer—these assets can be issued or traded anywhere by anyone, as long as they are denominated in a foreign currency. The largest markets for these assets are located in London, Hong Kong, Singapore, and the Caribbean.

Eurodollars and Eurobonds have become important sources of funds for many borrowers. For example, the corporations and governments of many emerging market economies have raised funds through these markets because they are

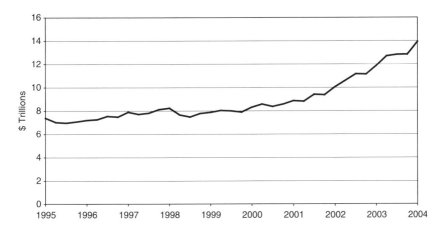

Figure 2.1
Cross-Country Bank Lending.
Source: The Bank of International Settlements.

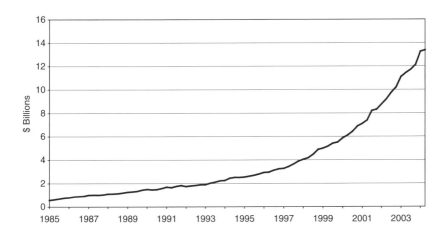

Figure 2.2
Cross-Country Bond Issues.
Source: The Bank of International Settlements.

attractive to foreign investors who would prefer to hold their assets in dollars or Euros as opposed to other more volatile and risky currencies. In addition, some countries leave Eurodollar accounts unregulated, making them attractive to certain savers and borrowers. (Such situations in the Caribbean and East Asia are often referred to as *offshore banking.*) As a result of these advantages, even the U.S. treasury and other U.S. corporations have taken to issuing Eurobonds dominated in dollars in foreign bond markets. To get a feel of how large these "Euromarkets" have become, here are a few facts. Eurodollar accounts now hold more than $5 trillion in deposits and are a $190 billion source of funds for U.S. banks. The Eurobond market is now home to 80 percent of the bond trade outside of the U.S., and the value of new Eurobond issues now has surpassed the value of new bond issues in the U.S. bond market.

While this fourth international lending boom has been driven by many of the same factors as previous booms—increases in trade, technology, and pro-trade government polices—there are at least three ways in which this latest boom is different from previous eras. First, the growth of international capital flows has not been driven by growth in industrialized countries, but by growth in poorer emerging economies, such as China. As late as 1990, net private capital flows to developing countries amounted to only $50 billion, but grew to more than $650 billion in 2006. These are net inflows, which hide the fact that while emerging economies are receiving large capital flows from rich countries, they are also sending large amounts of capital to rich countries. In fact, many developing countries are actually net lenders to developed countries. The largest example is China, which received $55 billion of net foreign investment in 2004 at the same time that it was holding more than $711 billion of foreign reserves, primarily U.S. T-Bonds.

Foreign investment can be broken into two categories. *Foreign direct investment* involves a corporation purchasing and operating capital within a foreign country, such as setting up a factory. *Foreign portfolio investment* refers the purchase of a domestic financial asset by a foreigner, such as a stock, bond, or bank deposit. Today, emerging economies account for 30 percent of foreign portfolio investment and more than 40 percent of foreign direct investment. These numbers were 10 percent and 15 percent in 1990, illustrating exactly how remarkable the growth in capital flows to emerging economies has been. This continues a process that began during the 1970s oil lending boom, but the recent lending boom appears to be much less dependent on a single commodity or a single region, though China and India are playing very large roles.

The second difference in this current boom is that during the first era of globalization (1880–1913), most foreign portfolio investment was in the form of bonds and flowed primarily to major borrowers such as railroads and governments. Today, foreign portfolio investment is increasingly flowing to a broad and diverse array of sectors in these recipient economies. In addition, foreign portfolio investment is much more heavily weighted toward stocks. This has in large part been driven by improved financial information about international corporations as well as by the rising importance of international institutional investors such insurance companies, mutual funds, and pension funds.

The third and final difference in this most recent lending boom is that it has been driven by improved information. As a result, the flow of foreign capital is increasingly determined by which countries are able to provide quality information and convince investors that they are an attractive place to invest, while those countries that cannot maintain investors' confidence fail to attract capital. In a world where capital is increasingly mobile, information-driven lending has had many positive implications: it increases the accountability of firms that do not act appropriately, it forces governments to focus on efficiency and maintain fiscal discipline, it acts to break down the economic and even political barriers between countries, and it compels financial systems and economies as a whole to become more efficient in order to compete for capital flows. The negative implication, however, is that confidence is often fleeting, and when a country loses investors' confidence, it will lose their capital as well, often very quickly and with devastating effects. Thus, in today's international financial system, capital mobility may increase financial volatility and economic insecurity. The role that international finance plays in economic volatility and business cycles is an important topic that is addressed at length later in this book (Chapters 9 and 10).

CASE STUDY: The Housing Market, Mortgages, and Securitization

Real estate has never been hotter than it has been over the last decade. Since 1997, nominal housing prices have increased by more than 100 percent in Australia, Britain, Ireland, Spain, and Sweden. In the U.S., nominal housing prices are up 95 percent between 1997 and 2006, the largest gain over any similar period in its history.

While a number of factors have played a role in fueling this boom, one of the most important is the ease by which individuals today can obtain a mortgage. Before the Great Depression, obtaining a home mortgage in the U.S. was not easy or cheap. Mortgages almost always had variable interest rates, high down payments (50 percent or more), and short maturities (5–10 years). A generation ago, families had to scrimp and save to stockpile the minimum 20 percent down payment needed to purchase most homes. In addition, households often had to pay sizeable *points* (fees associated with a mortgage which are calculated as a percentage of the money borrowed) and other fees that could significantly add to the costs of buying a house. Finally, the total funds available for mortgage lending were much more limited. Mortgages were almost solely provided by banks relying upon small deposits.

Much of this has changed, and now getting a mortgage and buying a house is considerably easier than it has ever been before. The down payments required from many families have fallen to 5 percent, and sometimes as low as 0 percent depending upon the circumstances. The costs associated with obtaining a mortgage have also fallen significantly, as can be seen in Figure 2.3, which presents the transaction costs (as a percentage of total mortgage loans) incurred by U.S.

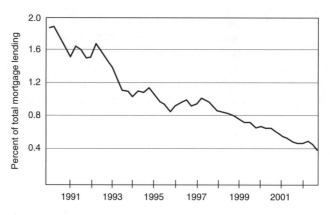

Figure 2.3
Initial Fees and Points for U.S. Mortgages.
Source: Federal Housing Finance Board at http://www.fnfb.gov.

mortgage borrowers. In addition, the creation of Internet banking as well as deregulation in the banking industry have expanded competition in the mortgage market, increasing the ease by which borrowers can shop around to get the best deal on a mortgage. Finally, financial development has dramatically increased the pool of funds available to finance mortgages. The result is that U.S. homeowners have choices in their mortgage lending that were previously unavailable. Because of this, mortgage debt, which was 20 percent of household income in 1949, has risen to 73 percent of income by 2001. In addition, 68 percent of households now own their own homes, creating a significant improvement in both their quality of life and their wealth.

Many of these developments in the mortgage market have been fueled by the explosive growth in the securitization of mortgages. *Securitization* refers to the process of transforming illiquid financial assets that are hard to resell into standardized financial instruments that are liquid. Individual mortgages are a classic example of a financial asset that is illiquid. This is because each mortgage is unique. Not only do individual mortgages differ in their default risk depending upon the credit risk of the borrower, but they are for nonstandard amounts, have different interest rates, are for different lengths of time, and are often paid-off early. All of these factors make mortgages unattractive to small savers or institutional investors. As a result, until recently there was no secondary market for mortgages; a bank that issued a mortgage would simply hold it until it was paid-off by the borrower.

While an individual mortgage is heterogeneous, large pools of mortgages behave in predictable ways. If the pool is large enough, not only will risk be reduced through diversification, but a financial analyst can accurately quantify the risk of a pool of loans. In addition, the other drawbacks of mortgages—their nonstandard amounts, their varying lengths, the fact that they are often paid-off early—disappear if a large enough pool of loans is created where these irregularities average out. The securitization boom that began in the 1980s was driven by this fact that heterogeneous assets can be homogenized by pooling a large amount of them together. Financial analysts realized that they could issue bonds to raise money to buy large portfolios of mortgages and then use the proceeds from mortgage payments to make the interest payments on these bonds (and, of course, make some profit for themselves). The result was an explosion in reselling mortgages on secondary markets (today, over 75 percent of all mortgages are securitized) and an expansion in the number of bonds backed by securitized mortgages. Because these bonds are relatively safe and provide a higher return than many corporate bonds of similar risk, they are also very attractive to savers. Over time, there has also been an increase in the variety of financial instruments that can be created through securitization, such as bonds of varying risk (and interest rates) as well as options and other financial derivatives.

Securitization has been good for savers and for securities firms, and it has also been remarkably good for banks and for homeowners. By selling their mortgages to institutions that engage in securitization, banks have been able to make their balance sheets more liquid and have generated an important new source of revenue without assuming much risk. In addition, securitization has increased the supply of funds in the mortgage market, which has played a big role in driving down mortgage rates and the transaction costs associated with obtaining mortgages, while at the same time increasing the amount of mortgage lending. Figure 2.4 illustrates the rapid growth of mortgage lending in the U.S., which has grown to more than $10 trillion. Securitization has also increased the variety of mortgages available to homeowners, including interest-only mortgages and negative amortization loans (in which the buyer pays less than the full interest payment, with the shortfall added to the principal to be repaid at the end of the loan). Finally, securitization has led to the creation of a subprime mortgage market, where potential homebuyers with low credit ratings can obtain mortgages. Today, subprime lending accounts for 20 percent of all new mortgage lending and 10 percent of total mortgage lending, up from essentially zero a decade ago.

While securitization creates win-win-win-win situations, securitization was not possible before the use of computers and improved communication systems. Securitization is a technical exercise, and its financial ramifications are almost impossible to grasp with a calculator alone. Likewise, purchasing large enough pools of mortgages requires the communication of large amounts of information, the costs of which was prohibitively expensive until the 1980s when new information technologies became available.

Governments have also played a crucial role in facilitating securitization. In the U.S., one federal government agency has been created, the Government National Mortgage Association (GNMA, or Ginnie Mae), and two other private

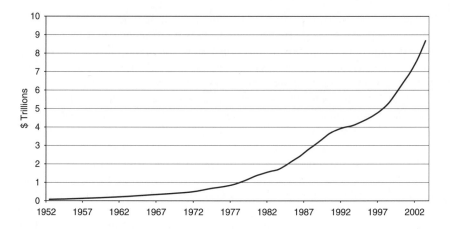

Figure 2.4
Outstanding Mortgage Loans in the U.S.
Source: Federal Reserve System, Flow of Funds Accounts, release Z.1 at http://www.federalreserve.gov/releases/Z1.

organizations have been sponsored and subsidized by the government, the Federal National Mortgage Association (FNMA, or Fannie Mae) and the Federal Home Loan Mortgage Corporation (FHLMC, or Freddie Mac), to help securitize mortgages. These organizations both securitize mortgages themselves as well as provide default insurance on mortgages that are securitized by other private securities companies. By 2003, Fannie Mae and Freddie Mac either held or guaranteed 43 percent of all mortgages. The rationale behind government involvement in the mortgage market is to encourage home ownership by reducing the costs and reducing the risk of mortgages (primarily by increasing maturities and encouraging fixed rate mortgages loans). This is exactly what has happened over the last 70 years.

Financial development in U.S. mortgage markets has outpaced mortgage market development in other economies. According to Green and Wachter (2005), in some countries—such as the U.K., Canada, and Japan—considerably less securitization takes place, with banks still the primary source of mortgage lending. As a result, mortgages tend to be of variable rate and not fixed, lending limits are often imposed, and consumer choice is limited. Other countries—such as Germany and Denmark—have high levels of securitization and large mortgage markets, but are regulated in such a way as to limit the credit risk to lenders, which limits the flexibility consumers have in choosing different types of mortgages. Finally, countries such as France, Italy, and South Korea have small and relatively underdeveloped mortgage and securitization markets, either because of government regulation or because of underdeveloped bond and stock markets.

Today, securitization has moved to other financial assets. Commercial loans, consumer loans, car loans, and credit card loans are all being securitized. Japan has securitized the bad loans in their banking system associated with their decade long banking crisis. Even the rock star David Bowie has securitized his music catalog and the royalties that he earns from it.

CASE STUDY: Hedge Funds

Financial development has not just led to the creation of new financial instruments, but to new financial institutions as well. One new type of institution that has received a great deal of attention is hedge funds. *Hedge funds* are private, international, and unregulated investment institutions that specialize in *short selling* (selling borrowed assets in the hope that these assets will fall in value and can be bought back at a profit) and maximizing *leverage* (purchasing assets with borrowed funds) in ways that generate significant speculative profits. Because the minimum amount needed to invest in a hedge fund is typically $10 million, the primary investors in hedge funds are major banks, pension funds, and other investment funds.

Hedge funds, contrary to their name, take on speculative risk in order to maximize returns. Most hedge funds utilize highly technical trading strategies that emphasize the use of financial derivatives such as options and futures contracts. Hedge funds typically make large, undiversified bets in which they place a significant share of their resources in only a small number of positions at one time. In addition, hedge funds attempt to remain fairly liquid so that they are able to swoop in and fully exploit short-term profit opportunities when they arise.

The growth of hedge funds has been remarkable. This growth has been fueled by their exceptional profitability. Figure 2.5 presents the number of hedge funds and their total assets. Hedge fund assets were up by 17 percent in 2004, which is roughly on par with their growth since the late 1980s. Today, hedge funds have more than $1 trillion in assets and are responsible for half of all trades in U.S. and British stock markets. While their returns and growth have been remarkable, it has been their focus on short selling that has gained them much of their notoriety, because hedge funds typically do well when asset prices are falling and other investment funds are doing badly. Dr. Mahathir Mohamad, former Prime Minister of Malaysia, has referred to hedge funds as the "highwaymen of the global economy." This is because of their penchant, in his opinion, for robbing from the poor, in this case from the less developed and emerging economies with more volatile financial markets where hedge funds do much of their business.

In fact, hedge funds have been blamed not just for taking advantage of economic crises, but for creating them in the first place. The most cited example of such an event was the European Monetary System crisis in 1992. The European Monetary System was a system of fixed exchange rates that predated the European Monetary Union. In 1992, George Soros, manager of the Quantum hedge fund, realized

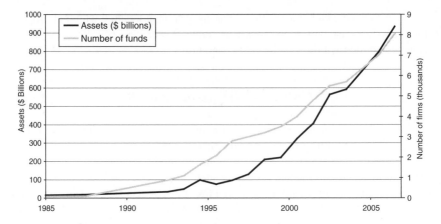

Figure 2.5
Hedge Fund Assets versus Number of Hedge Funds.
Source: The Hedge Fund Association at http://www.thehfa.org/pressreleases.cfm.

that because of looser monetary and fiscal policies, interest rates in Britain were unsustainably lower than those in Germany. The result was a profit opportunity for investors to borrow money in Britain, sell their pounds for deutschemarks, then invest these funds in Germany. Soros also realized that this situation could not last and that if enough people began selling pounds and buying deutschemarks, Britain would eventually have to devalue the pound. Before this happened, Soros bet heavily against the pound by short selling British assets, while at the same time writing public editorials that the pound was unsustainably overvalued. In essence, he was actively encouraging flight from the pound from which he stood to benefit. In the end, investors fled the pound, Britain was forced to devalue, and Soros made more than $1 billion. Many applauded Soros as someone who represents the best of capitalism: someone who was more astute and aggressive than his competitors. But others, including members of the British government, viewed this episode as a manufactured crisis that would never had taken place if Soros and other investment funds had not manipulated markets and sparked panic. Similar (though unsubstantiated) charges were made against hedge funds and Soros during the East Asian crisis, which is discussed in more detail later in Chapter 9.

Things do not always work out so profitably for hedge funds, however, and because of their riskiness, when things go bad, they go very bad. The best example of this was the collapse of one of the best-known hedge funds, Long Term Capital Management (LTCM), the directors of which included two Nobel Prize winning economists, Myron Scholes and Robert Merton. In 1997, LTCM had heavily invested in Russian bonds and sold short U.S. T-bonds on a bet that the interest rate difference between the two, or the *spread*, was too large and would narrow over time. Instead, a financial crisis struck Russia in August of 1998 and the spread between Russian bonds and T-bonds actually increased, resulting in huge losses suffered by LTCM. By September of 1998, LTCM was facing the fact that they would have to liquidate their $80 billion asset portfolio in order to make payments to their creditors. Many market watchers became worried that this massive sell-off could drive down asset prices and spark a financial panic across the globe, particularly because many of the investors in LTCM were large U.S. banks that would have suffered significant losses, maybe critically large, by losing their LTCM stakes. Thus, there was the potential that the collapse of LTCM could have had ripple effects that would significantly disrupt financial markets and international banking systems across the globe. In the end, the Federal Reserve helped negotiate a rescue plan in which LTCM's debts were restructured in return for an additional $3.6 billion infusion of funds from LTCM's investors. LTCM did eventually liquidate its assets and it no longer exists today. A crisis was averted, but not without significant losses to investors and significant risk to the financial system as a whole. (More on LTCM in Chapter 9, which discusses currency crises and contagion.)

Numerous questions about hedge funds remain. Do such large, unregulated investment institutions really encourage more and more efficient financial intermediation? Or are they a sign of how modern finance has become self-predatory, creating a suicidal and inherently unstable form of capitalism? And should governments attempt to more strictly regulate hedge funds before the next crisis occurs? These questions will become more pressing as smaller investors begin to participate in hedge fund finance. *Fund of funds* institutions, which are mutual funds that hold stakes in a variety of hedge funds, are beginning to offer smaller investors the chance to participate in the hedge funds sector in a way that allows for more diversification (but still potentially very risky).

Conclusions

Over the last 25 years, financial systems in industrialized and emerging economies have expanded faster than their economies as a whole. There are a number of factors that have contributed to this remarkable growth. First, information technology has improved the quantity and quality of information, which is the most crucial input into financial transactions. Also, as discussed in more detail later in this book, many governments have acted to deregulate and liberalize their financial markets, creating growth and innovation in financial systems that was previously impossible. In addition, the maturity of central banking has helped stabilize financial systems and have improved the efficiency of financial intermediation. Finally, helped in part by these first three factors, no other sector has taken such advantage of the new openness between countries that began after the fall of the Berlin

Wall in 1989 and the end of the Cold War. When people talk about globalization today, they are in large part talking about the ways that financial systems across the globe have become increasingly integrated. While there have been other eras during which large amounts of capital flowed between countries, this most recent era is distinctive because inflows and outflows are largely based upon the flow of information and the maintenance of confidence. More importantly, this era is distinctive because capital is flowing to a broader range of countries, including both the poor and the rich, and to a broader array of sectors within these economies, making its potential impact on growth much larger.

Financial development has taken place to such an extent that it is safe to say that many modern economies have become "financialized," meaning that their mechanisms, their growth, and their fluctuations are increasingly determined by the workings of their financial systems. While the growth benefits of this incredible financial development are clear, many of its potential costs are not as clear. One of the most common critiques of modern finance is the possibility (some would say probability) that financial development, particularly international capital flows, makes financial systems and economies more volatile. The result would be more frequent and severe recessions and even depressions. In order to understand the impact of finance on business cycles more thoroughly, it is important to take a thoughtful look at macroeconomic theory, which has had quite a bit to say about the workings of financial systems and their role in creating economic instability. This is where the next section of this book takes us.

PART II

MACROECONOMIC THEORY AND THE ROLE OF FINANCE

CHAPTER 3

Business Cycles and Early Macroeconomic Theories of Finance

Introduction

The study of macroeconomics is closely linked to the study of business cycles; in fact, the schism between macroeconomics and microeconomics first took place during the 1930s as economists struggled to explain the events now known as the Great Depression. Business cycles have garnered much attention from macroeconomists for two reasons. First, business cycles are costly. Recessions not only mean lost income, but they are also associated with higher suicide and homicide rates, higher crime rates, higher divorce rates, and declines in other measures of societal well-being. In addition to their short-term costs, economic contractions undermine the public's commitment to economic liberalism and possibly even to capitalism and democracy. Because of these costs, policies that can reduce macroeconomic volatility have the potential to enormously improve human welfare.

The other reason why business cycles receive so much attention from economists is that recessions and depressions come as close as macroeconomists can get to an economic experiment. During contractions, market functions begin to break down and, much like any piece of machinery, it is often easier to identify exactly how underlying mechanisms operate when they are not functioning properly than when they are. As a result, recessions and depression present unique learning opportunities for economists, offering them the chance to "peek under the hood" of an economy.

Financial volatility has always been associated with economic volatility, making the study of financial systems an integral component of the study of macroeconomics. Why are these two phenomena related? Does financial instability lead to recessions and depressions, or does economic volatility weaken financial systems, making them unstable? And if it is financial instability that is driving economic volatility, what is the process by which this occurs? To answer these questions, we have to develop a theory of how financial systems and macroeconomics operate. Without a theory, not only are we forced to guess about how business cycles work, but we also have no idea about what clues to look for that can help us determine their causes. In the words of Albert Einstein: "It is the theory which decides what we can observe" (Heisenberg (1971).

The purpose of this chapter is twofold. The first objective is to introduce the reader to some of the basic concepts and facts regarding business cycles. Included will be a case study of some of the empirical regularities (and irregularities) of business cycles in the U.S. and across countries, as well as a review of some of the financial variables that are the most closely watched indicators of future changes in economic activity.

The second purpose of this chapter is to review some of the first macroeconomic theories of business cycles. This includes a discussion of early monetary theories, the Classical model, and the Debt-Deflation model. These early theories are simple and focus on a single factor that drives business cycles. However, they point to factors that are potentially important elements of a more comprehensive explanation of business cycles. In fact, many of the elements that are highlighted in these early models reemerge as crucial components of modern financial macroeconomic theories of economic volatility.

Business Cycle Definitions

A *recession* is defined by economists as two or more consecutive quarters of negative GDP growth, while an *expansion* is two or more consecutive quarters of positive GDP growth. The *peak of an expansion* is the point in time at which the level of GDP reaches its maximum before a decline begins; thus, the peak of an expansion is the beginning of a recession. The *trough of a recession* is the point in time at which GDP reaches its lowest level before it begins to rise again; troughs mark the beginning of an expansion.

One problem with this working definition of a recession is that by defining a recession as a period in which growth is negative, it ignores periods in which growth is below trend but still slightly positive. These episodes are referred to as *growth recessions*, and while they are usually regarded as recessions by the public, they are not technically regarded as such by economists.

Table 3.1 presents a complete list of business cycles (measured peak to peak) in the U.S. and dated by the National Bureau of Economic Research (NBER), an economic research institution that is responsible for dating economic contractions and expansions. Looking at the postwar era, there have been ten recessions, the most recent beginning in April of 2001 and ending in November of that same year. This recession followed the longest expansion in U.S. history, which lasted more than 10 years from March 1991 to April 2001.

Table 3.1 Timing of U.S. Business Cycles

		Duration (in months) of		
Trough	Peak	Contraction	Expansion	Business Cycle
12/1854	06/1857		30	
12/1858	10/1860	18	22	40
06/1861	04/1865	8	46	54
12/1867	06/1869	32	18	50
12/1870	10/1873	18	34	52
03/1879	03/1882	65	36	101
05/1885	03/1887	38	22	60
04/1888	07/1890	13	27	40
05/1891	01/1893	10	20	30
06/1894	12/1895	17	18	35
06/1897	06/1899	18	24	42
12/1900	09/1902	18	21	39
08/1904	05/1907	23	33	56
06/1908	01/1910	13	19	32
01/1912	01/1913	24	12	36
12/1914	08/1918	23	44	67
03/1919	01/1920	7	10	17
07/1921	05/1923	18	22	40
07/1924	10/1926	14	27	41
11/1927	08/1929	13	21	34
03/1933	05/1937	43	50	93
06/1938	02/1945	13	80	93
10/1945	11/1948	8	37	45
10/1949	07/1953	11	45	56
05/1954	08/1957	10	39	49
04/1958	04/1960	8	24	32
02/1961	12/1969	10	106	116
11/1970	11/1973	11	36	47
03/1975	01/1980	16	58	74
07/1980	07/1981	6	12	18
11/1982	07/1990	16	92	108
03/1991	04/2001	8	120	128
11/2001		8		
		Averages length (in months)		
1854–2001 (32 cycles)		17	38	56
1854–1919 (16 cycles)		22	27	49
1919–1945 (6 cycles)		18	35	53
1945–2001 (10 cycles)		10	57	67

Source: National Bureau of Economic Research, www.nber.org/cycles.html.

A few other concepts and definitions are useful when characterizing the qualitative aspects of business cycles. A *procyclical* variable is a variable that has a positive correlation with GDP over the business cycle. Examples of procyclical variables include consumption, investment, and employment, each of which consistently rises as GDP rises and falls when GDP falls. A variable is referred to as *countercyclical* if it rises when GDP falls, such as unemployment or bankruptcy rates. An *acyclical* variable is one that has no consistent statistical correlation with changes in GDP.

Some variables are so consistently correlated with output that peaks and troughs in their movements can signal peaks and troughs in the movements of GDP. A *leading indicator* is a variable that peaks (troughs) before GDP peaks (troughs), while a *lagging indicator* is a variable that peaks (troughs) after GDP peaks (troughs). A *coincident indicator* is a variable that peaks and troughs at approximately the same time as GDP.

CASE STUDY: The Basic Facts of Business Cycles

Books have been filled with data and details about business cycles, but three important facts are crucial to understanding the behavior of business cycles both in the U.S. and internationally.

First, business cycles are not uniform. The word cycle implies a regular, symmetric process, which is not true of expansions and recessions. Business cycles vary considerably in terms of both their size and their duration. Referring back to Table 3.1, it is clear that recessionary episodes in the U.S. vary considerably in terms of their lengths. For example, the 1980 recession was the shortest contraction, which lasted only 6 months. It was quickly followed by the shortest expansion in U.S. history, which lasted only 12 months. The Great Depression, however, lasted 43 months, and the 1990s expansion lasted 120 months. Clearly, the length of past business cycles is not a reliable indicator of the length of future business cycles.

Business cycles are also not symmetrical. In the U.S., the average expansion is more than twice as long as the average recession. Figure 3.1 presents international data on the average length of expansions and recessions for a selection of industrialized countries. While there is considerable variation in the length of business cycles across countries, expansions last significantly longer than recessions across all of these countries.

On the other hand, recessions tend to be associated with much sharper changes in output than expansions. Figure 3.2 presents international data on the percentage change in industrial production during recessions and expansions. Here, there is more variability across countries, with a few countries having slightly larger output movements during expansions. However, it is typically the case that contractions

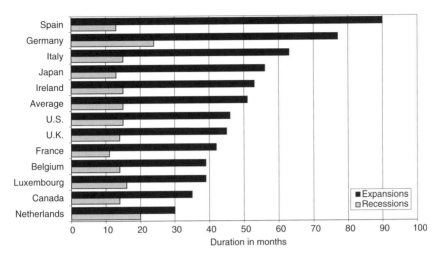

Figure 3.1
Average Duration of Expansions and Recessions, 1961–1993.
Source: Artis, Kontolemis, and Osborn, 1997.

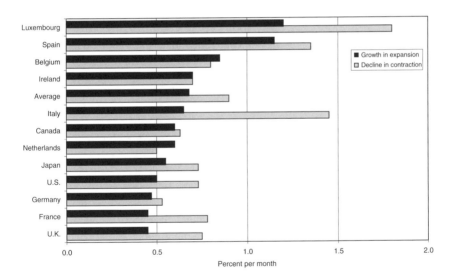

Figure 3.2
Monthly Percentage Increases and Decreases in Industrial Production Over the Business Cycle, 1961–1993.
Source: Artis, Kontolemis, and Osborn, 1997.

involve larger swings in production, and in some countries this difference is quite significant.

Second, business cycles in the U.S. and in other industrialized countries have changed over time, primarily because recessions have become less frequent. While historical macroeconomic data is difficult to obtain and often unreliable, the best analysis of historical business cycle data suggests that the output fluctuations associated with recessions are somewhat smaller than they were in the period before World War I: in the case of the U.S., roughly 20 percent smaller. In addition, recessions have also become shorter and less common. As can be seen from the bottom of Table 3.1, recessions were 8 months shorter over the 1945–2001 period than in any previous period, while expansions were 22 months longer. Longer expansions mean that recessions are less frequent. This observation has been referred to as duration stabilization and has been largely driven by two long expansions that took place between 1982 and 2001. In Chapter 7, questions regarding the ways that business cycles have changed over time will be revisited and examined in more detail, including a closer look at the role that financial development and improved public policies have possibly played in stabilizing the U.S. economy.

Third, far and away, the most volatile components of GDP are durables consumption and investment. Durables comprise only 8 percent of U.S. GDP, but according to David Romer (2001) account for nearly 16 percent of the changes in GDP during recessions. Durables are also a coincident indicator of peaks and troughs.

The three components of investment (residential, fixed nonresidential, and inventories) account for 16 percent of GDP on average, but account for 75 percent of changes in GDP during recessions. Changes in inventory alone account for 40 percent of these changes in GDP and are a leading indicator of GDP.

Financial Indicators of Business Cycles

Given the incredible volatility of durable consumption and investment, any plausible theory of business cycles has to explain why these components of GDP are so volatile. This is one of the primary reasons why financial systems have historically played such an important role in business cycle theory. One of the ways that durables and investment are different from other goods is that they are long-lived and provide benefits that incur over time, not just in the here and now. In addition, durables and investment tend to be large-ticket items. Both of these facts together mean that the funds used to obtain durables and investment goods are often obtained through financial intermediation. Thus, understanding how financial systems work is crucial to understanding the behavior of durables, investment, and aggregate output.

As evidence of how important financial indicators are to changes in business cycles, all of the major economic forecasting models include numerous variables that attempt to measure current and future financial conditions. The *Index of Leading Indicators*, which is comprised of ten of the most important and reliable leading economic indicators, is also heavily weighted with financial variables. Three of the ten leading indicators—the interest rate spread, the money supply, and stock prices—are clear indicators of financial conditions in financial markets and the banking system. Three other leading indicators—manufacturers' new orders for capital, manufacturers' orders for materials, and housing starts—are extremely sensitive to changes in financial conditions.

Let us look at the three financial leading indicators in the U.S. in more detail, beginning with the money supply. The money supply measure used in the Index of Leading Indicators is M2, which is strongly procyclical and a leading indicator. Procyclical movements in the money supply could reflect two different scenarios: either the central bank is actively expanding the money supply in order to spark an expansion, or the money supply is responding endogenously to increases in economic activity. These two scenarios are not mutually exclusive, but which of them is the most important explanation of why the money supply is so strongly procyclical is a matter of intense debate among economists; this is a debate that we will return to later.

The stock market is the most widely tracked financial indicator, not just by economists using the Index of Leading Indicators but by the public as well. Stock prices, as measured by broad stock indices such as the S&P 500 index, are strongly procyclical and a leading indicator. The problem with using stocks as an economic indicator, however, can be seen in Figure 3.3. Stock price volatility dwarfs the volatility of GDP. As a result, changes in stock prices generate a lot of false signals about future changes in output.

The final financial leading indicator is the interest rate spread. Both short-term and long-term interest rates are procyclical. There are a large number of interest rates that can be tracked, however, and some of them are more reliable indicators than others. Among the most reliable is the 3-month T-bill which has fallen during 10 of the last 11 recessions. Long-term interest rates typically move less reliably over the business cycle, which is problematic because these are the interest rates that have the most direct impact on investment decisions.

Both long-term and short-term interest rates also tend to be lagging indicators of turning points. The interest rate spread, however, is a leading indicator. This spread is calculated as the difference between the interest rate on 10-year T-bonds and the *federal funds rate*, which is the interest rate on overnight loans between banks. Thus, this interest rate spread measures the difference between long-term interest rates and short-term interest rates. There are two potential explanations for why this spread tends to increase before an expansion. First, the difference between long-term and short-term interest rates increases at the beginning of expansions as investment demand begins to pick up in anticipation of better economic conditions, but banks remain reluctant to lend. This increases the premium that must be paid to borrow long-term. The second explanation for why this spread increases before

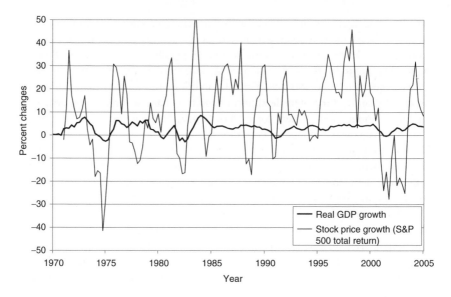

Figure 3.3
Volatility of GDP and Stock Prices in the U.S.

expansions is that monetary policy is a procyclical leading indicator of economic activity. As the money supply increases, short-term interest rates (particularly the federal funds rate) are driven lower while long-term interest rates remain constant or potentially increase in anticipation of higher future inflation.

The Sunspot Theory

One of the first theories regarding the causes of business cycles was proposed by W.S. Jevons (1884), who hypothesized that low sunspot activity on the surface of the sun diminished plant growth, reducing agricultural output (a hypothesis that has since been proved wrong by botanists) and aggregate output. Jevons believed that cyclical movements in sunspot activity drove business cycles. To support this claim, Jevons presented statistical evidence that business cycles lasted on average 10.43 years, from peak to peak, while sunspot cycles lasted an average of 10.45 years.

Unfortunately, there was a problem with Jevons' hypothesis. Later, new scientific evidence was presented that indicated that sunspot cycles actually lasted 11 years, seemingly disproving Jevons' theory. However, Jevons attempted to salvage his theory by positing that because his theory was so well known by farmers, they changed their planting behavior in anticipation of changes in sunspot activity, breaking the link between actual sunspot behavior and real economic activity.

At first glance, this episode hardly seems to amount to a great moment in the history of economics. On closer inspection, however, it is a seminal moment in the study of business cycles because Jevons was the first to suggest that business cycles can be *self-fulfilling*, or that the anticipation of future changes in economic activity can lead to changes in current behavior, which ensures that what is expected to happen actually does happen. This insight has become an important component of many modern macroeconomic theories, particularly those that emphasize the role of financial systems. Although Jevons' original theory has nothing to do with the behavior of financial systems, his idea that cyclical movements can be driven by self-fulfilling expectations later becomes an influential explanation of lending booms and busts as well as asset bubbles and crashes.

Early Monetary Theories

Before the Great Depression, most countries in the world were on the *gold standard*, an international monetary system which required that paper currency in circulation be backed by a fixed amount of gold held by the government. Under the gold standard, a country's gold holdings placed an upper limit on the quantity of money that could circulate in the economy. In addition, adherence to the gold standard meant that a country's money supply would fluctuate with its trade balance. Countries that were experiencing trade surpluses would enjoy gold inflows to pay for this surplus and could expand their money supply. On the other hand, countries that were experiencing trade deficits suffered from gold outflows and were forced to reduce their money supply.

Before Adam Smith, there was a general acceptance of the idea that the best way to promote the wealth and the power of nations was to increase their holdings of gold. This theory, referred to as *Mercantilism*, was based on the idea that gold determined the money supply and that the money supply determined the total value of trade and output within an economy. Accordingly, countries routinely engaged in policies that actively discouraged imports and encouraged exports in an attempt to generate large trade surpluses and gold inflows, believing that these actions by themselves would make them rich. Thus, Mercantilists viewed economic growth as a zero-sum game: a country could only get rich by running a trade surplus at the expense of their trade partners, requiring them to run trade deficits and get poorer.

Regarding business cycles, Mercantilists believed that maintaining stable growth in gold reserves was the key to maintaining stable output growth. Expansions were created when countries were able to establish the proper trade policies that generated trade surpluses: quotas, tariffs, subsidies, and taxes as well as foreign policies that ensured open foreign markets for their exports. On the other hand, recessions occurred when countries bought too many imports, ran trade deficits, and suffered from gold outflows and falling money supplies.

While Mercantilism placed its primary emphasis on monetary factors as being responsible for business cycles, the financial system itself played little role in this theory. A principal reason for this is that Mercantilists viewed the money supply very narrowly, as simply the total amount of currency and coins either in gold or backed by gold. Mercantilists believed that other financial assets played no role in determining the level of financial intermediation and economic activity. While unrealistically simplistic, the Mercantilist emphasis on the role of the money supply in determining economic volatility anticipates modern business cycle theories such as the Monetarist model (Chapter 4).

Ralph George Hawtrey (1913) developed a theory of business cycles that emphasized the role of financial systems while still adopting the Mercantilist position that changes in the trade balance drive business cycles. Hawtrey hypothesized that changes in the level of financial intermediation, particularly bank credit, fluctuate with the money supply and, under the gold standard, would also fluctuate with a country's trade balance. He argued that these changes in the supply of credit create fluctuations in investment and consumption that create business cycles.

Hawtrey believed that recessions begin when a country starts to run a trade deficit. As gold reserves fall, countries are forced to reduce their money supply. As opposed to the Mercantilists, who believed that reductions in the money supply directly reduce economic activity, Hawtrey believed that falls in the money supply are important because it reduces bank reserves and restricts the supply of bank credit. As financing becomes more difficult to obtain, firms are forced to reduce their investment levels and households are forced to reduce consumption. This reduces output and creates a recession. However, this recession does not last forever. As output falls, so too does a country's demand for imports. Eventually, the trade deficit disappears and turns into a trade surplus, leading to expansions in gold reserves, the money supply, credit, investment, consumption, and output. This expansion begins to increase the demand for imports and the whole process repeats itself. Thus, business cycles in Hawtrey's model are *endogenous*, or internally self-generating, and not the result of *exogenous*, or external, shocks.

On the basis of this theory, Hawtrey's prescription to end business cycles was simple: break the link between trade balances and financial intermediation by abandoning the gold standard. Of course, the gold standard was abandoned after World War II, yet business cycles have persisted, undermining Hawtrey's arguments. However, Hawtrey's emphasis on the role of changes in the supply of credit in generating macroeconomic fluctuations later proves to be influential in many modern business cycle and financial theories.

One final monetary theory was developed by Knut Wicksell (1936). Wicksell focused on how changes in the money supply lead to changes in interest rates that affect the level of financial intermediation and investment. In his model, reductions in the money supply drive up interest rates above the level required for savings to equal investment. This leads to a reduction in the quantity of investment demanded and a fall in output. By highlighting the role that the money supply plays in determining interest rates, this theory is another precursor to modern macroeconomic theories in which monetary policy plays a central role in creating economic instability.

The Classical Model

The Classical model is not a model in which financial systems play an important role in explaining either long-run growth or the causes of business cycles. However, its influence on economic history, the development of macroeconomic theory, and even economic policy today makes it impossible to have any reasonable understanding of modern macroeconomics and financial systems without first understanding the principles of Classical theory.

The fundamentals of the Classical model were laid out in the book that birthed the discipline of economics: Adam Smith's (1776) *An Inquiry into the Nature and Causes of the Wealth of Nations*. The Classical model was later refined by many of the founding fathers of economics, including David Ricardo, Jean-Baptiste Say, and John Stuart Mill.

The Classical model is based on three fundamental assumptions:

Perfect competition exists in all markets
This means that all firms are price takers, wages and prices are perfectly flexible, and perfect information exists about economic conditions. Perfectly competitive markets in which prices instantly adjust and markets always clear mean that when individuals act in their own self-interest, markets are efficient and societal welfare is maximized without the need of any administrator. This is what Smith meant by his use of the phrase "the invisible hand of the marketplace."

The economy is populated by representative agents, or individuals, who have the same preferences and act alike in every way
Combined with the assumption of perfect competition, the assumption of representative agents mean that macroeconomic behavior is determined by simply summing up the behavior of individuals. As a result, there is no real distinction in the Classical model between microeconomic behavior and macroeconomic behavior.

Real values and not nominal values are used when making economic decisions
In other words, individuals do not suffer from money illusion and are not fooled by changes in the price level alone into changing their behavior. Together, these three assumptions mean that changes in the money supply only affect prices and nominal variables; they do not have any impact on real variables. This classical principle

is referred to as *money neutrality* and implies that monetary policy determines the level of inflation, but plays no role in determining real economic activity and aggregate output.

In the Classical model, aggregate output is a function of three factors: the total quantity of capital, the total quantity of labor, and the aggregate productivity level of the economy. Aggregate output is completely determined by an economy's ability to produce goods, or by aggregate supply. The level of output that is consistent with the full employment of all of an economy's resources is referred to as the *natural rate of output*.

According to Classical economists, prices and aggregate demand adjusts to whatever the level of aggregate supply is so that markets always clear and output is always at the natural rate of output. In what is known as *Say's Law*, Jean Baptiste-Say argued that, "supply creates its own demand." Aggregate demand only influences the price level within an economy, and it has no impact on any of the real variables that determine welfare. As a result, aggregate demand is of minor consequence and standards of living are entirely determined by an economy's productive capacity.

If only changes in labor, capital, or productivity lead to changes in aggregate output, what are the potential sources of changes in these inputs? Classical economists believe that government policy plays a large role in shaping the incentives to acquire these three factors.

Regarding labor, the supply of labor changes with fluctuations in population (such as changes in immigration law). Taxes and government regulations affect both the incentives to work and the supply for labor. Taxes and regulation also affect the incentives for firms to hire new workers and the demand for labor. Policies that increase the supply and/or demand for labor increase the quantity of labor and aggregate output.

Taxes and regulations on firms also affect incentives to engage in investment, changing the demand for capital. They affect the attractiveness of savings, changing the supply of loanable funds that can be used to finance new capital and the price of financial intermediation. Policies that increase savings or the demand for investment lead to increases in the quantity of capital and aggregate output.

Finally, governments also play an important role in shaping *productivity*, or the efficiency in which capital and labor are used to produce output. Governments encourage new technologies through subsidizing education and through funding research and development projects. New technologies not only make existing capital and labor more productive, but also create incentives for firms to acquire more of these inputs. Governments can also shape aggregate productivity through the provision of infrastructure (roads, bridges, legal systems, law enforcement) and by ensuring access to natural resources (energy, water). Government policies that spur aggregate productivity lead to increases in aggregate output.

Finally, governments can encourage entrepreneurship by establishing property rights through the creation and enforcement of commercial law.

In the Classical model, there are a limited number of positive activities government should engage in, such as promoting aggregate productivity through education, research and development, and infrastructure. The government's role in the economy is primarily a negative one. Through its power to tax and regulate, governments are likely to reduce the incentives to hire and provide labor as well as the incentives to save and invest. Classical economists believe that governments are largely responsible for business cycles by enacting the policies that generate them. When governments reorientate their policies in a manner that favors the enhancement of capital, labor, and productivity, then productive capacity and aggregate supply increase, aggregate output rises, and expansions occur. On the other hand, when governments impose taxes and regulations that reduce the incentives to expand productive capacity, aggregate output shrinks, and recessions occur. Hence, the governing philosophy pushed by the Classical model and its adherents is one of *laissez-faire*, or "hands-off." The best government is the government that plays the smallest role in the macroeconomy. This conclusion is the direct result of the fundamental assumption in the Classical model that markets are perfectly competitive. As such, they work efficiently and maximize welfare and output if left alone. Any attempt to manipulate markets in an attempt to promote equity or some other objective has negative consequences that outweigh their potential benefits.

In the brief summary of the Classical model just presented, there was no discussion of financial markets, financial institutions, or the importance of financial intermediation in general. There are a number of reasons for this, all of them reflecting Classical economists' lack of interest in financial systems. First, the role of money in the Classical model is exclusively that of a medium of exchange. In other words, money is only used to facilitate trade, not as a financial asset. As a result, the Classical model ignores the importance of money in influencing financial intermediation, interest rates, and the level of credit in an economy, as well as how each of these factors potentially affects economic output.

Another important aspect of financial intermediation that the Classical model ignores is the problem of asymmetric and imperfect information. By assuming perfect information, the Classical model assumes away many of the problems associated with financial intermediation, essentially presuming that financial transactions are the same as any other economic transactions. By ignoring these complexities, the Classical model ignores many of the ways that financial systems fail to operate efficiently. Thus, Classical economists never considered the positive roles that governments can potentially play in minimizing market failure and enhancing economic efficiency.

Finally, the Classical model assumes that those who have funds to lend are immediately matched up with those who want to borrow, although there is no real discussion in the model of exactly how this process takes place. In the Classical model, finance is finance, and it is efficient whether it takes place directly through financial markets or indirectly through banks and other financial intermediaries. In fact, in a Nobel Prize winning paper, Modigliani and Miller (1958) show that in a Classical model with perfectly competitive financial markets, the financial structure of firms, including their decisions to finance their operations using debt versus using equity, is irrelevant. This conclusion that both the process and the form of financial intermediation are immaterial to economic activity appears to directly contradict behavior in the real world. The argument that, for example, there is no difference between bond and stock financing is certainly no argument that any CEOs who want to keep their job would ever make in front of their stockholders.

The Debt-Deflation Theory

The last of the early macroeconomic theories that is discussed here was developed specifically to explain the Great Depression. In 1929, just days before the October stock market crash, Irving Fisher, a well-known economist and wealthy entrepreneur (inventor of the Rolodex), pronounced that stocks had reached a permanently high level from which they would never retreat. Over the next few weeks, the stock market collapsed and Fisher proceeded to lose most of his fortune. Fisher devoted himself to figuring out what went wrong. His hypothesis, described in Fisher (1933), became known as the Debt-Deflation theory.

Fisher lays the blame for business cycles entirely on financial systems; specifically, volatile lending and borrowing behavior. In Fisher's opinion, recessions begin during economic expansions. Lending booms typically accompany expansions, leading to a buildup in debt levels. As debt levels get larger, firms and households become more financially fragile and begin to worry about being able to meet their debt payments. At this point, a negative external shock, such as a drop in profits or a decrease in the money supply that puts upward pressure on interest rates, can significantly change market perceptions. This leads many market participants, particularly those who are the most highly indebted, to begin selling their assets. As others in the market begin to observe this selling, they begin to dump their assets as well and the panic selling of assets begins in earnest.

The farther asset prices drop, the worse the financial conditions of indebted firms and households become because the nominal value of their debt is fixed. Most debt contracts are not *indexed*, meaning that there are no clauses that allow the nominal value of the amount owed to adjust up and down with the aggregate price level or the value of other assets. As a result, the panic selling of assets reduces the real value of assets relative to fixed value of debt. This puts a severe strain on indebted firms and households, leading to even more panic selling and further financial deterioration. Eventually, many firms and households will become insolvent. Insolvency leads to widespread bankruptcies, which increases the number of bad loans held by lenders. As bad loans increase, the financial position of lenders deteriorate even more. Lenders are then forced to restrict the supply of loanable funds even further, potentially to the point of completely halting in financial intermediation. Without financial intermediation, investment and consumption fall precipitously, firms are forced to cut production, and a recession (or potentially a depression) occurs.

This recession will end eventually, but only after a significant recovery period. Eventually, asset prices will bottom out, financial positions will solidify, bankruptcies will stabilize, and lending will resume. However, such a process could take a very long period of time. Fisher argued that a better solution is to prevent financial collapse in the first place through the aggressive use of monetary policy during the initial phase of a contraction, using injections of money to try and stabilize asset prices and lending before things spin out of control.

Two aspects of this theory are worth expanding upon. First, Fisher believed that market participants naturally tend to overreact to market conditions, whether good or bad. During expansions, lenders tend to provide loans too easily and borrowers tend to take on too much debt, while during recessions lenders tend to pull back too much and borrowers tend to resort to panic selling too quickly. This question about how market participants formulate their expectations of the future and whether these expectations are in some sense irrational, meaning that they are not fully consistent with profit and utility maximizing behavior, later becomes one of the most important questions in modern macroeconomic and financial theory.

The other aspect of the Debt-Deflation theory that deserves particular attention is Fisher's insights into the potentially negative effects of deflation. Deflation, either in the form of decreases in the aggregate price level or in the form of asset deflation caused by panic selling, is exceptionally costly because nominal debt contracts are fixed. Deflation occurred during the Great Depression as well as during a number of other economic contractions in the U.S. and European history. Fisher's theory was the first to explain the potential relationship between deflation and economic downturns. However, the relationship between deflation and aggregate output is not necessarily consistent across countries or time. During periods of high debt or in highly indebted countries, small reductions in the aggregate price level can lead to large, discontinuous drops in aggregate output. On the other hand, during less indebted periods or in less indebted countries, small amounts of deflation may have little noticeable effect on the financial system and the economy.

Deflation can also be costly in ways not identified by Fisher. For example, deflation can lead to *disintermediation*, or the withdrawal of deposits from banks, because interest rates cannot fall significantly below zero. In a world of deflation and zero interest rates, people have little incentive to save their money in banks or in other financial instruments, usually preferring to hold their wealth as money. Zero interest rates also potentially reduce the ability of the central bank to use monetary policy to stimulate the economy because expansionary monetary policy cannot drive interest rates any lower (more on this in Chapter 7 when stabilization policy is discussed in more detail).

Fisher's Debt-Deflation theory, which emphasizes the macroeconomic importance of financial volatility, shares a number of important features with Keynes' general theory, discussed in the next chapter. In addition, the focus on the macroeconomic impact of indebtedness and the fragility of the balance sheets of firms and households later becomes the cornerstone of a group of modern macroeconomic theories known as New Institutional Theories of Finance (Chapters 5 and 6). The Debt-Deflation theory also provides important insight into modern economic crises such as the Great Recession in Japan (Chapter 8) and the East Asian Crisis (Chapter 9).

Conclusions

Because of their sizeable costs, one of the primary objectives of macroeconomic research over the last 80 years has been to understand business cycles so that they can be prevented in the future. Economists have tried to develop a theory of business cycles that fit the empirical facts as they are understood. Early macroeconomic theories identified various potential factors, many of them financial, which played important roles in generating business cycles: changes in the money supply, changes in the demand and supply of credit, volatile expectations, changes in taxes and government regulation, high levels of indebtedness, panic selling, and nominal debt contracts. However, none of the theories discussed in this chapter could be called a true macroeconomic model because each of these early theories narrowly focused on only one aspect of the economy or, as in the case of the Classical model, made no distinction between microeconomic and macroeconomic behavior.

It was left to later theories that were developed after the Great Depression to more fully examine financial systems and business cycles within a general equilibrium framework that is truly macroeconomic in scope. We turn to these models in the next chapter, where we will see that while many of these early theories were simplistic, they laid the foundation on which modern macroeconomics and a deeper understanding of financial systems are built.

CHAPTER 4

Keynesian, Monetarist, and Neoclassical Theories

Introduction

The Great Depression was truly a seminal event in the study of macroeconomics. During the Depression, unemployment rose to 25 percent. Income fell by an incredible 50 percent and did not return to 1929 levels until 1936. An event this cataclysmic demanded an explanation, and economists at the time had a very difficult time providing one. Formulating a coherent account of what caused the Great Depression and how to prevent another one from occurring became the principal focus of macroeconomic research for the next three decades.

Before the Great Depression, the study of economics primarily dealt with microeconomic issues; the study of macroeconomics, as exemplified by the Classical model, was really just the study of microeconomics with larger quantities. The Great Depression, however, convinced many that macroeconomics do not behave just like individual markets. These critics argued that early macroeconomic theories such as the Classical model fell into the logical trap known as the *fallacy of composition*: what is true for an individual is not necessarily true for an entire group. For example, if you study harder and your professor grades on a curve, you are likely to get a better grade. But if the entire class studies harder and your professor grades on the curve, nobody does any better. Likewise, while it might be possible for an individual to work harder in order to get themselves through hard economic times, could it also be the case that everyone working harder would not be enough to get an economy out of a depression?

Financial collapse played a large role in the Great Depression. Not only did stock values fall by 85 percent from their October 1929 peak, but real estate and other financial assets plummeted as well. In addition, nearly 25 percent of all banks failed—more than 10,000 banks in all. Bankruptcies reached record rates, while investment in new capital dropped to almost nothing. The fact that this financial collapse was even more severe than the Depression itself and preceded the falls in aggregate output presents a persuasive prima facie case in support of the argument that financial systems were the crucial factor in this macroeconomic disintegration.

The primary purpose of this chapter is to review five major groups of post-Depression macroeconomic theories: the Keynes' General Theory, Keynesian theory as represented by the IS–LM model, the post-Keynesian Financial Instability Hypothesis model, the Monetarist model, and Neoclassical models (including the Rational Expectations and Real Business Cycle models). Persistent disequilibrium in financial systems played a primary role in Keynes' General Theory. However, the importance of financial systems was later discounted by Keynesians as their focus shifted to equilibrium analysis using the IS–LM model. As Keynesians gained power within the study of macroeconomics, adherents of Keynes who believed in the primacy of finance (known as post-Keynesians), were marginalized within the macroeconomics discipline as a whole. As a result, post-Keynesian theories such as Hyman Minsky's Financial Instability Hypothesis received little attention from most macroeconomists. This trend toward ignoring financial institutions continued in the Monetarist model, where financial systems only react passively to the unstable money growth that drives changes in economic activity. The pinnacle in this trend toward discounting finance was the Neoclassical models developed during the 1970s and early 1980s. The Rational Expectations model, where business cycles are the result of the discretionary use of monetary and fiscal policy, and Real Business Cycle models, where all markets are perfectly competitive and financial systems are always efficient, have little to say about the role of finance in macroeconomics. The end result is that by the early 1980s, financial issues were largely ignored as a source of macroeconomic volatility and received little attention in mainstream macroeconomic research.

Keynes' General Theory

In 1999, 27 prominent economists, historians, educators, political scientists, and philosophers were asked the following questions: (1) What books published this century altered the direction of our society? and (2) Which books will have the most impact on thought and action in the years ahead? The most cited book was John Maynard Keynes' *The General Theory of Employment, Interest, and Money* (1936) because of its broad influence on the study of economics, its explanations of macroeconomic volatility, and the rationale it provided for more active government involvement in the economy. Keynes's General Theory is the first model to make a real distinction between microeconomics and macroeconomics. It is also the first to take a more general equilibrium perspective on macroeconomics and look at the interaction between the goods, labor, money, and financial asset markets simultaneously.

In addition to being an economist, a classically trained pianist, a philosopher, a mathematician, a member of the Bloomsbury literary group, and an influential member of the British Treasury during World Wars I and II, Keynes was also a self-made millionaire. Keynes earned his fortune speculating in the foreign exchange market (after he nearly went bankrupt twice). Keynes' hands-on experience in financial markets deeply influenced his view of macroeconomics, which is evident by the primary role that financial systems and speculation play in his theory of business cycles.

Keynes' insights into money and financial systems are crucial aspects of what separates his theory from the Classical model. In the Classical model, money was simply a medium of exchange and only used to facilitate trade in the present time. Keynes believed that money is first and foremost a financial asset that has an attractive feature. Holding money is less risky than holding other financial assets, whose prices are subject to large fluctuations in financial markets because of uncertainty about future profitability and future default. Because it is a financial asset, money has an impact on the supply and demand for other financial assets that are substitutive means of holding wealth, such as bonds and stocks. As a result, the supply of money does not just affect the price and quantity of trade, but it also affects the level of financial intermediation, stock prices, and interest rates.

An even more important difference between Keynes' theory and the Classical model is that the Classical model largely disregards the fact that finance takes place across time. Yesterday's debt is paid with today's profits and cash flows. By ignoring this, the Classical model also ignores the fact that financial intermediation is subject to imperfect information because the future is never perfectly known. With imperfect information comes the importance of *uncertainty*, or the fact that market participants have to make a hypothesis about future economic conditions when making transactions. Keynes believed that views of the future are based upon past and current experiences but are highly subjective, meaning that views of the future are held with varying degrees of confidence across individuals. In addition, the past is not always an accurate indicator of the future. As a result, fundamental uncertainty exists, which makes speculative behavior inherent within financial transactions.

Take for instance an investor's decision to purchase a stock. The return on a stock is dependent upon what happens to its price, which, in turn, is a function of both its fundamental attributes and of how many people view the stock favorably and choose to purchase it. When uncertainty exists and it is impossible to statistically estimate the "true" value of a stock, the stocks with the highest expected returns are the ones that the most people believe will have the highest expected returns. Keynes compared buying a stock to a beauty pageant, except in this case the judges vote not on which contestant is the most attractive, but on which contestant the other judges are likely to find most attractive. The fact that the best response of an individual speculator is dependent on the actions of others can lead to a sort of *herding behavior* where if a large enough group of speculators is doing something, there is an incentive for everyone else to follow them and do it as well. Herding behavior can cause markets to overreact to new information or changes in market conditions. During good times, this can lead to asset bubbles in which people continue to buy overvalued assets, implicitly counting on the fact that there is a "greater fool" to which any asset can be sold. During bad times, herding behavior can lead to panic and financial market crashes.

Speculative behavior also affects firms' decisions to invest in capital projects. Before a project can be undertaken, decision makers must form a forecast of future returns from this project. These future returns, however, are highly dependent upon future economic conditions, which in Keynes' opinion are unknowable. If managers of firms subscribe to a pessimistic view of the economy, then it is also reasonable to believe that these managers will act accordingly and economic activity will be lower, slowing the economy and making this firm's capital projects less profitable. Thus, if managers believe that the general view of the future is low, managers will also lower their own forecasts, reducing the chances of adopting new projects. If everyone does this, then few investment projects will be adopted and the economy will in fact slowdown. Thus, views pertaining to investment projects are self-fulfilling (harkening back to the Sunspot model), making economic performance very sensitive to changes not just in what people think, but to changes in what people think other people are thinking.

Keynes used the term *animal spirits* to refer to his notion that individual views of the future are inherently speculative, subjective, unstable, sensitive to changes in market perceptions, and self-fulfilling. In his opinion, views of the future often change in ways that are completely unrelated to changes in economic fundamentals, in part not only because of a lack of information about fundamentals, but also because of changes in perceptions about just how uncertain these fundamentals change over time. This means that views of the future are subject to large and unpredictable fluctuations. It is important to note, however, that Keynes did not necessarily consider behavior driven by animal spirits to be irrational. He viewed the animal spirits behavior as a response to a world where there is true uncertainty and it is impossible to reasonably estimate the probabilities of various outcomes. In Keynes' (1937) words, uncertainty means the following: "There is no scientific basis on which to form any calculable probability. We simply do not know." Thus, Keynes viewed economic decisions not as a poker game, where agents make choices based on certain probabilities, but as a game in which the rules are constantly changing and the probabilities are incalculable.

It is the existence of uncertainty and animal spirits that are ultimately responsible for the unpredictability and instability of financial markets, investment demand, and aggregate demand. In fact, Keynes argued that uncertainty and business confidence play a larger role in investment decisions than the interest rate, which in his opinion is a relatively small factor in the overall returns from an investment project. The primary reason that uncertainty is so important in finance is through its influence on stock prices. In Keynes' opinion, stock prices play at least as large a role in the decision to undertake investment projects as interest rates. Because changes in business confidence influence both the attractiveness of investment projects and the value of stock prices, investment demand in an economy is first and foremost a function of market participant's views of the future. No manager will undertake an investment project at any interest rate if he does not anticipate a profitable economic environment in the future. An important implication of this is that there is no guarantee that optimism will be at a level that will generate enough investment to get the economy to its natural rate of output. Instead, high savings when business confidence is low will lead to excess demand and lower output, regardless of the level of interest rates.

In Keynes' General Theory, similar to the Debt-Deflation theory, recessions actually begin during expansions, when animal spirits fuel the speculative behavior that creates lending, investment, and asset booms. These booms lead to highly leveraged financial conditions that make firms and households vulnerable to a perceived slowdown in the economy. Eventually, some piece of new information—a low profit report, slower cash flows, or worries about future macroeconomic conditions—reduces confidence among a few individuals, which quickly spreads to create a widespread loss of confidence. Pessimistic views of the future and increased uncertainty lead to a reduction in investment demand. Stock prices also begin to fall, leading to additional reductions in investment spending. These falls in investment spending are further exacerbated by a *multiplier effect*, where lower investment spending reduces aggregate income, which in turn forces households to reduce their spending and firms to reduce investment, which further decreases aggregate income. As a result, even a small initial decline in confidence and investment can lead to a large fall in aggregate demand.

Because of its role in transferring changes in perceived uncertainty to the rest of the economy, the financial system plays a primary role in creating aggregate demand instability in Keynes' General Theory. This is similar to the Debt-Deflation theory, without the emphasis on nominal debt contracts, but Keynes has a much more detailed description of how fluctuations in perceptions of uncertainty affect the entire economy, not just the financial sector.

Keynes' analysis, however, is much different than that in the Classical model, where unstable aggregate demand could not affect aggregate output because wages and prices would always adjust to return the economy to the level of output that is consistent with the full employment of its resources, or the natural rate of output. Keynes rejects the Classical idea of Say's Law by arguing that imperfect competition in the labor market prevents the supply side of the economy from quickly adjusting to volatile changes in aggregate demand. Keynes argued that in a world in which each worker differs in their skill level, workers do not negotiate for one aggregate wage in a perfectly competitive labor market but instead negotiate wages individually. In such a decentralized labor market, workers do not care about what real wage clears the labor market. Instead, they are worried about receiving wages that are comparable to what workers of similar skill level are receiving. As a result, there is no guarantee that the aggregate real wage will be at the level that is needed to equate labor supply with labor demand.

During a recession in which aggregate demand and the price level are falling, real wages will begin to rise unless workers accept reductions in their nominal wages. However, workers will be reluctant to do this unless they observe that other workers are reducing their nominal wages as well. If workers refuse to take nominal wage cuts until they observe others doing so, nominal wages will not fall until there is a significant increase in unemployment. This is because unemployment is the only threat firms can use to get workers to accept wage cuts. This inability to organize behavior is known as *coordination failure*, and it is one important reason behind why wages in the labor market are not perfectly flexible, but instead are "sticky." Sticky wages play a prominent role in Keynesian explanations of unemployment. Such labor market rigidities also explain how financial instability, which works through aggregate demand, creates long-lasting periods where output remains below the natural rate of output.

Another interesting implication of the General Theory and, specifically, of Keynes' theory of investment is the *paradox of thrift*. Any exogenous increase in savings (caused by, for instance, a change in tax policy) without an increase in business confidence and investment will lead to a fall in aggregate demand and output. Falls in aggregate output reduce confidence and further reduce output, leading to an economic contraction that is eventually large and sustained enough to reduce aggregate savings. In the end, any increase in savings without a matching increase in investment and aggregate output is not possible. This implies that any sort of exogenous shock to savings, either from a change in confidence or a change in government policy, can be a potential source of business cycles.

In Keynes' theory, recessions can end in one of three ways. First, business confidence could spontaneously rise. However, there is no guarantee that confidence will automatically rebound during a recession. In fact, it is quite possible that the longer a recession lasts, the more deeply uncertainty perceptions and pessimism set in, which can further depress business confidence and magnify the size of the contraction in output.

Second, Keynes believed that wages are not fixed, only sticky. If given enough time, workers will gradually reduce their nominal wage demands as they observe other similar workers taking nominal wage cuts. This will reduce real wages and move the economy back toward full employment. As employment rebounds, macroeconomic conditions will gradually improve to the point that the financial sector and eventually confidence in business conditions begin to rebound. The problem with this "wait and see" solution, however, is that there are no assurances about how long this process will take. Given the difficulties associated with coordination failure, it could take a very long time for wages to fully adjust. In Keynes' opinion, policy makers cannot afford to patiently wait for this process to work itself out in the long run because, in his words, "in the long-run we are all dead."

The third way out of a recession is for the government to use macroeconomic policy to stimulate aggregate demand and output during recessions. There are two broad options for doing this. The first is monetary policy. As mentioned before, Keynes believed that money is an asset. The opportunity cost, or price, of holding money is the interest rate. Just like any other commodity, an increase in the supply of money would decrease its price and drive down interest rates. In theory, lower interest rates would encourage investment directly and would also stimulate investment indirectly by driving up the price of stocks. After proposing this potential role for monetary policy, however, Keynes was quick to discount the use of monetary policy as a reliable means of ending recessions. One reason is that as mentioned before, Keynes did not believe that investment demand was sensitive to changes in interest rates—perceived uncertainty and business confidence play the predominant role. In addition, Keynes was skeptical about the ability of central bankers to conduct monetary policy in a timely and effective manner. On the basis of the performance of central banks during the Great Depression, Keynes possessed a skepticism that was understandable. The final reason Keynes largely dismissed monetary policy was because he recognized that households and banks increase their holdings of money as a precautionary measure during bad times. This is especially true when interest rates are low because there is a low opportunity cost to holding money. Low interest rates also make holding bonds unattractive because interest rates are likely to increase and that will reduce the value of any bonds being held. As a result of each of these considerations, any increase in the money supply during recessions is likely to be hoarded, leading to little change in interest rates, the stock market, investment, and aggregate demand. Keynes referred to this as a *liquidity trap*, and it severely limits the effectiveness of monetary policy when it is needed most.

If monetary policy is not reliable, fiscal policy is another option. Once again, Keynes was skeptical that tax cuts would significantly increase spending because households are most likely to save any tax cut during a recession. When the government increases its purchases of goods and services, however, all of this money is immediately spent and goes into stimulating aggregate expenditure. In Keynes' opinion, exactly what the government purchases is less important than the fact that the government is spending. This government spending will increase income, which will then encourage private spending, creating a *spending multiplier* in which the total increase in income is greater than the initial increase in govern-ment spending. If conducted at the appropriate scale, government purchases can increase aggregate demand, either directly or by increasing expectations, enough to return the economy to the natural rate of output. This is the reason why Keynes is associated with arguments for a larger and more active government. In fact, he is held by many to be the founding father of the modern welfare state.

Keynesian Economics and the IS–LM Model

Publication of *The General Theory* immediately set off an intense period of investigation into different aspects of Keynes' model. One challenge facing economists is that *The General Theory* is not completely clear on a number of important points. This is in part because Keynes largely resisted using equations and empirical data in his analysis, believing that economic processes were too complex to be described by simple equations and that appropriate empirical data were often unavailable and unreliable. Consequently, even before Keynes had put his thoughts down onto paper, other "Keynesian" economists had begun the process of trying to interpret exactly what they thought Keynes meant to say.

In addition to making Keynes' General Theory clear to economists, another objective of Keynesians was to make Keynes' ideas more accessible to policy makers and the public. One difficulty in achieving this goal is that the General Theory is a model of disequilibrium, which is more difficult to deal with in a tractable way than simple models of market equilibrium, such as the Classical theory. As a result, many Keynesians began to investigate how to model many of Keynes' key principles—such as wage stickiness and animal spirits—within a general equilibrium framework where unemployment and output shortfalls could persist even when the economy is in balance.

The most prominent and influential of these Keynesian equilibrium models is John Hicks' (1937) IS–LM model. Hicks developed a model of aggregate expenditure that explains how changes in the money market (the LM curve) and changes in the goods and capital markets (the IS curve) influence aggregate demand. This Keynesian IS–LM model is consistent with many of the basic principles of Keynes' model, but with three important differences that generally separate Keynes' theory from Keynesian theory. These differences ultimately served to minimize the role of financial systems in generating business cycles within Keynesian economics as compared to Keynes' General Theory.

The first difference is that, in the Keynesian IS–LM model, both prices and nominal wages are fixed, not just sticky. Thus, the IS–LM model is the best thought of as a model of the very short run before prices and nominal wages have had any chance to adjust. Fixed prices and nominal wages imply that the aggregate supply curve is completely horizontal at the current price level and that changes in output are exactly equal to the size of the change in aggregate demand. In other words, the Keynesian IS–LM model is a model of aggregate demand only, and nothing else, effectively ignoring the supply side of the economy.

While the Keynesian IS–LM model assumes nominal wage and price rigidity, it does not explain the source of these market failures. For example, there is no discussion of the microeconomic fundamentals of nominal wage and price rigidity, meaning that there is no discussion of why profit-maximizing firms and utility-maximizing individuals would choose to adjust nominal wages slowly. Maybe even more importantly, Keynesians completely ignore potential sources of market failure in financial markets. In the Keynesian capital market, interest rates instantly adjust so that savings always equals investment, just like in the Classical model. The only real difference between these models is that planned investment in the Keynesian model is a function of business confidence and subject to uncertainty, making it much more volatile than in the Classical model.

The second difference is that Keynesians believe that changes in aggregate demand are driven primarily by exogenous changes in consumption and not by changes in investment demand. Keynesians believe that the decisions of households to purchase durable consumption goods are very similar to the decisions made by firms to purchase investment goods, making them very sensitive to changes in perceived uncertainty and animal spirits. Because consumption is a larger fraction of aggregate output, Keynesians believe that it is the most important source of fluctuations in aggregate demand.

By switching the focus away from investment volatility and towards consumption volatility, Keynesians also switched the focus away from financial systems. Because finance plays a smaller role in consumption decisions than in investment decisions, Keynesians downplay the macroeconomic effects of volatility in stock and bond markets. In the Keynesian way of thinking, animal spirits have less to do with the inherent nature of financial speculation in stock and bond markets (leading to investment volatility) and more to do with uncertainty regarding future macroeconomic conditions and job security (generating consumption volatility). Thus, the financial system plays only a minor role in transmitting external changes in business confidence to the rest of the economy in the Keynesian model.

The third important difference between Keynes and Keynesians has to do with the role of monetary policy in stabilizing output. As mentioned previously, Keynes did not advocate the use of monetary policy to stabilize aggregate demand. This was in large part because of the liquidity trap, where individuals and financial intermediaries tend to hold onto money balances rather than circulate them during economic contractions. On the other hand, Keynesians spent a great deal of time examining and advocating the use of monetary policy because they believe that postwar central bankers are in the perfect position to freely conduct stabilization policy given their relative independence from the political constraints that typically complicate fiscal policy. Keynesians ignored the liquidity trap in the same manner as they ignored financial systems in general.

Keynesian interest in monetary policy was also spurred by the work of Arthur Phillips (1958). Phillips investigated the relationship between nominal wage inflation and unemployment growth between 1862 and 1957 in the U.K. He found that a very strong negative correlation existed between these two variables, referred to as the *Phillips' curve*. Keynesians immediately modified Phillips' work using U.S. data, but this time focusing on the relationship between price inflation and unemployment. Numerous studies identified a strong negative relationship between inflation and unemployment. Keynesians realized that this negative relationship was important empirical support for their model, because if recessions are driven by lower aggregate demand, aggregate prices should fall at the same time that unemployment rises. Thus, this modified Phillips curve is a strong evidence in favor of aggregate demand-driven business cycles. The Phillips curve also offered Keynesians a practical tool that could simplify the complexity of stabilization policy to a single inflation rate target. If a stable tradeoff between inflation and unemployment exists, then all that monetary policy makers have to do is adjust the money supply until inflation is at the appropriate level that achieves the desired unemployment rate.

The Financial Instability Hypothesis

Not all proponents of Keynes believed that the spirit of Keynes' work could be captured within models that largely ignored financial intermediation such as the IS–LM model. One group of renegade economists, known somewhat confusingly as *post-Keynesians* (to be distinguished from Keynesians in general), tried to reassert the role of financial systems as the primary factor in driving aggregate demand volatility and business cycles. The most influential of these post-Keynesian economists is Hyman Minsky (his collected works are published in Minsky, 1982), whose Financial Instability Hypothesis model owes quite a bit to both Keynes' original intent in the General Theory as well as Fisher's Debt-Deflation theory. While never achieving the influence of Keynesian IS–LM theory within the macroeconomics profession, Minsky's focus on financial fundamentals at the microeconomic level anticipates much of modern financial macroeconomics.

In the Financial Instability Hypothesis model, Minsky asserts that capitalist economies are inherently flawed and unstable because financial systems are inherently unstable. In Minsky's model, the choices managers make with regards to their financial structure have long-lasting effects on their financial stability. Specifically, Minsky believed that firms engage in three types of financial strategies. *Hedged finance* refers to situations where firms have cash flows that are greater than the service payments they have to make on their debt, which includes both interest and principal payments. Hedged finance is obviously a safe situation for a firm to find itself in. *Speculative finance* refers to situations where firms have cash flows greater than interest payments that they are required to make, but not enough to significantly reduce the principal they owe. As a result, under speculative finance, firms find themselves in a more precarious financial position. *Ponzi finance* is the most risky and occurs when cash flows are insufficient to meet interest payments so that firms have to accumulate additional debt over time. (The term Ponzi refers to Charles Ponzi, a famous swindler who used a "pyramid strategy" of paying off existing investors with the contributions of new investors without ever producing anything.) Ponzi finance allows a firm to avoid bankruptcy in the near term, but obviously cannot be pursued forever without eventual default.

Minsky believed that the financial strategies followed by firms change over time, sometimes as a result of conscious decision making and sometimes because of unforeseen changes in circumstances. Like Keynes, Minsky believed that the future is essentially unknowable and beliefs regarding the future are highly subjective. In fact, Minsky even goes further than Keynes in arguing that individuals often act irrationally, excessively exuberant during good times and excessively panicky during bad times. During periods of strong growth and rising profits, firms find it easier to repay debt, so they borrow more. This leads to increases in investment and further increases in growth. These actions also decrease the levels of hedge financing and increase the levels of speculative financing and even, to some extent, Ponzi financing. Eventually, this excessive optimism reaches a breaking point. A negative event occurs, possibly a single large default. Business confidence begins to evaporate, which leads to drops in credit, investment, profits, and output. Almost immediately, many firms that might have intended to engage in hedge or speculative financing find themselves in the financially fragile position of engaging in Ponzi finance. As lenders become stricter in their credit practices, lending falls and defaults begin to escalate. Panic selling of assets begins to occur and a process of financial collapse similar to that described in the Debt-Deflation theory takes place, dragging the entire economy down with it. Thus, psychology and financial fragility, as measured by the microeconomic financial fundamentals of firms play the primary roles in driving business cycles.

According to Minsky, the policy implications for governments in the face of financial fragility cannot be boiled down to simple rules. Central banks have to stand ready to serve as a lender of last resort in order to minimize financial collapse and insulate the broader economy from the effects of financial instability. However, central banks also have to worry about not encouraging speculation by always bailing lenders out. In addition, central banks have to worry about the inflationary pressures that are created by constantly issuing money to stabilize financial systems.

The most effective way governments can encourage economic stability is to strictly regulate financial systems in order to discourage speculative and Ponzi finance. However, because financial innovation is always taking place, any type of financial regulation implemented by governments aimed at limiting speculative and Ponzi financing will be circumvented over time. Governments have to be constantly vigilant and ready to adapt their practices in response to changes in market conditions. In addition, regulators have to pay close attention to the microeconomic financial conditions that exist at the firm level and watch for signs of Ponzi financing and financial fragility. By highlighting the importance of financial fundamentals, the Financial Instability Hypothesis model is a predecessor to New Institutional theories of finance (Chapters 5 and 6) that further develop many of Minsky's insights within more rigorous models that emphasize the microeconomic foundations of financial fragility.

The Monetarist Model

The 1950s and 1960s were an era in which Keynesianism dominated macroeconomic theory. The most powerful voice of dissent during this period was Milton Friedman, probably the second most influential economist of the 20th century and, like Keynes, a man of many talents. In addition to being a prominent conservative policy guru (Friedman has developed many influential public policy ideas, including privatization proposals such as school voucher programs), Friedman did groundbreaking work in the areas of law and economics, consumption theory, and economic history. Friedman is also the father of a school of macroeconomic thought referred to as Monetarism.

Monetarists have the following goal: reassert Classical principles in a model that better explains business cycles. A critical component of this Monetarist model is that while it accepts the Classical principle of money neutrality, it recognizes that it only holds in the long run. In the short run, Monetarists believe (like Keynesians) that fluctuations in aggregate demand can have real effects on output and drive business cycles. However, the Monetarist model is similar to the Classical model in that it minimizes the role of financial systems in creating this aggregate demand volatility. For example, just like in the Classical model, the Monetarist model assumes that money primarily serves as a medium of exchange and not as a financial asset as asserted by Keynes. As a result, monetary policy affects aggregate output directly, not through its impact on financial intermediation. While deemphasizing financial systems, Monetarists instead view the erratic monetary policies followed by misguided central bankers as the primary source of aggregate demand shocks that cause business cycles.

Principles of the Monetarist Model

Monetarists believe in three basic principles, each based on a traditional Classical principle but with some modification.

Prices and wages are perfectly flexible, but perfect information does not exist
Monetarists believe that perfect competition best describes the behavior of markets, but with the exception that perfect information about the money supply and the price level is impossible because of the secrecy of central banks. (Note here that Monetarists are only concerned with imperfect information regarding the price

level, they ignore imperfect information in financial transactions.) Imperfect information means that expectations of the future price level can have real effects on an economy if these expectations are wrong.

Monetarists believe that firms and households have *adaptive expectations.* Adaptive expectations mean that individuals are not forward-looking but are backward–looking, and only change their expectations of the future gradually based on what they have observed in the past. (An example of adaptive expectations at work can be seen on every college campus when the weather suddenly turns cold but many students continue to walk around in shorts and a T-shirt.) Because of this, nominal wages and the price level are slow to adjust in the Monetarist model to unforeseen changes in the money supply. Disequilibria in markets can exist not because of any real market imperfections as assumed by Keynesians, but because of incorrect expectations of what nominal wages and the price level should be to clear the market.

Implicit in this concept of adaptive expectations is a view of the world that is very different from the Keynesian view. Keynes viewed the future as unknowable because it will be different from the past. As a result, expectations of the future should have nothing to do with what has happened in the past. Monetarists believe that the future is like the past but we cannot observe it. The only way to estimate the possibilities of future outcomes is to watch what has already happened.

Changes in aggregate demand do not affect real output in the long run, but they do affect real output in the short run
Unlike Classical economists, Monetarists assert that money neutrality only holds in the long run. The reason, once again, has to do with imperfect information and price misperceptions. When the public is surprised by a change in the money supply, firms and workers are fooled into changing their real behavior, meaning money neutrality does not hold. However, firms and households eventually recognize their mistakes and gradually adjust their expectations. Wages and prices then adjust and return the labor and goods markets to equilibrium.

Consequently, changes in aggregate demand drive business cycle fluctuations. These fluctuations are not permanent but temporary deviations from the natural rate of output, which is determined by the full employment of capital, labor, and technology that is available in the economy. As a result, the natural rate of output is not some theoretically achievable level of output (like in the Keynesian view), but a level of output that the economy would achieve in the absence of any unexpected demand shocks.

Fluctuations in the money supply drive fluctuations in aggregate demand and are responsible for business cycles
Monetarists adhere to the Classical Quantity Theory of money demand and aggregate demand, which is based on the assumption that money primarily serves as a medium of exchange and that money is needed in order to conduct transactions.

This implies that there is a direct relationship between the amount of money in circulation and the level of nominal aggregate spending in an economy:

$$MV = PY \tag{4.1}$$

Here, V is velocity and represents the number of times a unit of money changes hands over a period of time. Y is real aggregate expenditure, P is the price level, and M is the money supply. In the Quantity Theory, any increase in the level of nominal expenditure (PY) has to be matched by either an increase in the supply of money (M) or a higher velocity of money (V) in order to support this higher volume of trade. The Quantity Theory is a theory of aggregate demand because it implies that a negative relationship exists between the price level and real expenditure, holding money and velocity constant (intuition: a higher price level reduces the real supply of money, which leads to a reduction in real expenditure). As a result, changes in this aggregate demand relationship only take place in response to a change in the money supply or a change in velocity. Monetarists believe that the demand for money and velocity are relatively stable if monetary policy is stable, so that changes in aggregate demand are almost exclusively the result of changes in the money supply.

Like the early monetary theories discussed in the last chapter, the Monetarist model asserts that economic fluctuations are largely the result of changes in the money supply that create fluctuations in aggregate demand. Unlike those early monetary theories, Monetarists do not rely on the gold standard but on adaptive expectations to explain why money has real effects. Expectation stickiness, not wage stickiness like in the Keynesian model, means that changes in aggregate demand have real effects on output and unemployment. Recessionary periods in which output growth is below the natural rate are the result of money growth being lower than anticipated. When this happens, the actual price level is lower than the expected price level, real wages become too high, and firms are forced to layoff workers and cut production. On the other hand, expansions in which output growth is above the natural rate are caused by higher than anticipated money growth, which lowers real wages and encourages employment and production.

However, any deviation from the natural rate will not last forever. In the case of a recession, eventually the public will realize that they have set their expected price level and real wage demands too high and will begin to accept nominal wage reductions that encourage employment and production; wages and prices adjust (in the absence of another change in the money supply) and the economy returns to its natural rate. This proposition that in the short-run monetary policy and changes in aggregate demand influence output, but in the long run the economy returns to its natural rate of output leaving only the level of inflation and other nominal variables changed, is referred to as the *natural rate hypothesis*.

Note that the natural rate hypothesis is inconsistent with the Keynesian Phillips curve in two ways. First, it asserts that there is no trade-off between unemployment and inflation in the long run. Second, it asserts that the trade-off between higher inflation and unemployment in the short run is unstable because how much unemployment falls in response to an increase in inflation depends upon the current level of price expectations, which can vary significantly over time.

How persistent recessions are depends on how quickly the public adjusts their expectations in the long run. In Monetarists' minds, the long run is a long period of time. According to Friedman, it can take up to 10 years before the real effects of an unexpected change in the money supply disappear and leave only higher prices. This process takes so long because the public never has perfect information about the extent of the change in the money supply; they can only learn about monetary policy by observing past inflation rates. This requires a great deal of time and leads to long response lags, providing monetary policy with a great deal of power to influence the macroeconomy.

If business cycles are caused by changes in the money supply, why then do central banks allow the money supply to move so irregularly? Friedman believed it was due to the misguided attempts of Keynesian central bankers to use monetary policy to control output. Yes, the central bank can increase output above the natural rate of output, but only in the short run, and only at the cost of higher inflation. If the central bank persists in increasing the money supply in order to prop up output (either because of a desire for higher output or because they have overestimated the natural rate of output), inflation will begin to accelerate, eventually reaching a point where the central bank will have to reverse course and cut the money supply in order to reduce inflation. Thus, monetary policy becomes a yo-yo, increasing and decreasing over time and creating, not eliminating, instability in the macroeconomy.

Monetarists feel that central banks can avoid these policy swings and eliminate business cycles by changing their goal from economic stabilization to monetary stabilization. In an influential address, Friedman (1968) argued that central banks should control what they can control by adopting a money growth rule that specifies that the money supply increases at a constant rate—for example, 5 percent each and every year. By doing this, not only will central banks be able to stabilize economic growth, but they will also be able to keep inflation at a low level, reducing the distortions created by inflation, eliminating a large source of uncertainty in the economy, and increasing economic efficiency. This would be a record of success that, in Friedman's opinion, is far superior to the record established by the active use of monetary policy.

In this Monetarist theory of business cycles, financial systems play a minor role. Because of its complete focus on monetary policy, financial market instability is ignored by Monetarists as a factor in business cycles because bond and stock markets play little role in the money creation process. Not only do financial markets have little impact on the money supply, but from the Monetarist perspective, the money supply has little direct impact on financial markets. This is because money is exclusively a medium of exchange in the Monetarist model and not a financial asset like in the Keynesian model. As a result, money is not an integral part of an individual's wealth portfolio and changes in the demand or supply for money lead to little substitution between money and stocks or money and bonds. Changes in the money supply only affect financial markets through its impact on overall macroeconomic performance.

Banks receive more attention from Monetarists because of their role in generating the money multiplier (see Chapter 2 for an explanation of the money multiplier process). However, things such as bank runs and bank failures are important factors in adding to macroeconomic volatility only because they reduce the money multiplier and change the money supply in unpredictable ways. There are two important policy implications of the Monetarist model that pertain to banks. First, while Monetarists do not believe that central banks should conduct monetary policy in an effort to stabilize the economy, there is an important role for central banks to serve as a lender of last resort in order to prevent banking panics and ensure the stability of the money supply. Thus, Monetarists believe that discretionary monetary policy is only appropriate when it is used to offset major economic disturbances that threaten the functioning of the banking and monetary systems. Second, in an effort to protect the stability of the money supply, Friedman proposed that banks be required to hold 100 percent of their deposits as reserves. This would eliminate the money multiplier and banks' role in creating monetary instability. Under a 100 percent reserve requirement, central banks would have complete control over the money supply and complete accountability for its movements, which is why Friedman found this proposal appealing. Of course, this regulation would also limit bank lending and financial intermediation, but given the limited importance of financial intermediation in Friedman's view, this is a small price to pay for greater monetary stability.

Another way to understand just how irrelevant financial systems are in the Monetarist model is to note that Monetarists do not make a distinction between the level of the money supply and the level of credit in an economy. In their model, an increase in the money supply would automatically increase the level of lending and credit within the banking system, spurring aggregate demand. There is no consideration of the ways that credit can expand without changes in the money supply, such as through financial innovation. There is also no consideration of circumstances in which the money supply might increase but banks would resist lending and refuse to expand credit, such as Keynes' liquidity trap. This distinction between the money supply and the level of credit becomes a crucial component of New Institutional theories of finance, which are examined in the next two chapters.

Neoclassical Theories

The rational expectations model

While Monetarists reasserted many Classical principles, Neoclassical models such as the Rational Expectations model and Real Business Cycle models took this revival of Classical economics even further. The Rational Expectations model extends Classical principles to the formation of expectations. In the Monetarist model, adaptive expectations make price expectations slow to adjust to changes in economic conditions. As a result, changes in monetary policy that affect the actual price level can fool firms and workers into thinking that real conditions have changed, leading them to produce more or less than they would if they had perfect information.

However, there is an inconsistency inherent in the assumption of adaptive expectations. The cornerstone of economics is the rational choice model, in which individuals make decisions based on weighing the benefits of an activity against its costs. For example, people are assumed to consume a good until the marginal benefit of another unit of the good equals the marginal cost of the next unit. The logical inconsistency in the Monetarist model is this: why do not people apply this same rational choice model to their formulation of expectations? Monetarists believe that individuals are rational and forward looking when making all of their other decisions but are not when selecting their expectations of the future. As a result, they are in conflict with a well-established microeconomic theory of utility and profit maximization.

The insight of rational expectations, which was first proposed by John Muth (1961), is that this dissonance between how individuals form their expectations and how individuals make their other decisions can be reconciled by simply assuming that agents form their expectations based on the rational choice model. In other words, *rational expectations* mean that individuals form their expectations by making an optimal forecast of the future using all currently available information. An "optimal forecast" means that they have a probability distribution of the likelihood of future events and take both mean and variance into account when forming their expectations. "All currently available information" does not mean perfect information because some information may not be publicly available and because some information may be prohibitively costly to obtain (i.e., the marginal cost of such information is greater than its marginal benefit). It does mean that while the public can still make errors, they do not make predictable, or systematic, errors based on the information that they have.

It is easy to miss how this view of the world is radically different from the Keynesian view of uncertainty and animal spirits. According to Keynesians, the future is unknowable—there is no probability distribution that governs future events, so changes in perceptions are governed by no simple rules. According to Rational

Expectations theory, however, the chance of future events occurring is the same as past events, so we can use the past to forecast the future using statistics. Thus, it is possible to form a probability distribution of the future based on the past. To reuse the analogy, Rational Expectation adherents believe that forecasting the future is similar to playing poker, in which today's actions should be governed by statistical probabilities. Keynesians believe that forecasting the future is impossible because the rules of the game are always changing, so today's actions reflect today's potentially biased view of the future.

The relatively simple insights of rational expectations revolutionized modern macroeconomics when Robert Lucas (1972) developed a macroeconomic model that incorporated both rational expectations and Friedman's natural rate hypothesis. In his Rational Expectations model, business cycles are temporary deviations from the natural rate of output caused by unanticipated changes in aggregate demand. For example, consider the effects of an unanticipated decrease in money growth by a central bank. This reduction in the money supply reduces aggregate demand. Firms mistakenly view this fall in aggregate demand, at least in part, as a decrease in the individual demand for their goods and respond by cutting production and reducing nominal wages and employment. As workers see their nominal wages fall, they mistakenly believe that this is also a reduction in their real wages and reduce their labor supply. Until firms and workers realize that the price of the goods they produce fell because aggregate demand fell, output and employment will remain below their natural rates and the economy will be in a recession. However, in a world of rational agents, this should not be a prolonged period of time. People will quickly realize that they have been operating under mistaken expectations. Firms and workers will adjust their production and labor supply accordingly, prices and wages will correct themselves, and the economy will return to its natural rate.

How can changes in aggregate demand be unanticipated if expectations are rational? Once again, remember that rational expectations do not mean perfect expectations. There are three very important reasons why changes in money policy are difficult to observe. First, most information on monetary policy only becomes available after a lag. Second, central banks often make temporary adjustments in the money supply to respond to temporary changes in market conditions, making it difficult to separate permanent changes in monetary policy from temporary changes in the money supply. Third, central banks have historically been very secretive organizations. Until recently, the Fed never released press statements indicating when they were changing the stance of monetary policy.

Rational expectations have radical implications for government policy. Systematic, or predictable, policies will always be anticipated by the public, who will adjust their expectations and their actions in anticipation of any change. The only way that a policy maker can influence real variables is if changes in policy are unanticipated by the public. In other words, the only way for policy makers to increase real output is for them to be secretive and unpredictable. The problem is that stabilization policy by its very nature cannot be unpredictable. Stabilization policy will not be able to stimulate output during recessions if everyone knows exactly how policymakers are going to respond beforehand.

In fact, if taken to its logical extreme, the Rational Expectations model implies *policy irrelevance*, or that all government policies that are observable will be completely ineffective. This does not hold just for monetary policy, but for fiscal policy as well. Consider a deficit-financed tax cut aimed at stimulating aggregate demand. If the public is rational, they will realize that these deficits will have to be paid for in the future with higher taxes (if not by themselves, then by their heirs). As a result, they will likely save this entire tax cut to pay for future tax increases and aggregate demand will change very little or not at all. Likewise, a deficit-financed increase in government spending will also be matched by an increase in household saving, leading to at most a minimal change in aggregate demand.

To summarize, the Rational Expectations model implies that if the past is a reliable indicator of the future, then the rational choice model can apply to the formation of expectations. In this case, monetary and fiscal policy cannot play a positive role in the economy. In fact, by being the largest source of economic uncertainty, changes in government policy destabilize the economy and drive swings in the business cycle. Because of this, rational expectation proponents strongly believe in *laissez-faire* fiscal policies and rules-based monetary policies.

Real business cycle models

Real Business Cycle models came to prominence in the 1980s with the seminal research of Finn Kydland and Edward Prescott (1982) and John Long and Charles Plosser (1983). Real Business Cycle models take the neoclassical revival to its logical, if circular, conclusion by returning to all of the fundamental principles of the Classical model. Real Business Cycle models assert that the natural rate hypothesis holds in the long run and in the short run because markets are perfectly competitive and individuals have perfect information. Aggregate demand is irrelevant to real economic activity and money neutrality always holds. Only aggregate supply, which is a function of the amount of labor, the amount of capital, and the aggregate level of productivity in an economy, determines the level of real output in an economy. As a result, in Real Business Cycle models, only changes in aggregate supply generate business cycles. Government policies that create market distortions and reduce the incentives to work, invest, or innovate play a prominent role in initiating fluctuations in output.

The main difference between the Classical model and a Real Business Cycle model is in the level of detail that is incorporated into the economic analysis. While both are models of perfect competition in which the economy is always in equilibrium, Real Business Cycle models are much more rigorously specified and explicitly include modern microeconomic principles such as dynamic marginal analysis and rational expectations. Real Business Cycle models are actually based on Neoclassical Growth models, which have been used extensively in macroeconomics since the 1950s to investigate issues related to growth across countries. Real Business Cycle advocates assert that the same models that economists use to investigate the long-run growth behavior of economies can be used to investigate their short-run cyclical behavior as well.

In Real Business Cycle models, recessions and expansions are driven by cyclical changes in aggregate productivity that shift aggregate supply. When a number of negative shocks from various sources occur simultaneously, output falls to a permanently lower level. The more frequent and the larger these shocks, the bigger the change in output will be.

Real Business Cycle proponents argue that productivity shocks come from three principal sources:

Changes in the prices of important inputs into production, such as the price of oil
Higher input prices increase the costs of production and also reduce the productivity of capital by making a portion of the capital stock too expensive to operate. Large increases in the price of oil proceeded recessions in the U.S. in 1973–1975, 1980, and 1990–1991. On the other hand, low oil prices such as those that existed throughout most of the 1980s and 1990s are typically associated with periods of increasing productivity and output. The price of other important raw materials such as steel, food, and coal also contribute to changes in aggregate productivity.

Changes in technology
While we typically think about changes in technology occurring at a constant rate, technology actually increases in fits and starts. Real Business Cycle proponents view the production of new technologies as a random, cyclical process that drives fluctuations in output.

Changes in government taxation and regulation
Taxes lower aggregate productivity by reducing the incentives to work, invest in new capital technologies, and invest in education. Government regulations are also highly distortionary. Worker safety standards, food and drug regulations, regulations on natural resource exploration, and many other government programs place constraints on markets and productivity. Another example of costly government regulation is the increased security precautions imposed after 9/11 aimed at improving security on airlines, roads, international travel, and so on, which have in all likelihood significantly reduced overall productivity within the U.S. economy. Given that government taxation and regulation change constantly and that government policy also influences the price of inputs (e.g., through foreign policy or trade policy), Real Business Cycle proponents view government as an important source of changes in aggregate productivity and business cycles.

One of the most important features of Real Business Cycle models is that business cycles are efficient, meaning that they do not represent lost output as suggested by aggregate demand theories of business cycles. Business cycles are an optimal response to changes in the natural rate of output caused by real changes in the economy. As a result, stabilization policy is unnecessary. Instead, government policy should focus on supply-side policies aimed at increasing the productive capacity of the economy. The best way to do this is to leave markets alone and follow a *laissez-faire* approach to government intervention in the economy.

One important similarity between the Rational Expectations model, Real Business Cycle models, and the Classical model is their complete disregard of financial systems. In these models in which markets operate efficiently, financial systems are not particularly interesting because prices are perfectly flexible, representative agents are homogenous, and savings is smoothly transformed into investment. Financial intermediation does not break down, and rises and falls in credit do not precede movements in the macroeconomy. Whatever financial volatility exists is a symptom of volatility in the real sectors of the economy, not vice versa.

The most extreme example of the irrelevance of finance in Neoclassical theory is the fact that money is always neutral in Real Business Cycle models and monetary policy has no impact on real macroeconomic activity. Central banks control inflation but they cannot influence output because the money supply only influences aggregate demand and not aggregate supply. As a result, Real Business Cycle proponents typically ignore monetary policy and its impact on financial systems, arguing for money growth rules that keep inflation low.

Thus, by the mid-1980s, which was the height of the Neoclassical revival, financial systems had been pushed to the extreme margins of macroeconomic research and financial systems were largely ignored in forecasting and policy analysis.

CASE STUDY: Explanations of the Great Depression

The Great Depression is the largest economic contraction in U.S. history. Table 4.1 provides some data on key macroeconomic variables during the Depression. Between 1929 and 1933, aggregate output fell by between 30 and 50 percent (depending on whether real GDP or industrial production is used as a measure) and unemployment rose to nearly 25 percent. At this same time, stock prices fell 85 percent, one-quarter of all banks failed, and bankruptcy rates skyrocketed.

If the average person today is asked to describe the Great Depression, after "bread lines" some of the most often used phrases would be "the stock market crash" and "banking crises," which indicate how widely recognized the role of the finance is in the crisis. Most observers at the time placed the primary responsibility for the crash on financial systems as well. Franklin Roosevelt in a 1933 address

Table 4.1   Key U.S. Macroeconomic Variables during the Great Depression

	Real GNP (in $ Billions)	Industrial Production Index	Unemployment Rate (%)	Stock Price Index	Bank Failures	Consumer Price Index
1928	98.2	100	4.2	153	498	100
1929	104.4	106	3.2	201	659	100
1930	95.1	85	8.7	161	1,350	97.4
1931	89.5	71	15.9	100	2,293	88.7
1932	76.4	56	23.6	36	1,453	79.7
1933	74.2	67	24.9	79	4,000	75.4
1934	80.8	70	21.7	78	57	78
1935	91.4	80	20.1	80	34	80.1
1936	100.9	94	16.9	112	44	80.9
1937	109.1	97	14.3	120	59	83.8
1938	103.2	75	19	80	54	82.3

Source: U.S. Department of Commerce, Historical Statistics of the United States; Board of Governors of the Federal Reserve System, Banking and Monetary Statistics (Washington, D.C.: National Capital Press, 1943).

stated that "Unrestrained financial exploitations which created fictitious values never justified by earnings have been one of the great causes of our present tragic condition." However, with the exception of Keynes' General Theory and the Financial Instability Hypothesis, the role of finance was downplayed by macroeconomic theories developed after the Great Depression.

As we discussed before, Keynes believed that the Depression was caused by a dramatic fall in aggregate demand driven by falls in business confidence that reduced investment. By creating the forum that fueled speculative behavior and the animal spirits that initiated this fall in aggregate demand, the financial system played a key role in both creating and propagating these shocks throughout the entire economy. Why exactly confidence fell so significantly in 1929 is unclear (just as actions motivated by animal spirits usually are), but Keynes focused on overbuilding, overproduction, over-indebtedness, and overvalued stock markets that built-up throughout the 1920s. This made the financial conditions of many borrowers and lenders extremely fragile, setting the stage for a dramatic reversal that could be triggered by even a minor piece of bad news.

Keynes believed that falling business confidence also played a role in the bank failures that plagued the U.S. economy during the Depression. As the Depression worsened, people began to panic and withdraw their savings from banks throughout the country. These bank runs not only led to bank failures, but those banks that did not fail were forced to severely restrict their lending, effectively halting financial intermediation and further reducing investment.

The falls in aggregate demand created by financial volatility and the falls in confidence had real effects on the economy because of wage inflexibility in the labor market. Consistent with this theory, nominal wages did not fall as fast as the price level during the early part of the Depression, leading to increases in unemployment.

Keynes believed that if aggregate demand could have been stabilized sooner, most reliably through increasing government spending, the Depression would have been much milder and considerably shorter. Instead, the federal government stubbornly stuck to its *laissez-faire* policies (Hoover even pushed through a budget that actually increased taxes and reduced government spending). Even the Federal Reserve refused to offset the falling money supply caused by the drop in the money multiplier as a result of the banking crisis.

Minsky's explanation of the Great Depression is similar to Keynes, but with an emphasis on the financing decisions made by firms at the microeconomic level. During the 1920s, a generally optimistic and expansive attitude led to booms in investment spending fueled by speculative and Ponzi financing. By the end of the decade, the balance sheets of most firms were heavily laden with debt that could not be serviced if even a minor decline in profitability took place. After the financial collapse began in October of 1929, many firms immediately found themselves engaged in Ponzi financing, setting the stage for an unprecedented financial and economic collapse. (New Institutional views of the Great Depression, discussed in detail in the next chapter, mesh well with many aspects of the Financial Instability Hypothesis model's explanation.)

Keynesian explanations of the Great Depression differ from Keynes' General Theory mainly in regard to the channel by which animal spirits affected aggregate demand. Keynes believed that animal spirits are created within financial markets, are driven by speculation, and primarily affect investment demand through changing business confidence. Keynesians, however, believe that animal spirits are chiefly created in goods markets and are driven by households' fears regarding their future economic security. As a result, it is changes in consumer confidence which affect consumption demand that drive fluctuations in aggregate demand. The financial volatility associated with the Great Depression was not seen as a cause of the Great Depression by Keynesians, only a symptom of the general collapse.

One problem with Keynes' and Keynesian explanations of the Great Depression is that it is hard to understand how a 50-percent fall in aggregate output could be caused by pessimistic views of the future alone. If this were the case, why have not we seen depressions comparable to the Great Depression since the 1930s (surely we are not more optimistic than we used to be)? And what was the exact shock that occurred in 1929 that could explain such a large decline in confidence across many countries at once? It is hard to believe that the stock market crash alone was large enough to explain an economic contraction the size of the Great Depression. The stock market crash reduced wealth by roughly 75 percent of annual income in

1929. However, this decline in wealth alone is able to explain at most half of the fall in consumption demand. In addition, the stock market has fluctuated wildly since the Great Depression (e.g., the crash of 1987 was actually larger than the 1929 crash) but never with anywhere near such dire economic consequences. Thus, a number of questions regarding the Depression remain unanswered by Keynesians, largely because they lack a concrete model of exactly how views of the future are formed.

Monetarists believe that the Great Depression was caused by a fall in aggregate demand created by the Federal Reserve and the contractionary monetary policies that they followed before and during the Great Depression's early years. These reductions in the money supply reduced liquidity in the economy, which directly reduced spending. The falling money supply also played a role in triggering bank failures by making it impossible for banks to meet their withdrawal demands; these bank failures further reduced liquidity and aggregate demand. However, just as in the Keynesian model, the collapse of the financial system was primarily a symptom of the Depression, not its cause. Monetarists believe that if the Fed would have just committed itself to increasing the money supply sooner, the Depression would have come to a much quicker end.

Two problems exist with this Monetarist explanation. First, the Monetarist conclusion that a direct and constant relationship exists between the money supply and spending seems implausible to many. Does monetary policy really have the power by itself to reduce output by 50 percent? And if monetary policy is that powerful, why do people insist on adjusting their price expectations slowly and only by looking backwards, not looking forward?

The second problem has to do with the nature of the fall in the money supply during the Depression. Monetarists are quick to argue that the Federal Reserve was responsible for the fall in the money supply, but from Figure 4.1 it is clear that the Federal Reserve did little to change the monetary base during the Depression, but M1 still fell by roughly one-third. This was the result of increased precautionary money holdings by banks and the public, as evidenced by the fact that the currency-to-deposit and excess reserve-to-deposit ratios rose dramatically, as illustrated in Figure 4.2. As money demand went up, bank deposits, lending, and the money multiplier dropped precipitously, significantly reducing M1. Thus, it appears that much of the fall in the money supply was the result of the Great Depression, not necessarily caused by a change in monetary policy by the Fed. Critics of the Monetarist model argue that a large fraction of the postwar correlation between the money supply and aggregate output can be explained in this same way: it is not changes in the money supply that are changing output and financial conditions, but it is changes in output and financial conditions that lead to changes in the money supply. By ignoring the important microeconomic foundations of financial systems, Monetarists may be ignoring the real cause of economic volatility and focusing only on a symptom of the problem.

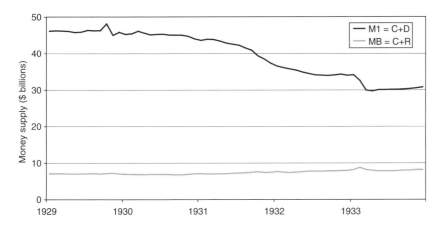

Figure 4.1
M1 and the Monetary Base in the U.S. during the Great Depression.
Source: U.S. Department of Commerce, Historical Statistics of the United States; Board of Governors of the Federal Reserve System, Banking and Monetary Statistics (Washington, D.C.: National Capital Press, 1943).

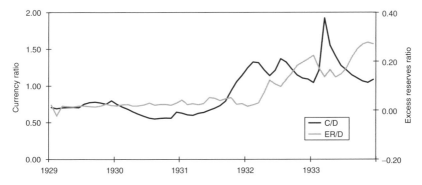

Figure 4.2
Currency-to-Deposit and Excess Reserves-to-Deposit Ratios in the U.S. (Data is for Federal Reserve Member Banks).
Source: U.S. Department of Commerce, Historical Statistics of the United States; Board of Governors of the Federal Reserve System, Banking and Monetary Statistics (Washington, D.C.: National Capital Press, 1943).

The Rational Expectations model also relies on the decline in the money supply to explain the Great Depression. In this explanation, the fall in the money supply was unexpected, fooling workers into demanding higher real wages and firms into thinking the price of their goods had fallen, together reducing production and aggregate output. A number of problems exist with this explanation, however.

Most importantly, it stretches credulity to think that a contraction as large and protracted as the Great Depression could be caused by a misunderstanding. It is also hard to understand how such a large fall in the money supply could be unexpected, fooling firms and workers for such a long period of time. This is not to say that expectations must be irrational; it does indicate that some form of market failure must have played a role in the Depression. The financial system is one important sector of the economy that is subject to such failures.

The proponents of Real Business Cycle models have long tried to identify a real supply shock or series of shocks that reduced aggregate productivity and initiated the Great Depression, but without much success. Some have focused on the effects of the Smoot-Hawley export tariffs imposed at the beginning of the Great Depression, which increased import tariffs by 40 percent. At the time, however, exports were only 7 percent of U.S. GDP, making it unlikely that these tariffs can explain even a small fraction of the large contraction in GDP. This leaves Real Business Cycle models with no persuasive explanation of why the Great Depression occurred, let alone why financial systems were particularly volatile over this period.

Conclusions

In the words of Keynes (1936): "the tendency to transform doing well into a speculative investment boom is the basic instability in a capitalist system." Spurred by the financial collapse Keynes witnessed during the Great Depression, financial systems and their role in feeding animal spirits and creating investment volatility were crucial components of his General Theory. Some postwar economists, such as Minsky in his Financial Instability Hypothesis, stayed relatively true to Keynes' vision and emphasized uncertainty and the role of financial fragility in creating and magnifying the size of business cycles. But most subsequent theories incrementally marginalized the role of finance in mainstream macroeconomics.

Postwar macroeconomic theories have made many vital contributions to our understanding of macroeconomics. Keynesians, using the IS–LM model, not only made Keynes more accessible by creating equilibrium models in which persistent shortfalls in output below the natural rate of output existed, but they also provided important insights into how monetary policy and fiscal policy could be used to stabilize the economy. Monetarism not only reasserted important Classical principles through the natural rate hypothesis, but took a skeptical look at the conduct of monetary policy that was a much needed antidote to overconfident Keynesian policy makers. Much the same can be said about the Rational Expectations model, which forced macroeconomists to consider more carefully how people form their expectations of the future and the role these expectations play in economic instability and the impact of economic policy. Finally, Real Business Cycle models have encouraged economists to pay more attention to supply factors such as productivity, capacity utilization, and input prices when investigating business cycles. They have also made economists think more carefully about the microeconomic foundations of the macroeconomic models they develop by emphasizing microeconomic principles such as utility maximization, profit maximization, and market equilibrium.

Even given these contributions, however, the dominant postwar models of Keynesianism, Monetarism, and Neoclassical theories have important shortcomings when it comes to providing a complete and persuasive explanation of economic contractions. The best example of this is their lack of a convincing explanation of the Great Depression. One important reason behind these shortcomings is a general lack of understanding about the microeconomic foundations of financial systems and how market failure in finance driven by uncertainty creates the kind of instability that can explain recessions and depressions. Instead, Keynesian, Monetarist, and Neoclassical models focus solely on changes in expectations and government policy, particularly monetary policy, as the cause of business cycles. These models simply assumed that financial intermediation always takes place smoothly and efficiently. This glaring omission in macroeconomic theory lasted until the mid-1980s, when new models were developed to better explain both the microeconomics behind financial intermediation and the fundamental causes of financial and macroeconomic instability. These new models, referred to as New Institutional theories of finance, are the subject of the next two chapters.

CHAPTER 5

New Institutional Theories of Finance: Models of Risk and the Costs of Credit Intermediation

Introduction

With the exception of Keynes' General Theory, the mainstream macroeconomic theories developed after the Great Depression stand in sharp contrast to earlier theories of business cycles in regard to the relatively minor role attributed to financial systems. What is paradoxical about this trend was that the importance of finance in macroeconomic theory was falling at the same time that its importance in the real economy was dramatically increasing.

However, this trend toward the minimization of finance in macroeconomic theory ended in the 1980s with a new group of models referred to as *New Institutional theories of finance*. New Institutional theories fall within a class of models known as New Keynesian models. *New Keynesian models* refer to a broad group of models that focus on investigating the macroeconomic effects of imperfect competition and market failure, particularly in explaining how market failure can amplify small exogenous shocks into large business cycles. While market failures, such as price and wage rigidity or financial market disequilibrium, have been a part of macroeconomic theory since Keynes' General Theory, they were typically investigated within ad hoc models that simply assumed certain things about the way that markets work, with no real analysis of why these market failures exist or how it could result from rational behavior. All New Keynesian models share the goal of developing more rigorous models of market failure with better microeconomic foundations. Adding microeconomic foundations means that market failure in New Keynesian theories occurs as a result of firms and households engaging in optimizing behavior. As a result, New Keynesian models incorporate important Neoclassical concepts such as rational expectations (from the Rational Expectations model), the natural rate hypothesis (from Monetarists), and dynamic marginal analysis (from Real Business Cycle models). The problem with these previous Neoclassical models was that they had a difficult time explaining large and persistent contractions, such as the Great Depression. New Keynesian models aim to show that even after adopting these Neoclassical principles, Keynesian results such as persistent unemployment and shortfalls of output below the natural rate of output can still exist, providing a comprehensive and plausible explanation of business cycles.

New Institutional theories of finance, which focus on market failure within the financial system, are a crucial component of this broad New Keynesian research agenda and are the focus of both this chapter and the next chapter. This chapter will introduce some of the basic principles of New Institutional theories. It will also develop one of its most important groups of models, referred to as Financial Accelerator models, which examine the microeconomic fundamentals behind how changes in the costs of credit intermediation magnify economic volatility.

What is Meant by "New Institutional" Theories of Finance?

Four important observations about financial systems are shared by all New Institutional theories of finance:

The study of the macroeconomic implications of finance has to begin with the study of the microeconomic behavior of banks, financial markets, firms, and households There is a great deal of heterogeneity among those who participate in finance. Not every firm and household shares the same default risk, just like not every lender shares the same willingness to accept risk when making loans. To simply assume uniform representative agents, as Neoclassical and even Keynesian macroeconomic models have done, and focus only on finance from a macroeconomic perspective means that the complexity of the interactions between individuals in the financial system get ignored and many important macroeconomic implications are missed. For example, many microeconomic details of financing, such as measures of risk and leverage, get ignored in representative agent models. By focusing on heterogeneity and microlevel financial fundamentals, New Institutional theories provide much deeper insight into the process of financial intermediation and its macroeconomic impact. (For this insight, New Institutional theories owe a debt to Fisher's Debt-Deflation theory and Minsky's Financial Instability Hypothesis model, as argued in detail in Fazzari, 1992.)

When examining financial activity, the primary focus should be on the provision of credit and not just on the total amount of liquidity or the money supply There is an important distinction to be made between liquidity and credit. Liquidity refers to the total amount of loanable funds that are potentially available to a financial institution or in the financial system as a whole. Liquidity changes when there is a change in the funds available to lenders. This occurs when either the amount of savings changes within an economy, or when there is a change in the money supply (such as a change in the monetary base by the central bank, which involves the trade of an asset to the central bank in return for loanable funds). Liquidity is typically measured by a measure of the money supply such as M1 or M2.

On the other hand, credit is a more difficult thing to measure. *Credit* refers to the total amount of loanable funds that a financial institution or financial system is actually willing to provide. In other words, credit is based both on total liquidity and on the willingness of financial institutions to make a loan. During periods of pessimism, New Institution theories argue that it is possible for liquidity to be high but for the supply of credit to be low. Likewise, even if liquidity is tight (for instance, if the central bank is restricting money growth) it is possible that optimistic financial institutions could be increasing the credit available to borrowers.

This leads to another important distinction between credit and liquidity: because the willingness to lend is a key component of credit, perceived default risk plays a crucial role in determining credit, even more than the interest rate. Default risk can change when there is a change in the financial position of a borrower, when there is a change in the profitability of the project a borrower wishes to undertake, or when there is a change in the borrower's commitment to repaying. Just as importantly, perceived default risk can change when there is a change in the financial position of the lender. Finally, default risk can also change when there is a change in the expected future performance of the macroeconomy. Thus, the evaluation of risk is a complex process that is subject to a great deal of uncertainty. This means that the provision of credit is also likely to be volatile.

The most important reason that financial transactions are imperfectly competitive is that financial information is imperfect

Since Adam Smith it has been recognized that the principal reason that financial markets are not perfectly competitive is that imperfect and asymmetric information exists between borrowers and lenders. If you remember our discussion in Chapter 1, *asymmetric information* in the context of financial transactions refers to the fact that borrowers always have better information about their own credit worthiness than lenders. In the case of firms, they have better knowledge about the profitability of the projects they wish to undertake with the funds that they borrow. In the case of both firms and households, the borrower has better information about their financial health and their commitment to repay. As a result, the provision of credit is reliant upon the availability of good information—along with liquidity, it is the principal input in the creation of credit. When a borrower can provide reliable information that convinces the lender that they are unlikely to default, then loans will be made available. If the borrower is unable to do this, either because of a lack of a credit history or because of the existence of information that indicates they have a high risk of default, then credit will not be provided.

Asymmetric information distorts the incentives that lenders and borrowers face when making a transaction, and as a result increases default risk in two important ways. The first has to do with the fact that individual borrowers who have high default risks are the ones who are most likely to seek loans. The reason for this is clear: risky borrowers are those who are most likely to gamble with both their own funds and other's funds, while conservative borrowers are less likely to suffer losses and need a loan. This problem, which takes place before any financial transaction takes place, is referred to as *adverse selection*. Because lenders are aware of adverse selection, they are more reluctant to provide credit to all borrowers because they do not have perfect information about who is an acceptable and unacceptable risk.

The second way that asymmetric information increases default risk is by encouraging more risky behavior by the borrower after credit has been provided. When credit is provided in the form of a loan, either from a bank or through a debt instrument such as a bond, the lender assumes some of the downside risk of the projects the borrower undertakes; if a project fails and the borrower defaults, then the lender is going to be out of a portion if not all of their money. However, the upside benefits of these projects are not shared so equally. If the project turns out to be a huge success and the borrower realizes large profits, they do not have to share any of these gains with the lender; they simply have to repay the loan. The incentive this creates for borrowers is obvious. When borrowers are able to allocate some of the downside risk of a project to others while keeping all of the upside benefits of a project for themselves, it encourages borrowers to engage in riskier behavior than they otherwise would. This incentive problem is known as *moral hazard*. Moral hazard is one of the fundamental problems in finance. In fact, when you consider the fact that most financial institutions are in some ways both borrowers and lenders (for instance, banks make loans but also take deposits) it is possible for financial institutions to be victims of moral hazard at the same time that they are guilty of engaging in moral hazard.

Adverse selection and moral hazard are important factors in determining the supply of credit. Because these problems are the result of asymmetric information, the poorer the quality of information that is available on a borrower, the more likely it is that a lender will limit the borrower's credit or increase the price the borrower will have to pay for credit. In the real world, this means that newer, smaller firms that have not had time to establish a credit history and do not have the resources to provide a large amount of financial information to lenders are likely to receive less credit on costlier terms. One of the important functions of banks is to overcome these problems and obtain information about these small borrowers so that they can obtain sufficient credit. Banks have traditionally done this in a couple of ways. One way is by establishing long-term relationships with small borrowers that allows borrowers to build a credit history. Another is through becoming experts in monitoring borrowers by becoming familiar with the local community in which borrowers operate and with the individuals that their borrowers work with. When firms borrow, they have better knowledge about the profitability of the projects they wish to undertake with the funds that they borrow.

There is no mechanism to ensure that the supply of credit equals the demand for credit. As a result, disequilibrium in the financial market is persistent, maybe even permanent

Because risk perceptions, and not just interest rates, determine the supply of credit, there is no mechanism to eliminate a shortage of credit during a period of pessimism. When financial institutions perceive higher than acceptable risk in making new loans, they are reluctant to extend credit regardless of the interest rate. In essence, there are risk externalities associated with lending so that the usual price mechanisms of financial markets do not guarantee equilibrium. This market failure has important implications for the efficiency and stability of financial intermediation, which is where we turn now.

The Financial Accelerator Model and the Role of Credit in Business Cycles

What role do asymmetric information and imperfectly competitive financial markets play in generating macroeconomic instability? One of the most influential models of how imperfectly competitive financial markets propagate business cycles was developed by Ben Bernanke and Mark Gertler in a series of papers (Bernanke and Gertler, 1987, 1989, 1990, 1995). In their *Financial Accelerator model*, the financial fundamentals of borrowers and lenders affect bankruptcy risk, which in turn affects the costs of credit and the aggregate level of credit. As a result, even small microeconomic changes in the balance sheets of firms, households, and banks can have a significant impact on macroeconomic behavior.

To understand why financial fundamentals play such a big role in the provision of credit, Bernanke and Gertler focus on the costs that borrowers and lenders incur in a financial transaction, what they refer to as the *cost of credit intermediation*. From the perspective of borrowers, the cost of credit intermediation is in part determined by the interest rate, but not entirely. The costs of providing information are also a big consideration in any financial transaction because information is expensive. Not only do borrowers have to obtain and organize basic financial information to provide to perspective lenders before a loan, but they also have to incur *monitoring costs*, or the costs of periodically providing additional information to a lender over the life of a loan. Borrowers might also have to provide collateral or *compensating balances* (deposits made by the borrower which are held by the lender), which have an opportunity cost associated with them. In the case of a bond or stock issue, there are significant underwriting costs that are incurred by borrowers when an investment bank sells these bonds to the public.

In addition, lenders also incur significant costs of credit intermediation as resources are needed to monitor borrowers by organizing and analyzing financial and credit history data. These costs incurred by lenders are passed on to borrowers either directly through fees or indirectly through higher interest rates.

Because of the sizeable costs associated with credit intermediation, firms prefer to finance investment projects internally, meaning from their own retained earnings. Of course, it is not possible for most firms to finance their own projects completely, which is why most firms rely to some extent on external finance, even though it is more expensive. Financial theory predicts that firms have a hierarchy of finance that they follow. After exhausting their internal finance, firms prefer to issue debt through financial markets. However, the bond option is available to only the largest firms that are raising large amounts of funds and that have established credit records. Other firms are forced to get their financing through banks, usually at a significantly higher cost than bonds. Firms that cannot raise enough through debt move to equity, which has the significant downsides that it dilutes ownership and profits and may signal to outside investors that the firm thinks its stock price is overvalued.

Bernanke and Gertler's principal insight is that the cost of credit intermediation, and thus the overall level of credit in an economy, is a function of the financial fundamentals of both borrowers and the lenders. While naive financial analysts focus simply on the debt levels of borrowers, it should be clear that debt levels are not the determining factor in the default risk of borrowers, and hence their credit worthiness. Even if a borrower has a high level of debt, they can still attract credit if they have a large asset base that can be collateralized. Instead, it is net worth, or total assets minus total debt obligations, which is the principal factor in determining the default risk of a borrower. In addition, other financial variables such as cash flow also play a smaller but important role in shaping the financial fundamentals and default risk of borrowers.

To see how changes in net worth affect the costs of credit intermediation and aggregate output, consider the effects of a change in the net worth of borrowers. Assume that a recession occurs that hurts firms' sales and reduces their net worth. A fall in net worth increases the bankruptcy risk of these firms. This will lead to an increase in the cost of obtaining future credit for these borrowers, either because lenders want to increase interest rates or because lenders will demand more information, more collateral, more monitoring, more compensating balances, and so on; these higher costs of credit intermediation mean that some firms (and some households that would like to borrow to purchase durable consumption goods) cannot afford to obtain additional credit. This occurs at exactly the same time that, because of the recession, firms and households need credit the most. Lower credit reduces the demand for investment and consumption, ultimately serving to accelerate the speed and the size of the economic downturn. (Note that this process is similar to that in the Financial Instability Hypothesis of Minsky, but with much more detail regarding how these microeconomic conditions have macroeconomic effects.)

This process works from the other side of the financial transaction as well. A lender's willingness to extend credit is not only a function of the borrower's financial position but of their own financial position as well. Once again, consider the case of a recession that increases the default rates of borrowers that in turn reduces the net worth of banks. These capital losses force banks to reduce their risk exposure and move toward holding more liquid, less risky assets. If they are to engage in any new lending, banks are forced to charge higher interest rates and require more information, more collateral, and more monitoring. This increases the costs of credit intermediation and reduces the efficiency and the quantity of lending. Once again, this accelerates the speed and the size of the contraction in output.

This Financial Accelerator model has four important implications for business cycles. First, the financial accelerator process creates both changes in aggregate demand and changes in aggregate supply that play an important role in propagating business cycles. Let us consider a typical recession in the Financial Accelerator model, which is illustrated in Figure 5.1. It begins with an exogenous shock that reduces aggregate demand. This shock could come from an unexpected fall in the money supply (such as in the Monetarist or Rational Expectations model). This shock could also come from a change in confidence driven by animal spirits (such as in the Keynesian model), particularly a change in confidence driven by a change in the perceived risk of the overall financial system. (New Keynesians also do not rule out supply-initiated business cycles from exogenous changes in productivity.) Regardless of the source of the fall in aggregate demand, investment and consumption demand begin to fall, similar to the old Keynesian model. As aggregate demand falls, inflexible wages and prices in the labor and goods markets lead to falls in income and increases in unemployment.

This is when the financial accelerator kicks in. As the recession takes hold, firms and households see their cash flows slow down and their net worths fall, leading to an increase in defaults. These defaults reduce the net worth of banks and other lending institutions as well. As the net worth of borrowers and lenders fall, the costs of credit intermediation begin to rise. Firms and households are forced to cut back even further on their borrowing, which leads to another round of declines in investment, consumption, and aggregate demand. Just as importantly, firms are forced to cut back on their production because costlier credit increases the risks associated with producing more output, the reason being that excess inventories typically have to be financed by firms. As a result of this increase in the cost

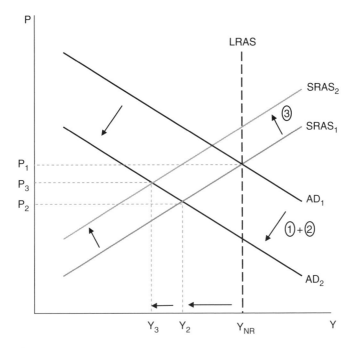

Figure 5.1
Recessions in the Financial Accelerator Model.

of production, coupled with reductions in capacity from lower investment and cutbacks in their labor force, aggregate supply begins to fall. This process continues in a downward spiral of sustained falls in aggregate demand and aggregate supply, creating a large and persistent recession.

How will recessions in the Financial Accelerator model end? Eventually, consumption and investment demand stabilize as firms and households have to replace capital and consumer durables that have worn out over time. In addition, wages and prices gradually adjust back toward equilibrium, which raises employment and aggregate output. As the economy stabilizes, lenders and firms reevaluate their risk assessments, which lead to a fall in the costs of credit intermediation and a resumption in borrowing. All of these things together move the economy back towards its natural rate. It is important to note, though, that exactly how much time this process takes is highly uncertain. It depends in part upon the flexibility of wages and prices. It also depends upon the flexibility of financial market participants in reevaluating risk perceptions and lowering the costs of credit intermediation. Even if the costs of credit intermediation fall quickly, credit may not be immediately restored if firms and households need to form new ties with lenders and insolvent borrowers have to reestablish their credit histories.

The second important implication of the Financial Accelerator model is that financial volatility does not initiate business cycles, but it does amplify them. Recessions begin with an exogenous shock that affects the financial fundamentals of borrowers and lenders. This shock could be a nominal shock from a change in aggregate demand or even a real shock in the form of a change in productivity that shifts aggregate supply. Once a shock occurs, regardless of its source, the financial accelerator magnifies otherwise small shocks into large swings in aggregate output.

Third, the financial accelerator effect is both nonlinear and asymmetric. It is nonlinear because the financial accelerator is likely to be more powerful during larger downturns, when net worths have fallen the most and cash flows are very tight, and the need for credit is at its most extreme. It is asymmetric because it amplifies recessions but is unlikely to have the same impact during expansions. This stems from the fact that firms are likely to be more sensitive to increases in the costs of credit intermediation during recessions when the returns on their investment projects are falling than they would be to any fall in the costs of credit during an expansion when profits are high and credit is easy. Thus, the financial accelerator is most likely to play a role during large recessions than during small downturns or expansions. This prediction of asymmetry is consistent with what we observe in the real world. As we discussed in Chapter 2, business cycles are asymmetric across countries, with recessions being considerably shorter than expansions but the changes in output that occur during recessions being considerably sharper.

The fourth implication of the Financial Accelerator model is that the effects of financial instability are not felt the same by all borrowers. For large corporations with high net worths, established credit records, and large sources of internal finance (through retained earnings), financial fundamentals and the financial accelerator play little role in determining their levels of credit and investment. However, smaller firms without established financial channels and without adequate capital will find that their credit and investment fluctuate significantly with their net worths and other measures of financial soundness. As illustrated in Matsuyama (2007), these changes in the composition of credit between firms and industries can have long-term implications for investment and productivity, even leading to booms or busts in specific industries. For these same reasons, changes in net worth disproportionately affect poorer households and their demand for durable consumption goods. Likewise, smaller lenders, such as banks, are the most likely to restrict their credit during recessions because of the impact of even a few defaults on their smaller asset portfolios. The reason that Classical and Neoclassical theories of finance are incapable of explaining the role of finance in generating business cycles is because they ignore these kinds of heterogeneity in financial intermediation.

The Financial Accelerator and Monetary Policy

How does monetary policy affect the macroeconomy? Explaining the fundamentals behind why changes in the money supply have real effects on the economy, or the *monetary transmission mechanism*, is crucial to understanding both the potential power of monetary policy and whether monetary policy can be used to effectively stabilize output and smooth business cycles. While this topic is investigated more fully in Chapter 7, it is worth briefly discussing here a few of the important implications of the Financial Accelerator model for the conduct of monetary policy.

In the traditional theory of the monetary transmission mechanism, an increase in the money supply increases the amount of liquidity in the financial system, which reduces interest rates; lower interest rates in turn stimulate consumption, investment, and aggregate output. However, in New Institutional theories such as the Financial Accelerator model, interest rates are only one component of the costs of credit. A reduction in interest rates may not significantly reduce the costs of credit intermediation if the other costs associated with lending remain high. This is particularly true during recessions and other times of pessimism when high levels of perceived risk may lead to a "pessimism trap" in which reductions in interest rates do not stimulate lending. Monetary policy in the Financial Accelerator model is also complicated by the fact that it disproportionally affects small firms and small banks, creating significant distributional and equality considerations for policy makers to consider.

Multiple questions are raised by these insights, all centering around alternative avenues by which monetary policy can affect economic activity other than through changing interest rates.

Do increases in the money supply reduce the default risk of banks and some firms, stimulating credit and aggregate output? Do increases in the money supply drive up asset prices and increase the amount of collateral that firms can use to reduce their costs of credit? Does monetary policy work through changes in aggregate demand or does it primarily work through aggregate supply by changing the risks associated with production? Or could it be that traditional instruments of monetary policy are largely ineffective and central banks need to investigate the use of other tools such as regulatory policy (e.g., loosening bank capital requirements during recessions)? Each of these questions, and others like them, are explored more fully in Chapter 7, which deals with new research on stabilization policy in theory and in practice.

The Empirical Evidence on the Financial Accelerator Model

Attempts to empirically evaluate the Financial Accelerator model have fallen into three categories:

Firm-level studies of financial stability
Unfortunately, firm-level financial data is difficult to obtain. However, some data from manufacturing firms in the U.S. have been available that clearly supports the conclusion that small firms play a disproportionately large role in business cycles. Figure 5.2 presents data on the volatility of total manufacturing sales compared to the volatility of sales of the smallest one-third and largest one-third of manufacturing firms. The volatility of small firm sales is particularly pronounced at business cycle turning points in 1981, 1982, and 1991. Clearly, small firms account for a disproportionate share of the volatility in total sales over the business cycle.

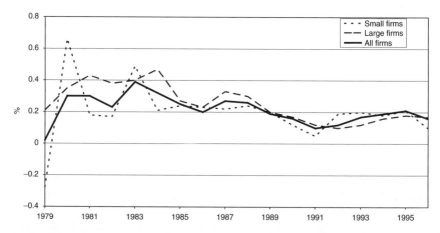

Figure 5.2
Volatility of Sales in Small and Large Manufacturing Firms in the U.S.
Source: Stanca, 2002.

Bernanke, Gertler, and Gilchrist (1996) conducted an exhaustive investigation of financial data from U.S. manufacturing firms and found that about one-third of the changes in aggregate income can be explained by differences in the financial fundamentals of small firms (less than $250 million in assets) relative to large firms. In other words, firms with weaker balance sheets play a disproportionately large role in explaining aggregate instability, just as the Financial Accelerator model would predict. This same result holds if instead of grouping firms based on size, firms are grouped according to the extent of their reliance on bank finance, as opposed to internal finance, bonds, or equity finance. This result is also consistent with the Financial Accelerator model because bank-dependent firms are more likely to be smaller, newer, have lower net worth, and be more sensitive to changes in the costs of credit intermediation. While their results are based on data from manufacturing firms alone, it is important to note that in other industries, small firms are actually more prevalent. By the authors' definition of small firms, 45 percent of manufacturing firms are small, as compared to 75 percent of wholesale and retail firms, 88 percent of service firms, and 90 percent of construction firms. As a result, if firm-level financial data were available for all of these industries, it is likely that we would find an even larger role for the financial fundamentals of small firms in explaining aggregate fluctuations.

Gilchrist and Himmelberg (1995) investigate the relationship between cash flows and investment. They find that a Neoclassical model of investment fits the behavior of large U.S. firms with access to bond markets very well. However, this Neoclassical model only explains half of the changes in investment for small firms without access to bond markets. This indicates that credit market imperfections play a significant role in the investment levels of financially weaker firms.

Fazzari, Hubbard, and Peterson (1988) use data from U.S. manufacturing firms but focus on the differences between firms that can rely on internal finance and those firms that have to rely to some extent on financing their activities externally through banks or financial markets. Interestingly, all sizes of firms rely primarily on internal finance, with smaller firms relying on it the most. For example, the smallest firms (less than $10 million in assets) had retention ratios (which is the ratio of retained earnings to total earnings) of 80 percent, while the largest firms (greater than $1 billion in assets) had retention ratios of 50 percent. Fazzari, Hubbard, and Peterson find that those firms with the highest retention ratios (i.e., those firms that have exhausted all of their internal finance and have to rely more heavily on external finance) had investment levels that were the most sensitive to various measures of cash flows and overall financial health. On the other hand, firms with low retention ratios (i.e., firms with little demand for external finance) and more liquid balance sheets had more stable investment levels. These findings are robust to changes in the time period, firm size, firm age, and other measures of economic activity. These conclusions are entirely consistent with the predictions of the Financial Accelerator model.

Studies investigating the impact of financial fundamentals on macroeconomic fluctuations

Numerous studies have found significant correlations between changes in the levels of aggregate financial activity and the behavior of aggregate investment, consumption, inventories, and employment (see Bernanke, Gertler, and Gilchrist [1996] for a complete review of these studies). In one particular study, Stanca (2002) found that the average debt-to-asset ratio and the interest payments-to-cash flow ratio for U.S. manufacturing firms are strongly procyclical. The variances of these ratios are strongly procyclical as well. This indicates that both leverage and the dispersion of leverage rise during an expansion as firms take on more debt and lenders are eager to extend it. During contractions, however, firms are forced to reduce their amount of debt, either through reducing their demand for credit or because they are cut off by lenders. Lower borrowing impacts investment and amplifies swings in output. Once again, Stanca finds that the cyclical movements in debt are stronger for small firms and weaker for large firms.

Additional evidence on the costs of credit intermediation is found in the data on interest rate spreads. Figure 5.3 presents the interest rate spread between bonds rated Baa (bonds with relatively high default risk) and the U.S. 10-year treasury bonds (T-bonds; bonds with zero default risk). As this figure illustrates, this spread is negatively related to growth in commercial credit, indicating that changes in perceived risk and the costs of credit intermediation play a significant role in credit fluctuations. Similar results are found when examining the commercial paper

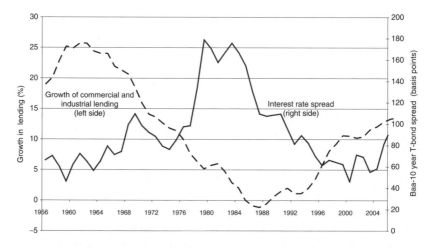

Figure 5.3
Interest Rate Spread and Commercial Lending in the U.S.
Source: Board of Governors of the Federal Reserve System Release H15 Historical Data.

market. Friedman and Kuttner (1993) find that the interest rate spread between commercial paper and treasury bills (T-bills) is a significant predictor of real economic activity. (They also find that changes in the quantity of commercial paper are also significant, even after controlling for movements in the interest rate spread. This indicates that factors in addition to the price of credit are driving changes in real activity—more on this in the next chapter.) The authors find that it is changes in cash flows and default risk that are the most significant predictors of movements in interest rates spreads and the quantity of credit in the commercial paper market.

Finally, some empirical studies have found that financial fundamentals do not just affect business cycle behavior, they also affect growth. Beck *et al.* (2004) find that countries with higher levels of financial development see higher growth in industries with a higher concentration of small firms, exactly as New Institutional theory would predict.

Changes in the terms and composition of lending over the business cycle
Asea and Bloomberg (1998) looked at over 2 million bank loan applications in the U.S. between 1977 and 1993. They find that the costs of credit intermediation are strongly countercyclical, with risk premiums and collateral requirements rising during recessions and falling during expansions. Likewise, Lang and Nakamura (1995) find that the number of bank loans made above the prime rate (i.e., loans made to borrowers with a higher possibility of default) falls during a recession. These studies, and others like them, suggest that the costs of credit intermediation are countercyclical and reduce the quantity demanded of credit during recessions.

Kayshap, Stein, and Wilcox (1993) investigate how financial markets and bank lending respond to changes in the money supply. Their results indicate that when the Fed cuts the money supply, the quantity of commercial paper rises but there is little change in the quantity of bank loans provided. They interpret this as follows: when the Fed tightens bank credit, higher costs of credit intermediation force higher quality borrowers to move away from banks and towards direct finance through commercial paper, leaving lower quality borrowers to complete for bank credit at costlier terms. Gertler and Gilchrist (1993) find similar evidence regarding the effects of changes in the money supply on small firms. They find that U.S. bank loans to small manufacturing firms and households fall relative to the bank loans to large manufacturing firms during periods of contractionary monetary policy. Likewise, other studies find that the volume of private bonds issued by small firms falls sharply relative to the public offerings of bonds by large firms during contractions. All of these studies suggest important reasons why small firms' financial positions and their access to credit are so volatile over the business cycle and why the financial accelerator provides crucial insights into macroeconomic volatility.

CASE STUDY: A New Institutional Explanation of the Great Depression

In Chapter 4, Keynes', Keynesian, Monetarist, and Neoclassical explanations of the Great Depression were examined. The Keynesian and Monetarist models in particular were developed around the goal of trying to provide a convincing explanation of the Great Depression. However, each of these theories' explanations has significant inadequacies, leaving them short of being fully persuasive.

The Great Depression has also become one of the focal points of empirical research conducted by proponents of New Institutional theories, particularly Ben Bernanke, in an attempt to address the shortcomings of previous macroeconomic theory. (Bernanke was appointed by President Bush as the chairman of the Federal Reserve Board in 2005, and began his tenure in this important role in January of 2006.) In his research, Bernanke argues that the best way to understand the Great Depression, particularly the depth and persistence of the contraction in output, is to view it first and foremost as a financial crisis. It is impossible to do this without understanding the fundamentals of financial systems in the U.S. and internationally.

In a series of papers (Bernanke, 1983, 1995; Bernanke and Gertler, 1987; Bernanke and James, 1991; Bernanke and Lown, 1991), Bernanke contends that the shock that initiated the Great Depression was a sustained fall in the money supply that began in 1928. However, Bernanke differs from Monetarists in that he believes that the primary reason the money supply fell was not the ignorance of the Fed but because of the U.S. commitment to a flawed gold standard.

Under the gold standard that was reinstated after World War I, a country experiencing a trade deficit suffered a gold outflow that reduced its money supply, precipitating lower prices and reequilibrating its balance of trade. However, the gold standard was not symmetric because a trade surplus did not have to lead to the opposite occurring. Many countries tried to follow *beggar-thy-neighbor* trade policies, in which they manipulated their money supplies in order to maintain a permanent trade surplus. To do this, a country running a trade surplus would *sterilize* their gold inflows, meaning they would increase their gold holdings without increasing their money supply. Sterilizing gold inflows prevented rising inflation, which would discourage exports, encourage imports, and dissipate trade surpluses.

While a beggar-thy-neighbor policy might be a logical strategy for one country to follow in isolation, it is a destabilizing policy if every country tries to do it at the same time. In the late 1920s, the effects of widespread commitments to beggar-thy-neighbor policies were disastrous. While trade deficit countries were forced to reduce their money supplies, trade surplus countries kept their money supplies constant (or in the case of the U.S., actually decreasing their money supply as

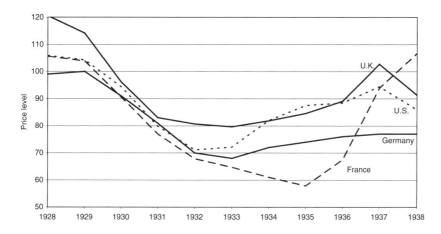

Figure 5.4
Wholesale Prices in Four Countries.
Source: Federal Reserve Archival System for Economic Research, http://fraser.stlouisfed.org.

they received gold inflows). The result was worldwide deflation. In the U.S., this deflation was made worse by waves of banking panics that took place in the early 1930s, which increased money holdings and reduced the money multiplier, the money supply, and prices despite the fact that the Fed belatedly tried to reverse course by increasing the monetary base. In the end, wholesale prices worldwide fell by more than 40 percent between 1929 and 1932 and by similar levels in other countries, as can be seen in Figure 5.4. This process continued unabated across countries until, one-by-one, they abandoned the gold standard. The U.S. was one of the last to leave the gold standard, hanging on until 1933.

Why was deflation so costly during the Great Depression? In perfectly competitive markets in which prices and wages are perfectly flexible, deflation would not be costly and changes in the money supply would be neutral. Keynes argued that wage inflexibility was the primary reason why deflation was costly, driving up real wages and unemployment.

Deflation can be costly for other reasons as well. Irving Fisher noted that financial prices are also not perfectly flexible. His Debt-Deflation theory, which was discussed in Chapter 3, highlights the macroeconomic implications of nominal debt contracts that are not indexed. When nominal debt contracts are fixed, a fall in the price level increases the real value of debt at the same time that it reduces the real value of assets that are used as collateral. This increases default rates among borrowers. As banks and financial market participants see the number of defaulted or delinquent loans in their portfolio rise, they readjust their risk perceptions, reduce their lending, and sell their less liquid assets for more liquid assets. Of course, if a large number of asset holders do this at once, it further sparks panic selling, further depresses asset prices, and further weakens lenders' and borrowers' financial positions. The end result is a vicious cycle that can lead to financial collapse. As a result, Fisher believed that financial fundamentals and the effects that deflation had on these fundamentals were the key to understanding the depth and the duration of the Great Depression. This belief is shared with Minsky's Financial Instability Hypothesis model as well as with the Financial Accelerator model.

The Debt-Deflation theory and the Financial Instability model are important influences on New Institutional theories of finance, but there are two primary differences. First, the Financial Accelerator model more carefully develops the microeconomic foundations of financial volatility. Second, the Financial Accelerator model emphasizes price mechanisms and how the financial fundamentals of borrowers and lenders affect the costs of credit intermediation. On the other hand, the Debt-Deflation theory and the Financial Instability Hypothesis emphasize reductions in the supply of credit (regardless of what a borrower is willing to pay) caused by bankruptcy fears and weakening financial positions.

The macroeconomic and firm-level financial data from the era supports the hypothesis that financial fundamentals played a crucial role in explaining behavior during the Great Depression. Looking at the macroeconomic financial data, there is ample evidence of widespread financial weakness in the U.S. economy before and during the Depression, particularly among banks. The 1920s were not a good time for U.S. banks because of declines in agricultural prices. Particularly hard hit were rural banks, which were typically small and undiversified. In fact, over 6,000 banks failed in the 1920s. However, these problems did not stop lenders from rapidly expanding credit; total debt roughly doubled over the decade. As the Great Depression and deflation struck, the aggregate debt-to-income ratio jumped from 9 percent in 1929 to 19.8 percent in 1932 and half of all farm loans became delinquent. Likewise, small firms with capital of between $50,000 and $100,000 lost one-third of their total capital from losses in 1932 alone, leading to a large number of defaults among firms (Calomiris, 1993). Homeowners were also widely in default. In Cleveland, Indianapolis, and Birmingham, more than half of all home mortgages were in default. At the same time, three states and more than 300 cities were in default (Friedman, 2005).

Not only were banks subjected to large losses and reductions in their net worths because of these defaults, but as a result of the Fed's refusal to provide short-term lending to banks, the public lost confidence in banks, which led to massive deposit outflows. As a result of deflation, higher defaults, deposit outflows, and a lack of a true lender of last resort, banks that were highly leveraged and weak before the Great Depression began to fail at unprecedented rates. Between 1929 and 1933, nearly 10,000 banks (25 percent of the total) failed or suspended payments and nearly half of all banks disappeared (due to failure or merger).

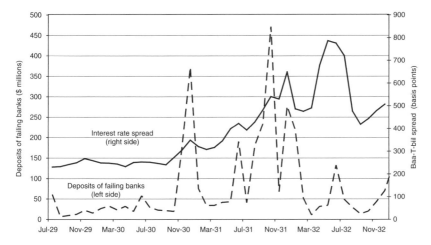

Figure 5.5
Interest Rate Spread and Banking Failures in the U.S.
Source: Bernake, 1983.

Looking at firm-level financial data, Bernanke (1983) examines the role that deflation and reductions in the net worth of lenders and borrowers played in increasing the costs of credit intermediation. There is ample evidence that the costs of credit intermediation rose in the U.S. during the Great Depression because of multiple factors. First, asset prices fell significantly during the Depression, even more than wholesale prices. For example, the stock market fell by nearly 85 percent between 1929 and 1932. This not only reduced the net worth of both borrowers and lenders, but it reduced the value of their collateral as well. Second, Figure 5.5 presents the interest rate spread between Baa bonds (corporate bonds of moderate risk) and U.S. T-bills. This spread is a measure of perceived default risk, and this spread increased dramatically during the Depression, closely following the deposits of banks that failed over the period. The larger the interest rate spread, the higher the costs of credit intermediation. Finally, bank runs forced banks to hold more excess reserves and more liquid assets to reduce their bankruptcy risk, increasing their costs of providing credit. The fact that the share of bank lending in total lending fell during the Depression is strong evidence that the costs of bank lending increased significantly. Of course, nonbank lending through debt or equity markets was not available to many small borrowers, meaning that small firms and households were disproportionally hit hard by higher costs of credit intermediation.

Another piece of empirical evidence comes from credit surveys that were conducted during this time, which indicate that a broad cross-section of firms felt the negative effects of the higher costs of credit intermediation. These surveys, which are reviewed by Bernanke (1983), indicate that obtaining credit was difficult and costly both during and after the Depression, particularly for small firms and households. In one of these surveys, 75 percent of firms reported that they could not obtain credit through their regular channels during the 1933–1938 period, which is after the worst of the Depression had already passed.

An important question remains: did financial instability serve as the primary cause of the Great Depression, or was financial collapse just one symptom of the greater macroeconomic contraction as argued by Classical and Neoclassical economists? One way to address this question is to look at the timing of various aspects of the financial crisis. Banking failures, drops in the stock market, drops in the bond markets, and changes in credit all preceded changes in aggregate output. Bernanke (1983) presents econometric evidence that changes in the deposits of failing banks and changes in the liabilities of failing firms are both significant predictors of changes in investment and production, controlling for lagged changes in output and other monetary factors.

The Great Depression was an international phenomenon; world output fell by nearly 50 percent between 1928 and 1932, and a number of countries experienced financial collapse. A great deal of international evidence suggests that financial systems played an integral role in driving, and not just responding to, the Great Depression in other nations, just as it did in the U.S. Bernanke and James (1991) present econometric evidence that banking panics had a significant and persistent effect on production and investment across countries. For example, in 1932, countries experiencing banking crises saw industrial production fall by 16 percent, while countries that avoided banking crises saw industrial production fall by only 2 percent. They also present empirical evidence that those countries that experienced banking crises were those countries that were on the gold standard and experienced the most deflation. In addition, countries that suffered from a banking crisis had weak financial fundamentals in their banking system across a variety of measures before the crisis began. For example, banking crisis countries had higher levels of short-term foreign-denominated debt, often referred to as "hot money" because of the ease by which depositors can withdraw these funds. Crisis country banks also were smaller and undiversified (like in the U.S.) and had large amounts of equity holdings, which are very risky because of the volatility of stock prices. Finally, macroeconomic indicators in banking crisis countries were weak before the Great Depression began; growth was low, unemployment high, and debt levels large.

Conclusions

New Institutional theories of finance are consistent with Keynes' emphasis on the importance of market failures in financial systems, but use models with more persuasive microeconomic foundations behind them. The Financial Accelerator model has played an important role in changing the study of macroeconomics by focusing on financial systems as the key to transmitting and amplifying small shocks throughout the economy and driving business cycles.

The Financial Accelerator model is best characterized by its four most important conclusions. First, firm-level measures of net worth and cash flows along with other macroeconomic measures of financial fundamentals are crucial to determining default risk, and it is changes in default risk that determine the costs of credit intermediation and changes in the quantity of credit. Thus, like old Keynesians, New Keynesians believe that changes in perceptions and confidence are crucial in generating economic instability. However, unlike the Keynesian model in which beliefs were highly subjective and not necessarily related to changes in fundamentals, changes in beliefs about the future in the Financial Accelerator model are rational responses to changes in the financial conditions of borrowers and lenders that affect their default risk.

Second, fluctuations in the costs of credit intermediation and in the quantity of credit are highly persistent, especially during recessions, and most likely to impact small borrowers and lenders. Contractions in credit are persistent because the balance sheet fundamentals of borrowers and lenders only change slowly; as a result, risk perceptions only change slowly. In addition, after a contraction in credit it takes a long time for borrowers to reestablish credit links and rehabilitate damaged credit histories. Because these factors are most likely to affect small lenders and small borrowers, smaller banks are most likely to restrict credit and small firms and households are most likely to suffer sustained losses of credit and persistent reductions in production during recessions.

Third, persistent changes in risk perceptions and the costs of credit intermediation not only affect consumption and investment demand, but they also increase the risk of production and reduce productive capacity. As a result, both changes in aggregate demand and changes in aggregate supply are responsible for fluctuations in output over the business cycle in the Financial Accelerator model. In other words, the propagation of business cycles are both demand and supply driven, making them more complex than in previous macroeconomic models.

Finally, because the mechanisms of financial markets and business cycles are complex, monetary policy can have different effects under different circumstances. During a contraction driven by higher-risk perceptions, an economy could be caught in a pessimism trap during which an increase in money growth that would stimulate output growth at other times would have little or no impact on output. Likewise, different monetary policy tools could have different effects at different times. A traditional open market operation might have little impact on lending during a recession. On the other hand, an increase in discount lending directed toward small banks, which are most likely to lend to small borrowers, might be more effective during a recession in reducing the costs of credit intermediation and stimulating lending.

The Financial Accelerator model is not the only New Institutional theory of finance. The next chapter discusses another group of New Institutional theories, known as models of credit rationing, which reach many of the same conclusions as the Financial Accelerator model, albeit for different reasons. The distinct under-pinnings of these models lead to additional insights into the importance of financial fundamentals and highlight alternative channels through which financial systems breed business cycles.

CHAPTER 6

New Institutional Theories of Finance: Models of Credit Rationing

Introduction

While the Financial Accelerator model provides important insights into the interplay between financial systems and business cycles, it is not without its shortcomings. Various economists have raised three important critiques. First, and most importantly, there is extensive empirical evidence that investment demand is inelastic to changes in interest rates (see Chirinko [1993] for a comprehensive review of this evidence). Figure 6.1 illustrates the relatively weak negative correlation between changes in interest rates and changes in investment. If investment demand is not sensitive to interest rates, why would investment demand be sensitive to changes in the cost of credit intermediation? There is no existing empirical evidence that borrowers are responsive enough to changes in the costs of credit to explain the large volatility of investment (see Mojon, Smets, and Vermeulen, 2002).

The second problem is that banks use a number of nonprice commitments to reduce risk, such as requiring collateral and asking for co-signers on loans. These terms are not a direct factor in the costs incurred by a borrower (e.g., a firm can still use their collateral in production during the life of a loan), but they are still conditions that are difficult to meet. As a result, borrowers often find that their credit is limited regardless of the price they are willing to pay for it; in other words, they are credit constrained, not price constrained.

Finally, the Financial Accelerator model argues that as risk rises during recessions, the costs of credit intermediation rise as well, part of which takes the form of an increase in the interest rates charged to borrowers. However, higher interest rates (both real and nominal) exacerbate default risk through three channels.

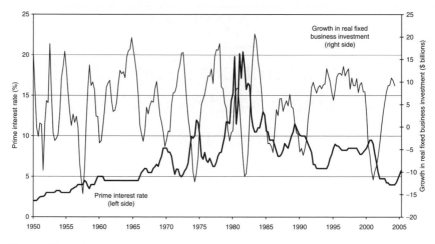

Figure 6.1
Interest Rates and Investment in the U.S.
Source: Federal Reserve Economic Data [FRED], http://research.stlouisfed.org/fred2.

First, higher interest rates increase the debt-servicing burden on borrowers, making payments harder to meet. Second, higher interest rates mean that more high-risk borrowers are likely to apply for credit. As we discussed in the previous chapter, this problem is referred to as *adverse selection*. Third, higher interest rates mean that borrowers that have already received credit are more likely to engage in riskier activities to cover their higher interest payments; this problem is referred to as *moral hazard*. Because of these concerns about bankruptcy risk during times when perceived risk is already high, lenders may be very reluctant to increase interest rates or other costs that figure into the costs of credit intermediation during recessions. If lenders are reluctant to pass the higher costs of lending onto borrowers, the channel by which the Financial Accelerator mechanism works breaks down.

These problems have not caused economists to completely dismiss the Financial Accelerator model, but they have encouraged economists to look for additional channels through which financial fundamentals and risk affect the macroeconomy. Another class of New Institutional theories of finance known as *models of credit rationing* focus on credit limits and other constraints lenders place on the quantity of credit made available to borrowers. These credit limits are a function of the financial strength of borrowers and lenders. As a result, credit constraints fluctuate over the business cycle and amplify economic fluctuations. This chapter reviews these models of credit rationing and examines the role of credit constraints in financial and economic activity.

Two Models of Credit Rationing

Models of credit rationing share many of the same features as the Financial Accelerator model. These models emphasize the importance of asymmetric information and the heterogeneity of borrowers and lenders. Because lenders have imperfect information about borrowers, there is always uncertainty regarding default risk, forcing lenders to form expectations of the default risk associated with each borrower. These risk perceptions are usually based on two factors. First, the financial fundamentals of an individual borrower, primarily the borrower's net worth and cash flows. Second, how future macroeconomic conditions might affect the borrower's balance sheet. The financial fundamentals of lenders are important as well and influence the supply of credit because more fragile lenders must assume less risk. Because of the importance of risk perceptions in the provision of credit, disequilibrium is a persistent, if not a permanent, aspect of financial markets and changes in financial fundamentals drive changes in lending, investment, and consumption within an economy.

What models of credit rationing and the Financial Accelerator model disagree about is the channel by which changes in the net worth of borrowers and lenders affect the market for credit. In the Financial Accelerator model, credit is price rationed, meaning that changes in the price of credit lead to fluctuations in its quantity. These changes in price are driven by changes in the cost of credit intermediation, which rise as the financial fundamentals of lenders and borrowers deteriorate (which occurs during a recession). As the costs of credit intermediation rise, borrowers reduce their quantity demanded of credit and lenders increase their quantity supplied of credit, leading to excess demand in the credit market.

As discussed in the introduction to this chapter, there are reasons to be skeptical that price-based mechanisms drive changes in the quantity of credit. In contrast, models of credit rationing assert that credit is quantity rationed, meaning that lenders impose nominal quantity limits (i.e., credit ceilings) on the amount of credit they are willing to provide to any individual borrower regardless of the price that borrower is willing to pay. These credit limits fluctuate as the financial fundamentals of lenders and borrowers change over the business cycle.

There are two models that explain why lenders prefer to impose credit limits instead of changing the price of credit. The first model was proposed by Stiglitz and Weiss (1981) in their model of credit rationing, which is one of the most influential papers in modern macroeconomics. Stiglitz and Weiss argue that the effective return a lender receives on a loan is more complicated than just the nominal interest rate alone. The effects of changes in interest rates on the default rates of borrowers must also be considered. In Stiglitz and Weiss' model, increases in interest rates increase the default risk of individual borrowers and the default risk on the lender's entire portfolio because of the incentive problems created by moral hazard and adverse selection. (In addition to this effect, other authors, such as Minsky [1982] stress the fact that higher interest rates increase default risk because of its impact on debt service payments that need to be met by borrowers.) As a result of these risk externalities, lenders are reluctant to change interest rates. Interest rates are likely to be inflexible, or "sticky," particularly during periods of high risk. The result is persistent disequilibrium in the credit market, where many borrowers are willing to pay higher interest rates to receive credit but lenders will not provide it.

To see why risk externalities lead to the imposition of credit constraints, consider a recession during which the perceived default risks of borrowers rise. Because of this higher risk, lenders, particularly banks that serve the smallest and most risky borrowers, want to cut back on their lending. Increasing interest rates, however, only increases the default risk of their portfolio by encouraging a riskier pool of borrowers to apply for loans (adverse selection) and by encouraging current customers to engage in riskier behavior (moral hazard). This would occur at the same time that the lender's default fears are at their highest. The only other option available to lenders is to restrict their lending at current interest rates. They do this by imposing a credit limit on each of their individual borrowers. The size of this credit limit depends upon the expected default risk of the individual borrower, which in turn depends upon the borrower's financial fundamentals. Borrowers who have lower net worth or more volatile cash flows are the most likely to suffer from tighter credit ceilings, especially during recessions. In other words, those borrowers who are the most financially fragile are the most likely to have their credit reduced at the point when they are the most desperate for it. These tighter credit limits reduce investment, consumption, and magnify contractions in aggregate output.

Using a similar model, Stiglitz and Greenwald (2003) show that changes in the financial fundamentals of lenders can also affect the credit constraints imposed on borrowers. A negative shock to the wealth of lenders forces lenders to reduce the riskiness of their portfolios. Given the problems of moral hazard and adverse selection, lenders reduce their lending by tightening credit limits as opposed to raising interest rates. Tightening is particularly pronounced for those borrowers with the weakest balance sheets.

The other model of credit rationing that has received considerable attention from economists was developed by Kiyotaki and Moore (1995). In this model, lenders require that all of the loans they provide be fully backed with collateral, imposing a credit limit on borrowers that is equal to the total value of their assets. (If the collateral required is less than 100 percent of a loan, credit constraints still have an important, but smaller, impact on credit.) Under these conditions, it is not changes in cash flows or net worth that change the credit constraints that borrower's face, but it is changes in the price of the borrower's assets that tighten or loosen these constraints.

To understand the implications of collateral constraints in this model, consider a typical recession during which asset prices fall. Borrowers not only see their net worths fall but they also see the value of their collateral drop, tightening their credit limits. This forces reductions in investment and consumption that create a feedback loop in which reductions in aggregate output lead to continued reductions in asset prices and credit, which in turn leads to additional falls in output. Because these falls in asset prices are persistent, the reductions in credit, investment, and output are also highly persistent.

While the mechanisms of the Financial Accelerator model and models of credit rationing are different, their macroeconomic implications are similar. First, credit rationing amplifies economic fluctuations, but it does not initiate them. Any shock that affects net worths, cash flows, and asset prices can trigger a business cycle, regardless of whether it is a shock that primarily affects aggregate supply (such as a productivity shock) or a shock that shifts aggregate demand (such as a change in the money supply). In fact, it is possible that recessions are self-fulfilling when worries about a recession lead firms and households to reduce their investment and consumption spontaneously. Some of these small shocks can even come from changes in asset prices, particularly housing prices. Iacoviello (2005) shows that in a model with credit constraints, real spending closely follows changes in housing prices and unexpected changes in inflation. Credit rationing transmits and amplifies otherwise inconsequential shocks through the financial system to other sectors of the macroeconomy.

Second, credit rationing reduces aggregate demand by reducing investment and consumption, but it also reduces aggregate supply by reducing capacity and increasing the risks associated with production (e.g., by increasing the costs of holding inventories that have to be externally financed). As a result, changes in both aggregate demand and aggregate supply play a role in amplifying business cycles regardless of the source of the shock that initiated the cycle. In models of credit rationing, recessions look very much like the typical recession in the Financial Accelerator model discussed in Chapter 5 (see Figure 5.1) but with changes in credit limits responsible for reducing credit and not changes in the costs of credit intermediation. Recessions end when net worths and asset prices stabilize. At that point, lenders reevaluate their risk appraisals and gradually loosen credit constraints, increasing borrowing, consumption, and investment. Exactly how much time this process takes is dependent upon the flexibility of prices and wages as well as the flexibility of risk perceptions. Given the persistence of financial fundamentals such as net worth and asset prices, this process is not likely to take place very quickly.

Third, credit rationing has asymmetric effects on business cycles. Credit constraints are unlikely to be binding during expansions, but likely to be binding during recessions. The effects of credit constraints are also nonlinear because they do not have an impact on lending until the ceiling is reached. As a result, a small negative shock to a borrower's wealth will not have any effect on their credit until borrowers are up against their credit limit. Once that limit is reached, another small shock of similar size will lead to a significant interruption of credit. In a model of credit rationing, Mankiw (1986) shows that when borrowers are near their credit limits, a small increase in interest rates leads to a large and discontinuous drop in credit.

Fourth, business cycles do not have the same impact on all borrowers. Once again, the most financially fragile borrowers—small firms, new firms, and households—are the most likely to be credit constrained and more likely to see their credit and investment levels fluctuate with their financial fundamentals. Likewise, the most financially fragile lenders, particularly small banks, are most likely to impose credit constraints and change these credit constraints over the business cycle.

There are two additional business cycle implications of credit rationing that do not necessarily hold in the Financial Accelerator model. The first is that under credit rationing, interest rates are unlikely to reflect the actual availability of credit in the financial system. Because higher interest rates encourage moral hazard and adverse selection, lenders are reluctant to increase interest rates during recessions. Because lower interest rates mean reduced profits, lenders are reluctant to cut interest rates during recessions. As a result, interest rates are inflexible and slow to adjust to changes in macroeconomic performance. Figure 6.2 presents the bank prime loan interest rate and real output growth in the U.S. between 1950 and 2005. Note that changes in interest rates are much smoother than changes in output. In addition, the prime rate is weakly procyclical, rising during expansions and

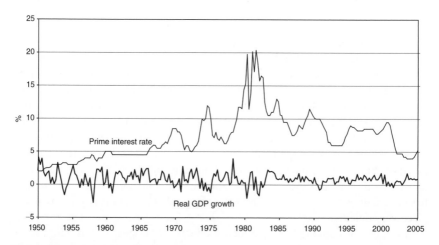

Figure 6.2
Interest Rates and Real Growth in the U.S.
Source: Federal Reserve Economic Data [FRED], http://research.stlouisfed.org/fred2.

falling during recessions. This could be interpreted as lenders taking advantage of expansions (when risk is low) to increase interest rates and reducing interest rates during recessions (when risk is high) in order to reduce risk exposure.

By emphasizing changes in the supply of credit (quantity rationing) as opposed to changes in price (price rationing), models of credit rationing are more similar to the Financial Instability Hypothesis model and the Debt-Deflation theory. These earlier financial models also focused on credit limits that are imposed regardless of what borrowers are willing to pay.

The difference between credit rationing and price rationing in models of credit rationing and the Financial Accelerator model also highlights a similarity between these two models. In both of these models, the traditional monetary transmission mechanism that relies on changes in interest rates to change the demand for investment and consumption is rendered ineffective. Under credit rationing, monetary policy can only affect economic activity if it changes the supply of credit and loosens the credit limits that lenders have placed on borrowers. A more complete discussion of stabilization policy, the monetary transmission mechanism, and the implications of credit rationing for monetary policy are included in the next chapter.

The other distinctive feature of models of credit rationing relates to the fact that most firms are simultaneously consumers and purchasers, borrowers and lenders. Firms borrow when they purchase investment goods or inputs from their suppliers and they lend to their customers in the form of consumer credit and accounts payable. As a result, as pointed out by Stiglitz and Greenwald (2003), credit chains are created throughout an economy that link suppliers with producers and firms with other firms and households. These credit chains ease the flow of funds and improve economic efficiency, but they also create another transmission mechanism by which small changes in credit constraints can significantly affect output. If one firm experiences a fall in net worth and tighter credit limits, it is forced to cut back on the credit it provides to its customers. This leads these firms to reduce their demand for goods and services, cut production, and tighten the credit limits they place on their customers as well. In other words, credit chains imply credit limit chains, and a negative wealth shock to only a small handful of firms can have a sizeable macroeconomic impact, particularly on aggregate supply.

Equity Rationing

To this point our discussion has focused on the effects of changes in interest rates on risk, meaning that the focus has been on credit rationing by banks and other financial institutions as well as by bond markets. But rationing may occur in stock markets as well, adding an additional layer of complexity and power to the propagation of shocks in financial systems.

Equity rationing is imposed both internally and externally. Regarding internal equity rationing, quantity limits are often self-imposed by the managers of firms, even though equity has the significant advantage that there is no bankruptcy risk associated with it. Managers impose equity limits because new stock issues dilute the return on existing equity, the maximization of which is management's primary responsibility. Also, issuing new equity may send unwanted signals to markets and shareholders that the managers think that the stock price is overvalued.

Equity rationing is also imposed externally by lenders through equity markets. Hellmann and Stiglitz (2000) present a model in which equity rationing takes place among investors when heterogeneous firms have private information about their investment projects. Because of the existence of asymmetric information, adverse selection and moral hazard are created. When investors reduce the price they bid on a stock (which increases the cost of equity to firms), it causes a riskier pool of firms to issue equity (adverse selection) and also encourages firms that already have equity financing to engage in riskier investment projects to increase their returns (moral hazard). As a result, investor's equity ration individual firms by placing limits on the amount of equity they are willing to hold.

The most interesting aspect of Hellmann and Stiglitz's model is that competition exists between banks and equity investors for low-risk borrowers. In this model, credit rationing interacts with equity rationing to make each of these problems worse. If banks increase interest rates during periods of higher perceived risk, they know that the lowest-risk firms will go to stock markets to finance their investments. As a result, the fiercer the competition that banks face from equity lenders, the more they are forced to maintain stable interest rates and credit ration. Likewise, equity investors know that if they reduce stock prices during periods of high risk, the lowest-risk firms will go to banks for their financing. As a result, the stronger the competition that equity investors face from banks, the more that they equity ration. Thus, this model reaches the surprising conclusion that more competitive financial systems may actually have more credit and equity rationing than financial systems in which bank borrowers and equity borrowers are segmented into different markets.

In contrast to Hellmann and Stiglitz, De Meza and Webb (1987) show that if credit-rationed borrowers can switch to equity, which is not rationed, then asymmetric information can actually lead to more investment than is socially optimal, opposite of what is found in traditional models of credit rationing. Taken together, these two models indicate that there are important feedback effects between credit rationing and equity rationing. This is because any increase in interest rates by banks leads firms with low-risk investment projects to switch to equity. As a result, banks keep interest rates low so that it is actually below the socially optimal rate, leading to overinvestment. These interactions have the potential to create multiple new channels in which market failure in financial markets takes place and by which small shocks that affect the net worths of lenders and borrowers are transmitted and amplified by financial systems.

Empirical Evidence on Models of Credit Rationing

Many of the empirical studies cited in the last chapter as evidence supporting the Financial Accelerator model could also be interpreted as evidence of the existence of widespread credit rationing. Specifically, the findings are that (1) changes in financial fundamentals are significant in explaining changes in consumption, investment, and aggregate output (Beck *et al.*, 2004; Bernanke, Gertler, and Gilchrist, 1998; Stanca, 2002); (2) the credit, sales, and investment of new and small firms are more volatile than large and established firms (Gilchrist and Himmelberg, 1995; Bernanke, Gertler, and Gilchrist, 1996); and (3) firms that more heavily rely on external finance from banks have more volatile credit (Fazzari, Hubbard, and Peterson, 1988; Gertler and Gilchrist, 1993; Kayshap, Stein, and Wilcox, 1993). In another study cited in the previous chapter, Friedman and Kuttner (1993) find that while the price of lending (as measured by the interest spread between commercial paper and T-bills) is the most significant predictor of aggregate output and financial activity, the quantity of commercial paper is also significant in predicting changes in real activity. This indicates that both price rationing (costs of credit intermediation) and quantity rationing (credit rationing) are significant factors in shaping lending.

In addition, much of Ben Bernanke's work on the Great Depression cited in the previous chapter also applies to models of credit rationing. Bernanke argues that deflation reduced net worths, increased the costs of credit intermediation, and reduced credit and aggregate output. However, deflation also reduced the value of collateral, which served to tighten credit constraints. One piece of evidence noted by Bernanke that is consistent with credit rationing is his reference to credit surveys conducted from 1933 to 1938, which reported that 75 percent of firms claimed they could not obtain credit through regular channels even after the worst of the depression was over. Note that, contrary to the Financial Accelerator model, interest rates were at historic lows during the Great Depression, meaning that credit was cheap but still hard to obtain, which indicates that credit rationing was prevalent.

A few additional empirical studies on credit rationing are worth examining. There have been some studies that have looked at the loan applications of firms. Levenson and Willard (2000) find that 6.4 percent of small U.S. firms (500 or fewer employees) that applied for financing between 1987 and 1988 did not get as much credit as they applied for. In addition to these firms, 2.2 percent of firms were initially denied credit and had to reapply before receiving it. Credit-rationed firms were smaller, younger, and more likely to be owned by their founder. While the number of credit-rationed firms is not large, it is important to note that the 1987–1988 period was not a recessionary period when credit limits would have been tight. In a larger sample of firms, Perez (1998) looked at 5,000 U.S. firms between 1981 and 1991 and found econometric evidence of persistent excess demand for credit across small, medium, and large firms.

Taking a different approach, Nilsen (2002) examines the role of trade credit (or account payable loans) between suppliers and purchasers in the manufacturing industry. Trade credit comprises 13 percent of total liabilities for manufacturing firms, but is used by nearly 60 percent of small firms. He finds that during periods of tight money growth, both small and large firms with lower bond ratings use more trade credit, while firms with higher bond ratings rely more heavily on bank loans. This suggests four things. First, credit rationing by banks plays an important role in determining not just the quantity of lending but the types of lending, especially during periods when overall credit is tight. Second, all firms with higher credit risk are subject to being credit rationed, not just small firms. Third, monetary policy affects real economic activity through changing credit constraints, not through changing interest rates. Finally, credit chains between suppliers and consumers mean that credit constrained firms are linked in ways that magnify the macroeconomic effects of changes in the financial position of even a small number of firms.

CASE STUDY: The Role of U.S. Banking Regulations in Credit Rationing

Government regulations play an important role in shaping the incentives lenders face when making a loan. Some government regulations have had the unintended consequence of encouraging lenders to tighten credit limits on borrowers.

One example of this was Regulation Q, which was enacted as a part of banking reform in 1933 and gave the Federal Reserve the power to impose interest rate ceilings on bank deposits. The intent of Regulation Q was to help banks by providing them with a low-cost source of funds. By providing cheap funding, the federal government was also attempting to discourage moral hazard and encourage banks to engage in safer lending practices. This worked fine when the Federal Reserve pegged interest rates at low levels during World War II. After the war, however, interest rates throughout the economy began to rise and depositors found themselves with more attractive alternatives than the low interest rates paid on bank deposits mandated under Regulation Q. The result was sustained disintermediation in the banking system. Deposit outflows picked up pace in the 1960s when new financial instruments with higher interest rates became available to savers such as negotiable certificates of deposit, money market accounts, and Eurodollar accounts. The final blow to banks under Regulation Q came during the 1970s when high inflation led to significantly higher interest rates and unsustainable levels of disintermediation throughout the banking system. In the end, Regulation Q encouraged 30 years of disintermediation that limited bank lending. Wojnilower (1980) presents case studies of the credit cycles that occurred throughout this period and argues that banks responded to disintermediation by credit rationing, particularly among small banks with no alternative channels for raising funds. Credit rationing was particularly acute during periods of higher perceived default risk. Regulation Q was finally revoked as a part of a financial deregulation movement in 1986.

A current banking regulation that potentially encourages credit rationing is the Basel accord of 1988. This agreement, negotiated amongst the largest industrialized economies, sets international capital adequacy standards on international banks, which are then voluntarily enforced by national regulators. The broadest of these standards requires banks to hold at least 8 percent of their risk-weighted assets as capital. "Risk weighted" means that assets are weighted according to which of four categories the asset fall into. (Activities that do not directly show up on a bank's balance sheet, such as some trading or option activities, are counted at the full value of the potential obligation the bank could incur.) Those assets that have the highest risk, such as consumer and corporate lending, are weighted by 100 percent of their value. Other assets that have lower risk, such as collateralized mortgages or holdings of municipal bonds, are weighted at less than 100 percent of their value. One justification for imposing these capital requirements is that bank capital provides a buffer against bad loans. Another justification is that capital requirements increase the stake owners have in the bank, reducing moral hazard incentives that encourage banks to engage in riskier lending behavior.

The Basel agreement, however, has had the unintended consequence of tightening bank credit during economic downturns. During a recession, banks see their bad loans rise and their net worths and capital fall. Given that recessions are a poor time to raise new capital, banks that are nearing their capital adequacy limits are forced to restrict their lending, especially in the most risky categories: consumer and corporate lending. These banks, for the reasons discussed earlier in this chapter, may choose to restrict their lending by imposing or tightening credit limits on their borrowers.

The 1990–1991 recession, which took place soon after the Basel agreement was enacted, is an example of how a "capital crunch" can lead to a "credit crunch." During the 1980s, U.S. banks suffered from both a boom/bust cycle in the real estate market, which played a significant role in the Savings and Loan crisis, and the Latin American debt crisis, in which a large number of Latin American countries defaulted on their loan payments. Both of these factors significantly reduced bank capital just as the Basel agreement came into effect. As a result, banks with total assets totaling 25 percent of all banking assets found themselves short of meeting the Basel capital requirements. At the same time, a fall in the

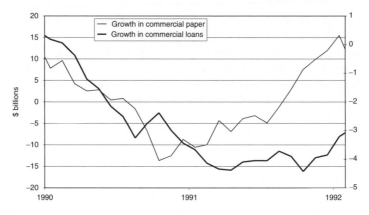

Figure 6.3
Commercial Loans and Commercial Paper in the U.S.
Source: Federal Reserve Economic Data [FRED], http://research.stlouisfed.org/fred2.

stock market (precipitated by the Gulf War and an increase in oil prices) increased the costs of new capital to banks. Together these factors forced banks to meet their new capital adequacy requirements by restricting credit. Figure 6.3 presents the growth of commercial loans and the growth of commercial paper issued over this period. The increase in commercial paper from late 1990 to early 1992 at the same time that bank loans were falling suggests that those firms with access to bond markets (firms with lower default risk) went there when banks were forced to restrict their lending, leaving those firms without access to the bond market to suffer from tighter credit limits imposed by banks. Bernanke and Lown (1991) present econometric evidence which indicates that changes in bank capital played a role in the contraction of credit, investment, and consumption during the recession, each of which were slow to rebound even after the Gulf War had ended and oil prices returned to previous levels.

Another unintended consequence of the Basel agreement is that instead or reducing moral hazard, it may actually increase moral hazard behavior by encouraging banks to engage in the riskiest activities within each of the four risk categories. For example, if all corporate lending is weighted by 100 percent when calculating a bank's capital adequacy requirement, then all corporate lending is equally as costly regardless of the default risk of individual borrowers. As a result, banks may lend to riskier borrowers within each of these categories in an effort to earn higher returns for the same amount of capital, increasing the overall default risk that the bank faces.

Because of these problems with the Basel agreement, industrialized nations have been working on a new set of capital adequacy standards referred to as Basel 2, due to begin in January of 2008 (January of 2009 in the U.S.). Basel 2 aims to more

Table 6.1   Average Growth and Volatility of Growth and Employment

	Non-OECD		OECD	
Variable	*Mean (%)*	*Number of Countries*	*Mean (%)*	*Number of Countries*
Growth	0.7	163	2.7	23
Std. dev. of growth	6.1	163	2.6	23
(Median std. dev. growth)	5.2		2.2	
Std. dev. of employment	9.8	83	3.5	21

Source: Easterly, Islan and Stiglitz (2000).

closely link the capital requirements of lending activities with their actual risk by increasing the number of risk categories for assets and also by incorporating the specific default risk of individual borrowers into banks' capital requirement calculations. Basel 2 also aims to require more regulatory supervision of banks and increase banks' financial disclosure requirements. Because of the complexity of the regulations and the costs associated with imposing these regulations, the negotiations over Basel 2 have proceeded slowly and many details remain to be negotiated.

CASE STUDY: Credit Rationing in Less Developed Countries

Why is output growth not only lower but also more volatile in less developed countries (LDCs)? Table 6.1 presents data on average real output growth and the standard deviation of growth and employment in Organisation for Economic Co-operation and Development (OECD) (developed and emerging) and non-OECD (less developed) countries. While average growth in non-OECD countries is only one-fourth of that in OECD countries, output growth and employment are more than twice as volatile. While OECD countries spend 9 percent of the time in recession, non-OECD countries spend 20 percent of the time in recession.

A good deal of evidence suggests that financial systems have played an important role in the growth volatility of LDCs. In the 1990s, a number of economic crises were sparked by financial crises in LDCs and some OECD countries across the globe. During these financial crises, countries that had experienced remarkable levels of financial development and had been the recipients of high levels of foreign investment over the previous four decades saw economic conditions collapse in a matter of weeks as capital flight and financial panic ran rampant. One example of this was the East Asian crisis of 1997–1999, which will be discussed in more detail in Chapter 9.

Easterly, Islam, and Stiglitz (2001) investigate the financial aspects of economic volatility in LDCs. While it is hard to get firm-level financial data in these countries, macroeconomic data provides some clues to the factors that affect the net worths of lenders and borrowers, which in turn affect default risk and the levels of credit rationing. The authors obtain a number of noteworthy results. First, the LDCs that grew the fastest were countries that were more open, had higher levels of financial development as measured by their ratio of credit to GDP, and had higher levels of capital flows. In other words, financial development and openness increase growth. This might be because of the microeconomic incentives that more efficient financial systems create to save and invest, reducing the amount of credit rationing at the individual level. It is also possible that governments themselves are credit rationed in their access to sovereign debt on international financial markets. In this case, increased financial development may loosen any financial limits imposed by foreign investors.

The authors also find that measures of financial volatility, such as capital flow volatility, are closely correlated with output volatility across LDCs. The fact that financial volatility is correlated with output volatility is not surprising given what we know about the importance of financial systems in propagating business cycles. In addition, the authors find that measures of openness are also strongly correlated with growth volatility, which suggests that economic openness increases efficiency and growth, but also exposes economies to potential capital outflows that can destabilize financial fundamentals and real economic activity.

Finally, and most surprisingly, the authors find that financial development, as measured by a country's credit/GDP ratio, has a nonlinear effect on growth volatility. At low levels of financial development, financial development reduces economic volatility, presumably because it increases economic efficiency and allows firms and households to use credit to stabilize production and consumption. As the financial system becomes larger relative to the rest of the economy, however, the risk and inherent volatility associated with financial intermediation begins to dominate, increasing growth volatility. Figure 6.4 presents Easterly, Islam, and Stiglitz's estimated relationship between output volatility and the credit/GDP ratio. The turning point is roughly when the credit/GDP ratio reaches 100 percent.

Thus, it appears that openness and financial development have clear advantages in terms of growth and efficiency for LDCs, but this growth comes at a price. Financial development increases the importance of credit intermediation and financial fundamentals in determining economic performance, which are inherently unstable for the reasons that have been discussed over the last two chapters. Openness exposes already unstable financial systems to significant risk from capital flow reversals. As a result, development policies that place a heavy emphasis on financial development appear to be a high-reward, high-risk strategy for progress.

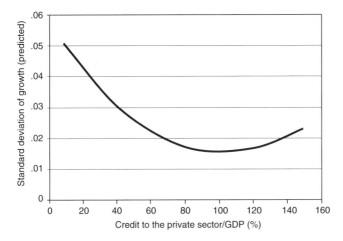

Figure 6.4
Growth Volatility and Private Sector Credit.
Source: Easterly, Islam, and Stiglitz, 2000.

Conclusions

Models of credit rationing stress the importance of understanding the microeconomics of financial intermediation and how changes in financial fundamentals affect risk perceptions and the provision of credit within an economy. In models of credit rationing, changes in interest rates change the risk assumed by lenders, creating externalities in the provision of credit. Lenders are reluctant to increase interest rates (or the price of shares in the case of equity lending) during periods of excess demand because higher lending costs increase default risk by (1) increasing debt-servicing burdens, (2) encouraging riskier borrowers to apply for funds (adverse selection), and (3) encouraging existing borrowers to engage in riskier activities (moral hazard). As a result, lenders are forced to ration the quantity of credit they provide to borrowers, either by imposing explicit credit limits or by imposing collateral requirements on their loans.

Because default risk and asset prices move opposite of aggregate output, credit constraints loosen during expansions and tighten during recessions, creating procyclical movements in lending that magnify changes in consumption, investment, and aggregate output over the business cycle. Models of credit rationing explain four important aspects of business cycles. First, credit rationing explains how persistent disequilibrium in financial markets creates persistent disequilibrium in other markets. Lending and borrowing does not just take place between banks and firms; instead firms, households, producers, suppliers, and customers are linked throughout an economy in a series of credit chains. Credit rationing can break links in these chains, creating long-lasting changes in credit that have ripple effects throughout the entire economy.

Second, credit rationing provides an explanation of the volatility of investment over the business cycle. Under credit rationing, investment is volatile not only because tighter credit limits affect investment demand, but also because tighter credit increases the risk associated with production. In other words, credit rationing implies that both aggregate demand and aggregate supply play a role in investment volatility and economic contractions.

Third, credit rationing implies asymmetry. Credit rationing is most likely to affect newer, smaller, and weaker borrowers and lenders. Business cycles are also asymmetric because credit rationing is more prevalent during recessions and has a significant macroeconomic impact only when firms approach their credit limits. This prediction of asymmetric and idiosyncratic business cycles is consistent with the international empirical regularities of business cycles. As a result, models of credit rationing highlight an important question economic forecasters must consider: How close are firms and households to their borrowing limits?

Fourth, and finally, credit rationing explains why monetary policy has different impacts under different circumstances. Credit rationing raises important questions about the monetary transmission mechanism by emphasizing the importance of changes in the provision of credit as opposed to the importance of changes in the level of interest rates. In fact, under credit rationing, interest rates are unlikely to reflect the actual lending conditions in the financial system, just like the low interest rates that existed during the Great Depression did not reflect how difficult it was to actually get credit. Models of credit rationing raise important questions about the effectiveness of stabilization policy, which leads to the primary topic of discussion in the next chapter of this book.

PART III

FINANCIAL VOLATILITY AND ECONOMIC [IN]STABILITY

CHAPTER 7

The Role of Financial Systems in Monetary and Stabilization Policy

Introduction

If the financial system is a primary cause of economic instability, can it also be part of the solution? The debate over whether monetary policy can be used to offset economic fluctuations has long been one of the primary topics of argument in macroeconomics. Because much of the impact of monetary policy is transmitted through financial systems, understanding the workings of financial systems is vital to understanding how monetary policy should and should not be used. As a result, the study of finance and monetary policy are closely linked, making it impossible to have a complete grasp of one without understanding the other.

Since Keynes, economists have generally acknowledged that money neutrality does not hold in the short run and that changes in the money supply have real effects. However, there has been quite a bit of disagreement as to why this is the case. Keynesians focus on price and wage rigidities while Monetarists and Neoclassical economists focus on the role of expectations and unanticipated changes in the money supply. Because of these different beliefs about how monetary policy works, there are also differing opinions regarding its potential usefulness in stabilizing output. Keynes himself was skeptical about the effectiveness of monetary policy because of questions about the competence of policy makers and worries about the liquidity trap. On the other hand, Keynesians believe in the Phillips curve and argue that timely countercyclical monetary policy can be used to offset the changes in aggregate demand that drive business cycles. Monetarist economists argue that while aggregate demand stabilization might work in theory, in the real world our understanding of the economy is too limited and monetary policy is too blunt a tool to work in practice; instead, its use is more likely to destabilize an economy than to stabilize it. Neoclassical economists, particularly Real Business

Cycle proponents, argue that business cycles are efficient and stabilization policy is unnecessary and counterproductive.

Recently, new issues have been raised regarding the questions of how monetary policy has real effects on the economy (the monetary transmission mechanism) and whether monetary policy can be effectively used to minimize macroeconomic volatility (stabilization policy). Because of the link between monetary policy and financial systems, new developments in our understanding of finance, specifically insights provided by New Institutional theories of finance, have important implications for our understanding of the proper role of monetary policy, its potential benefits, and its potential costs. This chapter reviews both old and new debates regarding both the potency and the appropriate conduct of monetary policy.

Why Does Money Matter? Traditional Theories of the Monetary Transmission Mechanism

Why is money not neutral? Traditional macroeconomic theories specify at least three channels by which monetary policy influences aggregate demand and real output. The first, and most widely accepted, is the *interest rate channel*: increases in the money supply increases liquidity in the financial system, which reduces both real and nominal interest rates; lower interest rates stimulate investment and consumption demand, aggregate demand, and aggregate output. This interest rate channel is the primary monetary transmission mechanism in the Keynesian model (specifically, the IS–LM model). In this model, an increase in the nominal money supply also increases the real supply of money because the aggregate price level is inflexible due to imperfect competition in the goods market. This drives down the opportunity cost of holding money, which is the nominal interest rate, and the real interest rate as well. Monetarists and Neoclassical theories make similar predictions but the market failure in these models is due to imperfect information. Individuals mistake unexpected changes in the nominal money supply for changes in the real money supply, which pushes down nominal and real interest rates. Regardless of the reason for the non-neutrality of money, however, each of these theories implicitly assumes that investment and consumption demand are sensitive to changes in interest rates and that monetary policy plays a central role in determining the level of real and nominal interest rates.

The second channel by which monetary policy affects real economic activity is the *wealth channel*. Interest rates also play a large role in the wealth channel, not by directly stimulating investment and consumption but indirectly by influencing the prices of long-term assets such as stocks, bonds, and real estate. An increase in the money supply drives down interest rates, which in turn drives up stock, bond, and real estate prices. As the value of these assets rise, households see their wealth rise and firms see the costs of financing investment through long-term securities fall. Because of this, investment, consumption, and aggregate demand rise. This wealth channel played a large role in Keynes' General Theory, but its importance was subsequently downplayed, along with other aspects of financial intermediation, in Keynesian models. However, the potential importance of the wealth effect has increased recently because of the dramatic rise in the size of stock and bond markets in financial intermediation and as a share of household wealth.

The third traditional channel is the *exchange rate channel*. Increases in the money supply put downward pressure on exchange rates (because of higher inflation and lower interest rates), making domestic goods cheaper relative to foreign goods. Over the long run, a lower exchange rate increases the demand for exports, reduces the demand for imports, reduces the trade deficit, and increases aggregate demand.

Two things are important to note about these three traditional channels of monetary policy. First, these channels are not mutually exclusive: monetary policy could operate through all three at the same time. Second, each of these channels operates only through their effects on aggregate demand.

These traditional monetary mechanisms are so widely accepted among economists, the public, and the media as to be almost accepted as law. One of the fundamental concepts any principles student learns is that central banks use monetary policy to control interest rates in order to control the economy. Journalists couch their discussions of monetary policy almost entirely in terms of interest rates. However, on closer inspection, it is not so clear that these three channels should be so naively accepted. Consider the interest rate channel first. We know that monetary policy primarily influences short-term interest rates. On a daily basis, the Federal Reserve adjusts the monetary base to target the *federal funds rate*, which is the interest rate on interbank lending of reserves (primarily overnight lending of reserves to meet reserve requirements). The federal funds rate in turn plays a role in influencing other short-term rates. However, it is unclear how a reduction in the overnight lending rate between banks should significantly reduce long-term interest rates, and it is long-term interest rates that are the true determinants of the financing costs of investment and consumption.

Another problem with the interest rate channel is that many studies have found that interest rates are not closely correlated with changes in investment levels, particularly fixed business investment (see Bernanke and Gertler, 1995). In addition, although Keynesian, Monetarist, and Neoclassical theories all accept the idea that it is the real interest rate that determines the costs of investment, empirical studies also show that nominal interest rates are more significant in predicting changes in investment than real interest rates (Stiglitz and Greenwald, 2003). To illustrate, Figure 7.1 presents real interest rates across four countries. Except during the oil price increases and inflation buildup of the 1970s, real interest rates have

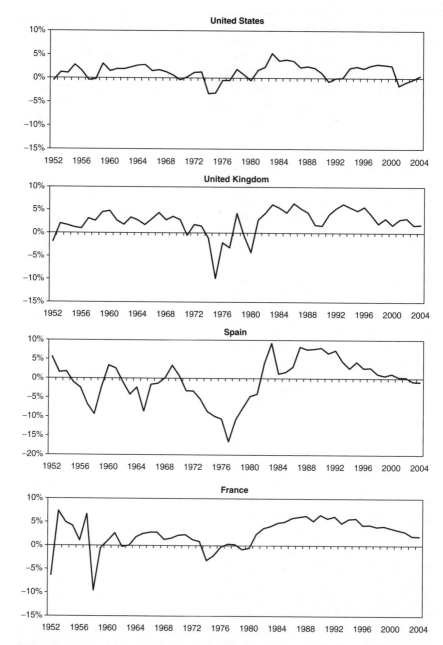

Figure 7.1
Real Interest Rates Across Four Countries.
Source: International Financial Statistics [IFS].

been relatively stable over time across these countries—much more stable than investment.

There are problems with the explanations provided by channels other than the interest rate channel as well. There is no consistent empirical evidence that monetary policy creates wealth effects in asset markets that are large enough to play any significant role in determining real economic activity. Likewise, there is little empirical evidence to support a strong role for the exchange rate channel, particularly because international trade plays a relatively small role in large economies such as the U.S. (where exports are only 11 percent of GDP and imports 12 percent of GDP).

Balance Sheet Channels and the Monetary Transmission Mechanism

New Institutional theories of finance offer an explanation for these anomalies and point to different ways in which monetary policy influences real output. In New Institutional theories, financial fundamentals and their effects on risk perceptions are the crucial determinants of fluctuations in credit and aggregate output. In these theories, monetary policy plays an important role in shaping financial intermediation through *balance sheet channels*, or the ways that monetary policy affects the financial fundamentals of borrowers and lenders. Changes in these financial fundamentals influence default risk, financial intermediation, and aggregate output.

There are many avenues through which monetary policy influences net worths, cash flows, and other financial fundamentals. One balance sheet channel comes from the influence of monetary policy on the costs of credit intermediation, as emphasized in the Financial Accelerator model. When the central bank increases the money supply and lowers interest rates, the profits and cash flows of borrowers increase. An increase in the money supply also improves the financial position of lenders by increasing liquidity and asset prices. Lenders respond to these improved fundamentals by reducing their lending rates as well as lowering other costs of credit intermediation, such as monitoring and collateral requirements. These lower costs of credit intermediation increase credit and spur consumption and investment.

Another balance sheet channel comes from the influence of monetary policy on the value of assets that are used as collateral, as emphasized in Kiyotaki and Moore's (1997) model of credit rationing. An increase in the money supply reduces interest rates, which increases the value of long-term assets such as stocks, bonds, and real estate—the kind of assets that are most likely to serve as collateral. Higher levels of collateral loosen credit constraints and increase the amount of credit in an economy.

A final balance sheet channel works through the risk externalities associated with changes in liquidity and interest rates. As illustrated by Stiglitz and Weiss' (1981) model of credit rationing, there are two risk externalities associated with financial intermediation: adverse selection and moral hazard. When the money supply increases and interest rates fall, these problems are lessened and the default risk associated with a lender's portfolio declines. As a result of lower risk, lenders loosen the credit limits they impose and increase their supply of credit, serving to stimulate aggregate output.

These channels are not mutually exclusive; in fact, not only may multiple balance sheet channels be working at the same time, but they may be working in conjunction with traditional monetary mechanisms such as the interest rate channel or the wealth channel. Regardless, the existence of balance sheet channels has a number of important implications for monetary policy and its impact on financial systems and the macroeconomy. First, the influence of monetary policy on interest rates remains important, but it is the impact of changes in interest rates on financial fundamentals and not their direct effect on the demand for investment and consumption that makes them important. This is an exceptionally important point because it provides an explanation for why there is no close empirical link between interest rates and investment or between interest rates and consumption. When changes in interest rates lead to changes in financial fundamentals during periods when balance sheets are otherwise strong, contractionary monetary policy has little effect. However, the same change in interest rates can have a large effect during periods of financial weakness and high perceived risk. This asymmetry breaks the empirical link between interest rates and macroeconomic variables. This is in distinct contrast with the traditional monetary transmission channels that emphasize changes in the quantity demanded of credit and not shifts in the supply of credit. This also explains why the real effects of monetary policy are persistent: even after interest rates begin to return to previous levels, their impact on financial fundamentals are long lasting.

Second, because monetary policy shifts the supply of credit, it not only affects aggregate demand but it also changes aggregate supply. For borrowers that are credit constrained, increases in the supply of credit reduces the risks associated with production by providing firms with "insurance" in the form of more accessible credit. Reductions in the risk of production encourage firms to produce more, increasing aggregate supply. As a result, just as New Institutional business cycles are driven by changes in both aggregate demand and aggregate supply, monetary policy can potentially stimulate output by working through both aggregate demand and aggregate supply.

Third, balance sheet channels predict that the effects of monetary policy are asymmetric and nonlinear for the same reason that credit rationing and the costs of credit intermediation have asymmetric and nonlinear effects on an economy. In the case of credit rationing, any change in the money supply has little impact on the supply of credit if borrowers have not reached their credit limits. However, once those limits are reached, even a small change in monetary policy can have a large impact on credit. In a similar fashion, changes in monetary policy have little impact on credit if risk perceptions are exceptionally high or if they are exceptionally low. As a result, New Institutional theories argue that the overall impact of monetary policy is often unpredictable, especially during extreme periods when it is most badly needed.

The fourth and final ramification for monetary policy is that these balance sheet channels are most likely to affect newer, smaller, and more bank-dependent firms and households. Likewise, small lenders such as banks will be most affected by changes in monetary policy. In other words, the firms, households, and banks with the weakest financial fundamentals are those that are most likely to see their credit fluctuate with monetary policy. This poses a significant equity concern for policy makers, who must consider these distributional effects if fairness and efficiency are to be objectives of monetary policy.

Empirical Studies of the Balance Sheet Channels of Monetary Transmission

In the previous two chapters, the empirical studies that were cited provided evidence that the financial fundamentals of borrowers and lenders are crucial determinants of credit and real economic activity. These studies are also indirect evidence supporting the existence of balance sheet channels for monetary policy. Two of these studies looked explicitly at monetary policy, particularly at its distributional impacts on borrowers. Kayshap, Stein, and Wilcox (1993) find that tighter monetary policies push higher quality borrowers into the commercial paper market, while lower quality borrowers without this option are left competing for limited bank loans. Gertler and Gilchrist (1993) find evidence that loans to small firms and households fall relative to bank loans to large firms during recessions and periods of contractionary monetary policy.

Two additional studies of monetary policy are of interest. Kayshap and Stein (2000) examine microeconomic data from U.S. commercial banks between 1976 and 1993 in order to investigate whether the financial fundamentals of banks affect their lending response to changes in monetary policy. They find that banks with less liquid assets relative to their total assets responded to changes in the money supply with larger changes in lending than banks with more liquid balance sheets. This effect is particularly strong among 95 percent of the smallest commercial banks, which are likely to have the weakest financial fundamentals regardless of the liquidity of their assets. These results suggest that the financial fundamentals of lenders and not just borrowers play a significant role in the transmission of monetary policy, as New Institutional theories would predict.

Finally, Barth and Ramey (2001) find that changes in the money supply have supply-side effects on real variables such as productivity, real wages, and output. Given that balance sheet channels work through both changes in aggregate demand and aggregate supply, this is also empirical evidence that is strongly consistent with New Institutional theories of the monetary transmission mechanism.

Is Monetary Policy Still Powerful? A Look at the Empirical Evidence

New Institutional theories of finance raise questions about the power of monetary policy to influence output, particularly during periods of rapid expansion or severe contraction. There are also other reasons that economists have begun to ask themselves whether monetary policy has lost some of its bite in recent years. Monetary transmission mechanisms primarily work through bank finance. The rapid pace of financial development over the last two decades has reduced the importance of bank finance through innovations such as new financial market instruments, the globalization of finance, and larger and more liquid financial markets. It can be argued that the falling importance of banks reduces the power of monetary policy (see Mayer, 2001). In addition, structural changes in the U.S. economy may have made the U.S. economy more stable, reducing the need for monetary policy as well as its ability to change output. These structural changes include: increases in the size of the service and nondurable sectors (which are more stable than the manufacturing sector), a more diverse manufacturing base, new management systems that reduce inventory volatility, and advances in information technology that have improved the speed and dissemination of information.

Unfortunately, investigating the strength of the monetary transmission mechanism is fraught with challenges, because it is difficult to separate a reduction in the power of monetary policy from an increase in the effectiveness of monetary policy. To understand why, consider a hypothetical example: pretend that monetary policy was perfectly effective and could be conducted with perfect foresight. In this case, aggregate output would be perfectly stable as the money supply increased and decreased to offset any potential shocks. However, a researcher investigating the monetary transmission mechanism would see that the money supply fluctuates while aggregate output does not—the correlation between the two is zero, so it appears that monetary policy is "ineffective." In other words, the problem is that while monetary policy influences output, changes in output also influence monetary policy, making it difficult to distinguish actual causation.

While the debate continues, the available empirical evidence suggests that monetary policy is as potent as ever. Romer and Romer (1994) investigate case studies of various business cycle episodes and find no evidence that financial innovation has changed the power of monetary policy over the long term. Likewise, Kuttner and Mosser (2002) review a series of papers on this topic and reach the conclusion

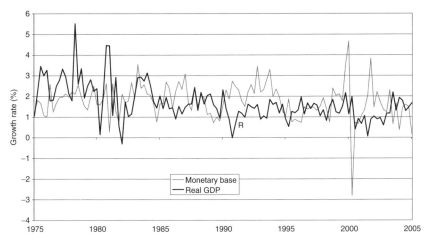

Figure 7.2
The Volatility of Growth in the Monetary Base and Real GDP in the U.S.
Source: Federal Reserve Economic Data [FRED], http://resear.stlouisfed.org/fred2.

that there is no empirical evidence that financial development or globalization have changed the impact of monetary policy. Finally, Boivin and Giannoni (2006) find that changes in the federal funds rate have become less correlated with changes in output and inflation over time. As can be seen in Figure 7.2, the same holds for the relationship between the growth rate of the monetary base and GDP growth, where the volatility of the monetary base has increased over time while the volatility of GDP has fallen. However, Boivin and Giannoni argue that this is not evidence of a lessening of the power of monetary policy but of the increased effectiveness of monetary policy. They provide empirical evidence that the Fed's response to changes in economic conditions has been more timely and larger—and also more decisive and effective. Coupled with other evidence that the economy is more flexible and responds more quickly to changes in monetary policy, these results suggest that the diminished correlation between indicators of monetary policy and output is an indication of the success, and not the failure, of recent monetary policy.

CASE STUDY: Monetary Policy During the 2001 Recession in the U.S.

The recession that lasted from March of 2001 to October of 2001 was one of the most unique in U.S. history: it was one of the weakest, with output only falling by 0.6 percent during the recession (as compared to an average fall of 2 percent), and also one of the shortest recessions, lasting only 8 months. However, growth during the 2-year period following the recession was slow and failed to match the strong recoveries that follow most recessions. In fact, unemployment continued to rise until mid-2003 (a "jobless recovery") and fixed business investment fell until mid-2002.

The Federal Reserve was very aggressive in attempting to prevent this downturn. Beginning in late 2000, well before the recession began, the Fed assertively loosened monetary policy and cut interest rates. Between late-2000 and mid-2003, M2 growth averaged 12 percent a year and the federal funds rate dropped from 6.5 to 1 percent.

One of the principal tools that the Fed uses to estimate the impact of changes in monetary policy is the Massachusetts Institute of Technology-Federal Reserve Board (MIT-FRB) model. This model is composed of more than 1,200 variables and more than 100 equations in which the relationships between variables are determined econometrically using historical data. According the MIT-FRB model, a 1 percent decrease in the federal funds rate typically increases GDP growth by 0.6 percent after 1 year and 1.7 percent over 2 years. This model also predicts that a 1 percent decrease in the federal funds rate should increase stock prices by 10 percent. Despite the Fed's aggressive actions, however, the actual results from this aggressive expansionary monetary policy fell far short of what the Fed's forecasting model predicted. In 2001, the Fed cut the federal funds rate by 2.5 percent, yet output growth was negative and the stock market fell by an additional 10 percent (as measured by S&P 500) on top of already significant losses suffered in 2000.

Why were the outcomes of the Fed's actions so far short of what their econometric models predicted? This question is a hard one to answer using only the interest rate channel of monetary policy as a point of reference. On the other hand, knowledge of the balance sheet channels of monetary policy provides some important insights into why this recession was so short, its slow growth aftermath was so persistent, and also into why monetary policy is both potentially weaker and stronger than it has ever been before.

Clearly, one of the most important reasons that the Fed's actions failed to have the desired preventative effect was the unprecedented level of economic uncertainty that characterized this period. Shocking corporate scandals involving Enron, WorldCom, Arthur Anderson accounting, Tyco, and numerous major stock brokers caused participants throughout the entire financial system to increase their perceived default risk of corporations. The terrorist attacks of 9/11 and the subsequent wars in Afghanistan and Iraq further fueled financial fears and weakened financial fundamentals. It is reasonable to argue that the Fed was caught in a "pessimism trap," where increases in the money supply and reductions in interest rates did not stimulate credit because of excessive levels of expected risk. The Fed appears to have found themselves in a situation in which they were "pushing on a string." Driving nominal interest rates to 40-year lows was still not enough to overcome high levels of perceived default risk and encourage lenders to increase credit.

Another factor hindering monetary policy was the dramatic drop in equity prices. Stock prices peaked in early 2000, beginning a dramatic and sustained bear market that lasted until 2003 (some would argue longer). As measured by the S&P 500 index, stock prices fell by 40 percent over this period. The drop was even larger in the technology sector: the technology-heavy NASDAQ stock index fell by 80 percent. These dramatic declines in stock prices reduced the net worths and cash flows of borrowers and lenders, reduced collateral (which tightened credit constraints), and increased risk by encouraging moral hazard and adverse selection. Together, these factors restricted credit significantly, which explains the −5.6 percent growth rate of business investment over the 2001–2002 period. This deterioration in financial fundamentals also weakened the expansionary impact of the Fed's monetary policy.

On the other hand, new innovations in the financial system also increased the power of monetary policy in new and different sectors of the economy. One of the things that made this recession unique was that it was accompanied by a boom in the real estate, housing, and mortgage sectors of the economy. New housing starts grew at a strong 2.2 percent during the recession year of 2001 and averaged more than 7 percent growth a year from 2002 to 2004.

In addition to fueling the housing boom, cheap mortgages sparked unprecedented levels of refinancing during the early 2000s. Figure 7.3 presents data on the dramatic increase in mortgage refinancing that began in 2001. Roughly 40 percent of all mortgages were refinanced between 2001 and 2003, totaling more than $2.5 trillion. Refinancing was not only a boon to mortgage lenders but, most

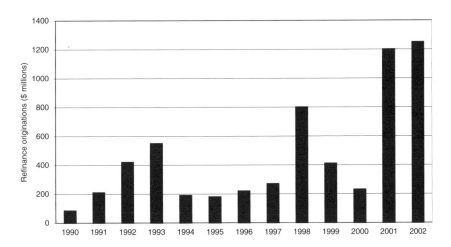

Figure 7.3
The Refinancing Boom in the U.S.
Source: Home Owners Alliance, 2002.

significantly, it increased the disposable income of homeowners and helped to stabilize aggregate demand in a way that is unique in U.S. business cycle history.

These housing and refinancing booms were initiated by the Fed's aggressive monetary expansion during the recession, which drove nominal interest rates to 40-year lows. However, these booms did not take place because of low interest rates alone. Financial innovation and development, particularly dramatic increases in the efficiency of mortgage markets because of securitization, played a huge role in providing households greater access to mortgage lending so that they could take advantage of these lower interest rates (see Chapter 2 for a more complete discussion of securitization). Securitization dramatically increased the levels of mortgage lending and loosened credit ceilings. Just as importantly, as can be seen in Figure 2.3 in Chapter 2, securitization reduced the transaction costs associated with financing and refinancing real estate. This historic fall in interest rates may not have had the impact on fixed business investment that the Fed anticipated, but this was largely offset by the incredibly positive response of the housing market. Thus, financial innovation helped to stabilize an otherwise weak economy and prevented the recession from being worse than it was.

The 2001 recession presents a cautionary tale for the Federal Reserve to use in guiding its future policy. Not only is it difficult for the Fed to accurately predict the impact of monetary policy during periods of turmoil, but it also appears that even the channels and sectors through which monetary policy works are continually changing as financial systems evolve.

Old Debates over the Effectiveness of Stabilization Policy

The traditional argument for the active use of government policy to stabilize output was first posited by Keynes and advanced by Keynesians. As discussed earlier, business cycles in the Keynesian model are caused by fluctuations in aggregate demand. Monetary policy and fiscal policy (changes in government spending and taxation) also influence aggregate demand. Hence, an enlightened policy maker should be able to use these policy tools in a timely manner to offset aggregate demand fluctuations and stabilize growth. In other words, proper monetary policy should *lean against the wind*, meaning that policy should work against the current momentum in the economy; during periods of slow growth, the central bank should increase the money supply, and during period of faster growth and rising prices, the central bank should reduce inflation by cutting money growth. Thus, the primary goal of monetary policy is to balance the benefits of higher output growth with the costs of higher inflation generated by the use of expansionary monetary policy in a way that is consistent with the Phillips curve. In the U.S., the federal government has committed itself to actively managing this trade-off between output and inflation in two separate laws enacted in 1946 and 1978. The

Employment Act of 1946 states that "it is the continuing policy and responsibility of the federal government... to promote maximum employment, production, and purchasing power."

The Keynesian belief in the efficacy of stabilization policy has met with pointed and sustained criticism over the years because of both theoretical and pragmatic problems with Keynesian prescriptions. The theoretical critiques begin with Friedman's *natural rate hypothesis* (see Chapter 4), which argues that the trade-off between inflation and output is not only temporary but also unstable. It is temporary because the money supply does not influence output in the long run; aggregate supply determines output in the long run, and monetary policy cannot affect aggregate supply according to Friedman. It is unstable because the trade-off between inflation and output changes as people change their expected price levels; if the public expects higher inflation (and adjusts wages accordingly), the central bank has to generate more inflation in order to get the same stimulative effect on output. Because of these two significant problems, Friedman and other Monetarists assert that the use of monetary policy to stabilize output is more likely to create high inflation and destabilize output than it is to offset business cycles. Instead, the discretionary powers of central banks should be revoked. Central banks should be committed by law to maintaining a constant rate of money growth that is consistent with a low rate of inflation.

Neoclassical economists take these arguments one step further. If the public has rational expectations, meaning they form their expectations in a forward-looking manner using all available information and do not make predictable errors, then monetary policy cannot influence aggregate demand at all unless it is unanticipated. Given that stabilization policy has to be systematic in order to be effective (in other words, any change in output must be met by a predictable policy response), it is impossible for a central bank to stabilize output. This outcome is often referred to as *policy irrelevance*. In addition, Neoclassical economists argue that even if the central bank never uses monetary policy to stabilize output, just the possibility of its use leads to higher inflation. This is because a low inflation policy is *time inconsistent*: the public knows that the central bank has an incentive to increase inflation in order to stimulate the economy, so they set their expected inflation rate higher than they would if the central bank's hands were tied. The central bank knows that the public will do this and is forced to match this higher expected inflation with higher actual inflation if it wants to avoid increasing wages and a decline in output.

Many of these same critics argue that while stabilization policy may not work in theory, it also does not work in practice. In fact, Keynes himself acknowledged that there were significant practical problems with the use of monetary policy. In his mind, the most significant of these was that policy makers at the Federal Reserve were incompetent and could not be counted on to act appropriately. While central bankers today are not incompetent, there are still significant limits to their knowledge. For example, it is widely acknowledged (as indicated by the variety of jokes about the certain uncertainty of economists) that the accuracy of economic forecasting is not very good. In the words of John Kenneth Gailbraith (*Wall Street Journal*, January 22, 1993): "There are two kinds of forecasters: those who don't know and those who don't know they don't know." One reason that forecasting is inaccurate is based on an observation by Robert Lucas now known as the *Lucas Critique*, which argues that because expectations may be impossible to predict in any given circumstance, any forecast of the future based on data from the past will be unreliable.

The inaccuracies of economic forecasting and the Lucas Critique raise important questions about stabilization policy because forecasting is crucial to the proper conduct of stabilization policy for two reasons. First, there are lags in monetary policy during the decision-making process, the money multiplier process, and the monetary transmission process that take an uncertain amount of time. As a result, accurate forecasts of downturns are critical so that policy can be enacted in a timely manner before a downturn actually begins. Second, the eventual effects of changes in policy must be understood in order for these policies to be conducted on the proper scale. If the effects of policy are not known or are different under different sets of expectations, it may be impossible to correctly predict the impact of stabilization policy on the economy. This would lead to variability in the timing and effectiveness of policy that would seriously diminish the ability of policy makers to stabilize output and would increase the chance that the policy enacted is wrong and destabilizing.

The final pragmatic problem with stabilization policy is that no government policy is formed in a vacuum. Instead, politics always play a role in shaping policy, sometimes in ways that advance interests other than stabilizing output. An example of this would be the pressure that is often placed on central banks to stimulate their economies before elections regardless of the actual need for such policies.

New Debates over the Effectiveness of Stabilization Policy

The development of New Institutional theories of finance have muddied the waters even more regarding the effectiveness of monetary policy in stabilizing business cycles. In these models, there is no direct link between the money supply and real economic activity. Instead, it is credit that is ultimately important. Monetary policy influences credit through its effects on the financial fundamentals of borrowers and lenders, but this link is tenuous. During times in which perceived risk is high, changes in the money supply may have little impact on credit regardless of how low the central bank drives interest rates. In addition, monetary policy has distributional effects that are inequitable because it primarily affects the level of credit that is available to smaller and weaker firms and restricts the credit supplied by smaller banks. Finally, New Institutional theories recognize that financial development plays a crucial role in the transmission of monetary policy and that the monetary transmission mechanism (along with the impact of monetary policy) can vary greatly over time. All these factors significantly complicate the conduct of monetary policy and increase the likelihood that the active use of monetary policy can become a source of instability, not the remedy for it.

While New Institutional theories raise significant questions about traditional monetary policy, they also raise the possibility that the monetary authorities can act to stabilize the financial system and the economy in other ways. For example, it is possible that the use of different monetary policy tools are more or less effective in certain situations. A traditional open market operation, in which the Fed buys and sells treasury securities from large banks, might be effective during a relatively stable period but have little effect on bank lending during a recession. On the other hand, an increase in discount lending directed toward small banks, which lend to small borrowers, might be ineffective during calm periods but very powerful during a recession in stimulating lending to those with the strongest unfulfilled demand for credit. If these small borrowers are linked to other firms in a series of credit chains, the aggregate impact of such a targeted monetary policy could be substantial.

Likewise, because monetary policy influences credit availability, it also influences the risk that firms face when they engage in production because lines of credit provide firms with insurance against changes in demand for their product. As a result, changes in monetary policy not only work through changes in the aggregate demand but through changes in aggregate supply as well. If expansionary monetary policy can reduce risk and increase credit enough to significantly alter aggregate supply, then it is much more potent than in Neoclassical and even Keynesian models where monetary policy influences aggregate demand alone.

Another way central banks can act to stabilize credit is through the use of their power to regulate banks. Like monetary policy, bank regulation affects financial fundamentals, risk perceptions, and the constraints and incentives that lenders face when extending credit. Recently, there has been a move across the world towards deregulating financial markets and financial intermediation. This process began in the U.S. during the early 1980s when restrictions on interest rates (Regulation Q), interstate banking, and bank asset holdings, among others, were removed. In their place, international capital adequacy requirements were imposed on banks through the Basel agreement (see Chapter 6 for more details). The theory behind these changes is that while deregulation increases the riskiness of banks because of moral hazard, stricter capital adequacy requirements provide a greater buffer against loan losses and increase the financial stake of owners, reducing the problem of moral hazard. Unfortunately, as discussed in Chapter 6, capital requirements get tighter during economic recessions, forcing banks to cut back on their lending during times when credit is needed the most. To alleviate this problem and help stabilize credit, monetary authorities could be given the power to loosen these capital constraints during downturns and increase them during expansions. The problem, of course, is that adjusting capital requirements might encourage more moral hazard lending. If central banks are given this power, however, it could be done in conjunction with other reforms aimed at increasing the safety of the banking system, such as tying banks' capital requirements more closely to the risk of specific borrowers and assets in their portfolio (this is one of the reforms adopted in Basel 2).

Central banks could also be given other powers of regulation that could be used to stabilize the provision of credit. Central banks could be given the power to tighten or loosen bank restrictions on short-term holdings of debt (particularly foreign-denominated debt, or *hot money*), on real estate and other holdings of speculative assets, and on rates of deposit expansion. In fact, there may even be a role for the imposition of interest rate controls by the monetary authority in order to discourage excessive lending during boom periods. Of course, each of these re-regulation ideas goes against the current trend toward deregulation. In addition, they require enlightened policy makers who can be trusted to use these tools judiciously, being aware of the potential efficiency and distributional impacts of government regulation. These are tough conditions for many countries, maybe all countries, to meet.

Finally, a debate is taking place over the appropriate goals of monetary policy and on whether policy makers should focus not only on inflation in goods and services but also in asset prices such as housing, bonds, and stocks. The idea here is that by taking a broader view of inflation, central banks can prevent speculation-driven asset bubbles before they begin by taking actions to dampen price increases in these assets. More on asset bubbles and monetary policy will be discussed in the next chapter.

CASE STUDY: Has Monetary Policy and/or Financial Development Played a Role in the Stabilization of U.S. Output?

A general consensus has been reached among economists that business cycles after World War II have been less severe than during earlier periods. In fact, this stabilization has been particularly pronounced over the last 20 years. This phenomenon has been referred to as "The Great Moderation," and has occurred not just in the U.S. but in all developed countries.

Christina Romer (1999) surveys the empirical evidence from the U.S. and reaches three conclusions. First, if the interwar period (1917–1940) is excluded (which includes the Great Depression and the two world wars), the variance of output in the postwar (1948–1997) period is about 20 percent smaller than it was

Table 7.1   Standard Deviations During Postwar Period in the U.S.

	Period	
	1948–1984	*1985–2004*
Real GDP Growth (%)	2.65	1.12
Industrial Production Growth (%)	5.85	2.43
Unemployment (%)	1.33	1.05

Source: U.S. Bureau Economic Analysis.

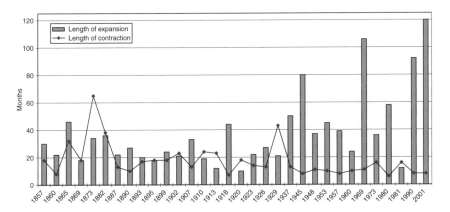

Figure 7.4
Length of Expansions and Contractions for U.S. Business Cycles.

in the prewar (1886–1916) period. Second, most of this decline in output volatility is driven by the period between 1985 and 2003. As can be seen in Table 7.1, output volatility from 1985 to 2004 was less than half of what it was in the early postwar period, with unemployment volatility falling significantly as well. Thus, while there has been output stabilization, this trend is recent and, because it is based on such a relatively short time period, somewhat tenuous. Romer's third conclusion is that while there is evidence of a decline in output volatility, there is even stronger evidence of a significant reduction in the frequency of recessions. Figure 7.4 presents data on the length of recessions and expansions from 1857 to 2003. While there does not appear to be any trend in the length of contractions, there has been a significant rise in the length of expansions. Comparing the prewar and postwar periods, postwar expansions have been more than 1.5 years longer on average. Longer expansions mean less frequent recessions: a phenomenon Diebold and Rudebusch (1999) refer to as *duration stabilization*. They report that only 20 percent of the time in the postwar period in the U.S. has been spent in recession, compared to 40 percent of the time in the prewar period.

Looking internationally, Summers (2005) reviews the cross-country evidence on macroeconomic volatility using data from G-7 countries and Australia. Output variability across these countries has fallen significantly since the 1980s, although the pace and the timing of this decline have varied significantly. In Australia, France, Italy, and the U.S., the decline occurred quite rapidly beginning in early to mid-1980s. On the other hand, in Canada, Germany, Japan, and the U.K., the decline was not consistent and the timing of the declines varied between the early 1970s to the late 1980s. However, the magnitude of the decrease in output volatility is approximately the same across countries: 50 percent lower during the Great Moderation than before 1980.

The question then is why have recessions moderated and become less frequent during the postwar era, particularly since 1980? Earlier, some of the structural changes in the U.S. economy that may have contributed to stability were discussed. Here, two additional explanations are of particular interest. The first is the role of financial development in improving output stability. An argument can be made that deregulation, the elimination of restrictions on interstate banking, deeper and more liquid financial markets, larger and more diverse banks, new securities such as derivatives, and the growth of securitization have all increased the availability of credit to firms and households. More credit leads to more stable consumption, investment, and production, meaning fewer and smaller business cycles. Financial innovation also helps spread risk more evenly, which stabilizes credit.

The benefits of financial development have been most obvious in the real estate market. As seen in Figure 7.5, a clear reduction in the volatility of residential

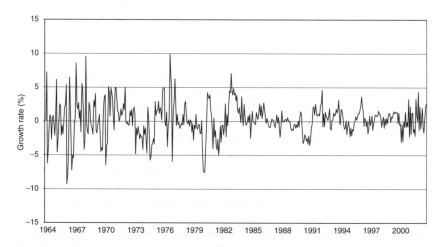

Figure 7.5
Growth of Residential Construction in the U.S.
Source: U.S. Census Bureau.

construction growth has occurred since the mid-1980s. Stock and Watson (2002) find that the standard deviation of residential construction has fallen by 64 percent since 1980. Financial development has played a key role in this by reducing mortgage costs, reducing collateral requirements, and increasing the credit available to even the riskiest of borrowers. Financial development has also fueled the boom in mortgage refinancing, which has also served as an automatic stabilizer of income during recessions. Peek and Wilcox (2006) find empirical evidence that increases in the securitization of mortgages is largely responsible for the decline in the volatility of residential construction and output.

One other study on the benefits of financial development was conducted by Aghion *et al.* (2005). They find that output volatility has a smaller impact on long-run growth in countries with higher levels of financial development. Thus, even if financial development does not reduce macroeconomic volatility, it appears to reduce the long-run costs of business cycles by allowing consumption, investment, and productivity return to their trend more quickly.

The other explanation of output stabilization that has received a great deal of attention from economists is the increased use of macroeconomic policy, particularly monetary policy. Before World War II, macroeconomic policy was limited. In the U.S., there was no federal income tax, government spending was only 2 percent of GDP, and the Federal Reserve was weak and decentralized. The role of the federal government in the economy expanded dramatically during the Great Depression, and this expansion accelerated during the World War II. Tax revenues and government spending greatly increased, and automatic stabilizers such as bank deposit insurance, unemployment insurance, social security, and welfare assistance were all implemented. In addition, the Federal Reserve was strengthened and power centralized within the Board of Governors in order to allow the Fed to better serve as a lender of last resort and more effectively manage monetary policy. One final ingredient in the rise of macroeconomic policy, and maybe the most crucial, was the development of Keynesian economics, which provided a theoretical rationale for the active use of fiscal and monetary policy to manage the economy and improve economic stability.

Romer and Romer (1994) quantify the impact of macroeconomic policy in the postwar era by identifying indicators of monetary and fiscal policy and then using these indicators to estimate how much output would have changed without their contributions. They find that the increased use and effectiveness of monetary policy is the most important factor in explaining both duration stabilization and the decline in output volatility. Automatic stabilizers also played a significant role, while discretionary fiscal policy played little role in improving stability. Stock and Watson (2002) find similar results which indicate that monetary policy has been responsible for one-quarter of the decline in postwar output volatility.

While monetary policy has contributed to the recent increase in macroeconomic stability by preventing and moderating some recessions, it is also important to recognize that it has been the cause of many recessions. In the words of Rudiger Dornbusch (1997): "None of the U.S. expansions of the past 40 years died in bed of old age; every one was murdered by the Federal Reserve." Unfortunately, the Federal Reserve's excessive use of expansionary monetary policy has created inflation cycles that have destabilized output. The most obvious example of this was the inflation explosion of the 1970s, when inflation rose above 10 percent because of the Fed's persistent commitment to stabilizing output by increasing the money supply in the face of rising oil prices. In 1981, the Fed was forced to severely cut money growth in order to reduce inflation, leading to the sharpest and deepest economic contraction in the U.S. since the Great Depression. In fact, declines in money growth have preceded six of the nine postwar recessions in the U.S.; in each case, the rationale for the decline was rising inflation. Romer and Romer (1994) estimate that output growth would not have been negative during the recessions of 1948–1949, 1969–1970, 1980, 1981–1982, and 1990–1991 except for the Fed's tightening of monetary policy. Blanchard and Simon (2001) support this conclusion by finding evidence that higher output volatility has been consistently correlated with higher inflation volatility over the postwar period. Thus, while monetary policy has helped to stabilize output and postpone recessions, its excessive use has led to higher inflation rates. This in turn has led to policy corrections that have destabilized output, offsetting much of the benefits that monetary policy could have contributed to economic stability.

It appears that the Fed and other central banks have learned from these past mistakes and this knowledge has greatly contributed to the Great Moderation. The significant decline in output volatility in the U.S. since the 1980s was proceeded by significant changes at the Federal Reserve. The election of Paul Volker and subsequently Alan Greenspan as chairmen placed cautious inflation-fighters in a key position of power at the Fed. This initiated a long period of low and steady inflation—both actual and expected inflation. Inflation declined from a high of 10 percent in 1981 to 3.3 percent in 1987, where it has remained roughly steady, or slightly falling, ever since. At the same time, the standard deviation of inflation fell from 4 percent in 1983 to 1 percent in 1986. These changes in the behavior of inflation have reduced output volatility by reducing inflation-related distortions and reducing economic uncertainty.

Summers (2005) argues that the declines in output volatility across G-7 countries and Australia were also associated with similar changes in monetary policy as occurred in the U.S. In each of these countries, increased output stability was proceeded or coincident with lower and less variable inflation. Other macroeconomic changes that took place, such as financial development, were not so consistently correlated with increases in macroeconomic stability across these countries. While this does not exclude the contribution of other factors, it is strong circumstantial evidence emphasizing that improved monetary policy has played the most crucial role in the Great Moderation.

Conclusions

It is tempting to damn the entire study of macroeconomics by saying that economists have not learned anything over the last 75 years about one of the major issues affecting economic welfare: how to prevent business cycles. It is true that there is as much, if not more, disagreement about the conduct and effectiveness of monetary policy today than there has ever been before. However, the fact that there is still disagreement does not mean that we have not learned anything. Sometimes a deeper understanding of an issue reveals the true complexity of it. This is what is happening with the study of stabilization and monetary policy.

As economists continue to investigate the monetary transmission mechanism, New Institutional theories illustrate how monetary policy can affect the economy in ways other than through its influence on interest rates. Specifically, these theories have shown how changes in monetary policy affect the financial fundamentals of borrowers and lenders, changing perceived risk that then affects the level of credit. Because these changes in financial fundamentals are long lasting, these balance sheet channels provide a persuasive explanation of why the real effects of monetary policy are so persistent. However, these balance sheet channels also raise questions about the effectiveness of monetary policy, because the relationship between the money supply, financial fundamentals, risk, and credit are not consistent. The relationships between these variables vary over the business cycle; for instance, during periods of exceptionally high perceived risk (such as during the 2001 recession), monetary policy might be largely ineffective (at least through traditional channels) in stimulating the provision of credit.

These same theories also tell us a great deal about the effects of financial innovation on the monetary transmission mechanism, but once again there is no clear-cut conclusion. Financial development has created new ways that monetary policy is influential. The best example of this is the growth of securitization in the mortgage market, which helped to amplify the impact of the Fed's low interest rate policy by fueling the refinancing boom of the early 2000s. However, financial development has also reduced the relative importance of bank finance and created more competitive and globalized financial markets that may act to minimize the real effects of changes in the money supply.

While monetary policy gets more complicated in theory, empirical studies of monetary policy provide us with more definitive conclusions. Existing empirical studies support the existence of balance sheet channels of monetary transmission and have generally found that monetary policy remains as powerful as it has been in the past, even if the channels through which it works have evolved over time. Likewise, the bulk of the empirical evidence suggests that monetary policy has played a significant role in moderating the size of recessions as well as in making them less frequent. In fact, while it is too short of a period of time to make any definitive conclusions, the evidence suggests that monetary policy has been particularly effective over the last 20 years. However, history also teaches us that the use of monetary policy often creates instability by generating inflation that central banks eventually have to deal with. As a result, the postwar period has been subject to policy-driven business cycles that are more moderate than before, but costly nonetheless. In the end, both the history of monetary policy and new research in financial macroeconomics remind us of the continued need for three things from both policy makers and economists: research, caution, and humility.

CHAPTER 8

Banking Crises and Asset Bubbles

Introduction

The purpose of this chapter is to investigate the nature and causes of two dramatic forms of financial collapse: banking crises and asset bubbles. A *banking crisis* refers to a situation in which numerous banks fail simultaneously, leading to a significant reduction in bank credit as well as other forms of financial interme- diation. Banks by their very nature are illiquid: they hold long-term assets (by lending for long term to firms and households) and short-term liabilities (through holding deposits and borrowing through short-term debt instruments). Because of this, banks are highly susceptible to failure, especially if their sources of funds dis- sipate quickly. This is the reason why in the era before deposit insurance, banking crises were typically precipitated by *bank runs*, or widespread deposit withdrawals fueled by the fear of bank failures.

Banking crises used to be considerably more common. Between 1867 and World War I, Friedman and Schwartz (1963) report that every recession but one in the U.S. was associated with a banking crisis. Compare this to the 1945–1971 period, during which Eichengreen and Arteta (2000) report that only a single banking crisis took place among 21 industrial and emerging economies. Because of their rarity over this period, many economists believed that banking crises were things of the past. Unfortunately, they were wrong. Between 1975 and 1997, 54 banking crises have occurred, and a number of these crises, such as the banking crisis in Japan, have been exceptionally long lasting and have had a large negative impact on macroeconomic performance. These banking crises have involved large fiscal costs for governments as well. Table 8.1 presents data from a study by Caprio and Klingbiel (2003), who identify the 15 largest banking crises since 1980 in terms of the costs incurred by governments in bailing-out and recapitalizing banks after a

Table 8.1　Worst Banking Crises Since 1980

Country	Crises Dates	Estimated Cost of Bailout (as Percentage of GDP)
Argentina[a]	1980–1982	55
Indonesia[a]	1997–1998	55
China	1990s	47
Jamaica[a]	1994	44
Chile[a]	1981–1983	42
Thailand[a]	1997	35
Macedonia	1993–1994	32
Israel	1977–1983	30
Turkey[a]	2000	30
Uruguay	1981–1984	29
Korea	1998	28
Cote d'Ivoire	1988–1991	25
Japan	1990s	24
Uruguay	1981–1984	24
Malaysia[a]	1997–1998	20

[a] Indicates a country with more than one banking crisis since 1980. The reported crises is the largest.
Source: Caprio and Klingbiel (2003).

crisis. Obviously, these costs are enormous. The reasons behind the recent return of banking crises are discussed in this chapter.

Unlike banking crises, asset bubbles in stock markets and real estate markets have never gone away. An *asset bubble* refers to a market in which the prices of assets rise above that which can be justified by the asset's financial fundamentals, which includes the characteristics of the asset itself—the expected return and the terms of the financial instrument—as well as the characteristics of the borrower— their credit history, their net worth, and their cash flows. In the words of Joseph Stiglitz (1990), asset bubbles are identified by the following: "If the reason that the price is high today is only because investors believe that the selling price is high tomorrow—when 'fundamental' factors do not seem to justify such a price—then a bubble exists." The problem with asset bubbles is that they burst, and these crashes are often associated with significant macroeconomic downturns, most obviously in 1929 stock market crash before the Great Depression but also more recently in Japan, East Asia, and in the U.S. before the 2001 recession.

Banking crises and asset bubbles should be studied together for two reasons. First, banking crises and asset bubbles often occur simultaneously (e.g., the Great Depression, Japan in the 1990s, the East Asian crisis of 1997). There are important feedback effects in which the existence of a banking crisis exacerbates the size of asset market crashes, and vice versa. Second, banking crises and asset bubbles are costly for many of the same reasons. Banking crises and asset crashes interrupt financial intermediation. In addition, both banking crises and asset crashes reduce wealth (in the case of a banking crisis, the losses to depositors are limited by the existence of deposit insurance). Lower wealth causes households and firms to reduce their demand for consumption and investment. Lower wealth also restricts borrowers' access to credit by reducing the strength of their financial fundamentals, also serving to reduce consumption and investment as well as production. In fact, just the fear alone of banking crises and asset market crashes can reduce both aggregate demand and aggregate supply by restricting credit.

The goal of this chapter is to answer three questions regarding banking crises and asset bubbles: Why do they occur?; How costly are they?; and Is it possible to prevent them?

The Causes and Prevention of Banking Crises

There are two broad categories of theories regarding the causes of banking crises. The first is known as *belief-based models of banking crises*. In these models, banking failures are driven by changes in expectations of future financial and macroeconomic conditions. These changes in expectations are not necessarily linked to any change in economic fundamentals. Charles Kindleberger (1978) was one of the first proponents of financial panic being the driving forces behind banking crises. On the basis of his reading of historical banking crisis episodes, he argues that banking is inherently unstable because individuals are subject to periodic manias and panics. In his view, people often act irrationally, changing their behavior not when anything real has changed in the economy but when they see (or believe they see) others changing their actions. This herding behavior (which is also an important aspect of the Keynesian concept of animal spirits) often leads speculators to withdraw deposits from banks based only on the fear that a bank run might occur and that they could be among the last-in-line to withdraw their deposits and lose their savings. This inherent fear leads to periodic bank runs and banking crises. Under this view, banking crises are self-fulfilling; once the belief that a banking crisis will occur becomes widely accepted, a banking crisis occurs regardless of the real financial fundamentals of banks.

While Kindleberger believes that irrationality is at the heart of banking crises, bank runs can also be driven by changes in the expectations of rational depositors. Diamond and Dybvig (1983) develop a rational expectations model of banking crises where the best response of one depositor depends upon what she believes other depositors will do. In the case of a bank run, the worst outcome for any depositor is to be among the last-in-line at the bank to withdrawing their deposits when a bank run occurs because there will be no money left. As a result, once a depositor believes that there is a sufficient possibility that others will begin to withdraw deposits (the authors show that this possibility does not have to be very high), self-fulfilling bank runs take place without any change in fundamentals. In other words, multiple equilibria in the banking system are possible, some of these equilibria are better than others (better meaning having more stable banks), and the public's current beliefs determine which equilibrium occurs.

If beliefs and expectations are so crucial to the operation of banking systems, can beliefs be shaped so that good equilibria are achieved? The obvious tool is government policy, particularly the provision of deposit insurance. If depositors are given a guarantee that there is no penalty for being the last-in-line when a bank fails, there is no incentive to withdraw money in anticipation of a crisis. In addition, the development of modern central banking and the seriousness with which it takes its role as a lender of last resort has also served to calm potential panics and reduce deposit volatility. The fact that banking runs and crises used to be quite common in the U.S. but have not occurred since the creation of federal deposit insurance and the strengthening of the Federal Reserve after the Great Depression is persuasive circumstantial evidence in support of belief-based models of banking crises.

However, this evidence is only circumstantial and does not prove the case. In fact, over the last two decades severe banking crises have taken place in countries and regions where deposit insurance was in place, such as Japan, East Asia, Scandinavia, and Argentina (in some of these cases deposit insurance was explicit, in others it was implicit). Clearly, something else is also going on here. Another category of banking crisis theories, referred to as *fundamentals-based models of banking crises*, focuses on changes in the financial fundamentals of banks. In these models, banking crises are both created by and the cause of fluctuations in net worth, cash flows, and bank profits that take place over the business cycle.

The first model of fundamentals-based banking crises was posited by Wesley Mitchell (1941), a modern version of which was developed by Allen and Gale (1998). In these models, there are two types of shocks to financial fundamentals that initiate banking crises. The first type of shocks are negative shocks to the net worths of banks. For example, both an increase in bankruptcy rates and falls in the market prices of assets significantly reduce the net worth of banks. In addition, as highlighted by the Debt-Deflation theory, deflation increases the real value of debt relative to assets when nominal debt contracts are not indexed, which increases bankruptcies among borrowers and reduces the net worth of banks in the process. Because inflation typically falls and bankruptcy risk rises during recessions, the probability of bank failures and banking crises fluctuates with the business cycle.

The other type of shocks that initiates fundamentals-based banking crises are shocks that reduce the profitability of banks—specifically, shocks that reduce the return on bank assets relative to the rates paid on liabilities. Such shocks include an unexpected increase in short-term interest rates (when the return on bank assets are fixed), higher real interest rates (which increases default rates by increasing moral hazard), an unexpected increase in inflation (which reduces the real return on bank assets), a decline in aggregate growth, and an unexpected depreciation of the exchange rate (which increases the value of foreign-denominated debt relative to domestic-denominated assets). In each of these cases, if banks have not adopted the proper risk-management strategies, bank profitability suffers and insolvency may occur. Because these types of shocks are often associated with changes in the macroeconomy, they provide additional explanations as to why the likelihood of a banking crisis rises during recessions and falls during expansions.

Fundamentals-based models of banking crises predict that banking crises are a potential symptom of business cycles. However, banking crises can also lead to business cycles. As emphasized in New Institutional theories of finance, banking crises affect the macroeconomy by weakening the financial fundamentals of both borrowers and lenders throughout the financial system, increasing default risk and reducing credit. As a result, a feedback loop exists where poor fundamentals in the banking system lead to poor macroeconomic performance, and vice versa. In certain circumstances, banking crises could be the result of a weak macroeconomy; in others, a banking crisis could precipitate a major macroeconomic contraction. Interestingly, U.S. history provides examples in which a banking crisis led an economic contraction (the panic of 1873) and in which an economic contraction led a banking crisis (the Great Depression).

Because the causes of banking crises are different in belief-based models than in fundamentals-based models of banking crises, their policy prescriptions regarding the prevention of crises are also different. In belief-based models, bank runs alone are the cause of banking crises, meaning deposit insurance and/or a strong lender of last resort are sufficient to prevent banking crises. However, in fundamentals-based models, deposit insurance and crisis lending might actually increase the probability of banking crises by encouraging moral hazard. When banks are allowed to use insured money to fund their lending or are bailed-out when they make a mistake, they are more likely to engage in riskier behavior than they otherwise would. Riskier behavior means more volatile financial fundamentals and a greater susceptibility to bank failures. Instead, fundamentals-based models argue that strict government regulation of banking systems aimed at reducing the riskiness of banking activities is the most reliable way to prevent banking crises. Appropriate regulations would include restrictions on risky asset holdings (particularly real estate and stock holdings), limits on the amount of loans allocated to single borrowers, limits on the levels of short-term foreign-denominated debt ("hot money"), restrictions on rates of deposit expansion, and even restrictions on interest rates (to minimize moral hazard). In addition, these theories argue in favor of the strictest reforms proposed in the Basel 2 agreement that more closely linked are the riskiness of specific bank assets to the amount of capital that must be held to back these assets (see Chapter 6 for a more detailed discussion of the Basel agreement and proposed reforms).

This leads to a persuasive explanation of why banking crises have once again become more common internationally since the 1980s. Fundamentals-based models argue that it is more than just a coincidence that the number of banking crises significantly increased after the widespread global financial deregulation of the 1980s. When restrictions on the behavior of banks were removed, banks engaged in riskier behavior and exposed themselves to the types of negative financial shocks that make them vulnerable to crises. This pattern of banking deregulation followed by banking system weakness was observed in the U.S. in the mid-1980s when the federal government was forced to spend roughly $200 billion to close insolvent Savings and Loan banks (S&Ls) after deregulation in the early 1980s. This pattern was also observed in Scandinavia (Sweden, Finland, and Norway) in the 1980s, and Japan, East Asia, and Argentina in the 1990s.

If a banking crisis appears imminent, fundamentals-based models of banking crises argue that aggressive action by a lender of last resort can provide liquidity to shaky banks and help stabilize financial fundamentals. Once a banking crisis begins, these models argue that the macroeconomic costs of a crisis can be minimized by prompt and aggressive government bailouts of insolvent banks. Bailouts are typically the best way to quickly get the banking system functioning again and reestablish credit because banking crises cannot end until the financial fundamentals of banks are restored. In addition, quick bailouts prevent banks from cheating taxpayers by making reckless loans to cronies in anticipation of an approaching bailout (such as what happened during the Mexican banking crisis in the late 1990s).

Of course, the problem with an aggressive lender of last resort and generous bailouts is that these things also encourage moral hazard and increase the probability of future banking crises. If banks, borrowers, and depositors can rely on the government to bail them out whenever things begin to go bad, they will engage in riskier behavior. To help illustrate how big a problem this might be, Table 8.2 presents a list of the financial bailouts provided by or organized by the U.S. government since 1980. It is not a stretch of imagination to believe that rational managers could look at this history and think that the government is implicitly providing their financial institutions with insurance for making high risk/high return loans. Whenever this attitude becomes prevalent in a banking system, banking crises are much more likely to occur.

Note in Table 8.2 that many of the Fed's intercessions in financial markets have been on behalf of institutions other than banks, such as the Fed's bailout of the Long Term Capital Management (LTCM) hedge fund and the Fed's big increase in liquidity after the '87 stock market crash and 9/11. With the advent of universal banking, which has allowed banks to become involved in all sectors of the financial system, the Fed's role as lender of last resort continues to broaden across financial institutions. For many observers this raises significant questions about the spread of moral hazard, particularly because financial innovation has led to the creation of new financial assets and institutions, such as hedge funds, that central banks cannot regulate but may feel obliged to rescue in the event of a financial emergency.

Table 8.2   U.S. Government Financial Bailouts, 1980–2000

Year(s)	Rescue	Rationale for Bailout
1982–1986	Latin American debt crisis	Federal government arranges relief package to limit losses to major U.S. banks
1984	Continental Illinois Bank	Federal Reserve, treasury, and FDIC organize bailout of bank and depositors
Late 1980s	Discount lending by Federal Reserve	Federal Reserve gives loans to 350 banks that later failed
October 1987	1987 stock market crash	Federal Reserve increases liquidity after a large 1-day drop to prevent further financial panic
1989–1992	S&L crisis	Federal government spends $250 billion to clean up S&L crisis driven by risky lending and bad management
1994–1995	Tequilla crisis	U.S. Treasury helps Mexico support the peso during a currency crisis in an effort to prevent further financial panic in the U.S. and Mexico
1997	East Asian financial crisis	U.S. government pushed for $200 billion IMF bailout of East Asian nations suffering from currency crises
1998	Long Term Capital Management bailout	Federal Reserve and treasury department organize a private sector bailout of the hedge fund in an effort to prevent financial panic
1999	Y2K crisis	Federal Reserve increased liquidity in response to fears of a Y2K crisis, which may have played some role in the stock market buildup of the late 1990s

Source: Phillips (2000).

Empirical Evidence on Banking Crises

What causes banking crises?

Directly testing belief-based models of banking crises is difficult because beliefs cannot be accurately measured, but also because these models do not predict any consistent relationship between measurable variables, such as financial fundamentals, and banking crises. In addition, in the modern era almost every industrialized or emerging economy has either explicit or implicit deposit insurance, and insurance can prevent self-fulfilling bank runs and limit the impact of changes in expectations.

A number of studies have attempted to test whether financial fundamentals play a role in banking crises and which of these fundamentals are most important in predicting them. Using data from 31 banking crises between 1980 and 1994, Demirgüç-Kunt and Detragiache (1998) identify the following factors as consistently significant predictors of both the probability and the severity of a banking crisis: slow output growth, high inflation, high real interest rates, balance of payment deficits (which lead to depreciation of the exchange rate), weak regulation enforcement, and, most interestingly, explicit deposit insurance. These results emphasize both the importance of financial fundamentals and the dangers of moral hazard.

Eichengreen and Arteta (2000) investigate 78 banking crisis episodes in 75 emerging economies. Unlike Demirgüç-Kunt and Detragiache, they fail to find that weaker government institutions or deposit insurance play a role in generating banking crises. However, they do find that crises occur in countries in which financial liberalization has recently taken place as well as in countries with high precrisis levels of credit growth and liabilities-to-asset ratios. This supports the argument that deregulation and the subsequent lending booms that often result play a significant role in the build-up to banking crises.

However, the fact that deregulation often leads to banking crises does not mean that regulation by itself can prevent banking crises. In an extensive cross-country study of data on bank regulation, Barth, Caprio, and Levine (2006) find that higher capital requirements and stricter regulatory supervision are not associated with higher bank efficiency or a lower likelihood of a experiencing a banking crisis. To explain this surprising result, the authors note that corruption in bank lending also tends to be correlated with stronger supervision in countries with weak legal and political institutions. Thus, it appears that strong regulation can actually lead to more corruption and lower efficiency without the proper institutions in place to regulate the regulators. The authors suggest that the best way to regulate both banks and regulators is to impose market discipline by making financial information more transparent to investors, who can then punish firms and countries that are not sufficiently vigilant. They find a positive relationship in cross-country banking data between timely and accurate financial information and banking efficiency.

Gorton (1988) examines the factors that affect the risk of holding bank deposits to investigate whether fundamentals or beliefs drive banking crises. Using U.S. banking data from 1873 to 1972, he reports that whenever the liabilities of failed corporations reach a threshold level, bank runs and banking crises occurred. The size of this threshold varies over time and depends upon the structure of the economy. For example, an increase in bankruptcies that would have caused a crisis in the U.S. before 1914 was significantly less likely to do so after the Federal Reserve was created or deposit insurance was implemented. Gorton's evidence supports the assertion that banking crises are primarily caused by changes in fundamentals and that they are a symptom, not the cause, of economic weakness.

One final study of interest comes from Dell'Ariccia, Detragiache, and Rajan (2005), who focus on the distributional effects of banking crises. They find that sectors of the economy that are more dependent on external finance (i.e., sectors that had the weakest financial fundamentals) performed worse during banking crises than other sectors. This result was strongest in situations where overall financial conditions are the weakest: in less developed countries, in countries with less developed financial systems, and when banking crises were most severe. These results, in conjunction with the other studies cited here, provide strong empirical evidence in favor of the hypothesis that financial fundamentals drive banking crises. In addition, these results are consistent with theories of New Institutional Finance that stress the importance of financial fundamentals in driving fluctuations in credit and business cycles. However, given the widespread implementation of deposit insurance and the lack of direct tests regarding the role of beliefs, the possibility of expectations-driven banking crises cannot be ruled out.

What are the costs of banking crises?

Numerous empirical studies have attempted to estimate the costs of banking crises. Their results have varied widely depending upon the size of the sample, the types of countries included, the time period investigated, the length of time investigated, how these costs are measured, and the method used to date the beginning and the end of the crises. That said, a few studies merit discussion. Investigating the effects of banking crises on growth, Demirgüç-Kunt, Detragiache, and Gupta (2000) estimate that growth falls by 4 percent on average following a crisis, but begins to recover after 1 year. The authors also find that both total credit and the number of bank loans falls during crises. On the other hand, Barro (2001) estimates that banking crises only reduce growth by 0.6 percent, which is significantly less than estimated in other studies.

Instead of focusing on the growth costs of banking crises, other studies attempt to estimate the output lost as a result of a crisis. Hutchinson and Neuberger (2005) estimate the costs of banking crises and find that during the 2–4 years following a crisis, output losses average 8–10 percent of precrisis GDP. Boyd, Kwak, and Smith (2005) investigate the costs of banking crises over a longer horizon. They find that 30 percent of countries that have experienced banking crises incurred no output losses. These countries were primarily developed economies. For those countries that did experience output losses, however, Boyd, *et al.* find that the average present value of output losses from trend output (i.e., from what the level of output would have been if the economy had continued at its precrisis growth rate) was between 60 and 300 percent of precrisis GDP. In addition, output remains below precrisis output for an average of 5 years, but in some cases much longer. Finally, the average cost to governments of a banking system bailout is roughly 8–10 percent of precrisis GDP. These results suggest that banking crises can have large and persistent costs in terms of lost output, but also that there is significant variability in the costs of crises across countries.

CASE STUDY: The Savings and Loan Crisis

Savings and Loan banks (S&Ls) are small, community-based financial institutions that have historically focused on raising funds through issuing savings accounts and using these funds to provide mortgages to homeowners. The S&L industry has traditionally been conservative, safe, and boring, making small but steady profits. This changed for the worse during the 1970s. As inflation gradually rose throughout the decade, S&Ls found themselves holding mortgages made in the 1960s with fixed nominal interest rates paying only 4–6 percent. This meant that as inflation rose to 13 percent by the end of the decade, the real interest rates S&Ls were receiving on these loans were negative. At the same time, S&Ls had to pay between 8 and 10 percent on their savings accounts in order to attract any deposits. This is obviously not a sustainable financial position, and by 1980 hundreds of S&Ls were insolvent. The Federal Savings and Loan Insurance Corporation (the FSLIC) did not possess nearly enough reserves to bailout S&Ls depositors, leaving the potential liability to fall on the federal government. The cost to U.S. taxpayers of closing these insolvent banks and paying-off depositors would have been roughly $15 billion in 1981.

President Reagan and Congress balked at these costs. Instead, in the words of Paul Krugman (1994), they chose to go "double or nothing" by deregulating S&Ls. The idea behind deregulation was to increase the efficiency of S&Ls and to put them on the same footing with commercial banks so that they could engage in higher return activities and become more profitable. The idea was that this would in turn improve their financial positions and reduce the need for bailouts.

Deregulation did appear to improve conditions in the industry for a while, but two huge problems emerged. First, though most S&L executives had very narrow experience in home mortgage lending, many S&Ls immediately began naively speculating in areas outside their expertise such as the oil industry (particularly S&Ls in Texas) and the commercial real estate market. This exposed these S&Ls to an incredible amount of risk. When oil prices fell and the real estate market cooled in the early 1980s, many more S&Ls became insolvent. Second, too often deregulation of the S&Ls meant no regulation of S&Ls. Many S&L executives engaged in deceit and outright fraud in an effort to increase returns and line their own pockets.

By the end of the 1980s, more than 1,000 S&Ls had failed. Deregulation had turned a $15 billion potential liability owed by the FSLIC in 1981 into a $166 billion problem by 1990 (roughly 2.7 percent of GDP at the time). This was a bill that was largely borne by U.S. taxpayers. The total economic costs of the S&L were even greater than this, however, as the crisis increased perceived risk throughout the financial system, which slowed the growth in credit and contributed to the 1991–1992 recession in the U.S.

The Causes and Prevention of Asset Bubbles

Asset bubbles and their subsequent busts have been a regular aspect of financial systems for as long as there has been finance. For example, the world's first stock

Table 8.3 Famous Bubbles in History

	Percentage Rise Bull Phase	Length of Up Phase (months)	Percentage Decline Peak to Trough	Length of Down Phase (months)
Tulips Holland (1634–1637)	+5900	36	−93	10
Mississippi shares France (1719–1721)	+6200	13	−99	13
South Sea shares Great Britain (1719–1720)	+1000	18	−84	6
U.S. stocks United States (1921–1932)	+497	95	−87	33
Mexican stocks Mexico (1978–1981)	+785	30	−73	18
Silver United States (1979–1982)	+710	12	−88	24
Hong Kong stocks Hong Kong (1970–1974)	+1200	28	−92	20
Taiwan stocks Taiwan (1986-1990)	+1168	40	−80	12
NASDAQ tech stocks United States (1999–2000)	733	60	−78	32
Japanese stocks Japan (1965–?)	+3720	288	—	—

Source: Cecchetti (2006).

exchange in Amsterdam was also the site of the world's first asset bubble during "Tulipmania." Table 8.3 presents examples of some of the most well-known asset booms and busts. Why is it that market participants cannot see that they are involved in a bubble before it bursts? It seems that, like many things in life, bubbles are usually only seen clearly in hindsight; at the time of the bubble, some argument can always be made that the price increases are justified, even if it is specious.

Like banking crises, there are two primary categories to which explanations of asset bubbles fall into: one that focuses on the role of beliefs and expectations and other that focuses on the role of financial fundamentals. The most influential proponent of belief-based asset bubbles is, once again, Charles Kindleberger (1989). In his investigation of historical bubbles in the U.S. and Europe, Kindleberger argues that financial market volatility is driven by three separate factors. First, speculative manias and panics are an inherent part of the market process. Speculation on asset appreciation and depreciation is necessary for markets to be efficient, but speculation can lead to market volatility when market participants become overly exuberant or pessimistic at different times. The second factor in market volatility is that speculation is often debt-financed. As a result, as argued in Minsky's Financial Instability Hypothesis model, investors can become quite highly leveraged during boom periods, making their returns very sensitive to even small changes, actual or anticipated, in the market. The final factor in market volatility according to Kindleberger is irrationality. In his opinion, which is generally consistent with the Keynesian idea of animal spirits, rationality is best thought of as "a long-run hypothesis." In the short run, investors often act irrationally, exhibiting herding behavior or "mob psychology" that causes investors to follow market leaders blindly regardless of what is true about the financial fundamentals of assets.

Because of these three factors, boom/bust cycles regularly play themselves out in financial systems. Kindleberger argues that booms usually start with either financial liberalization or a monetary expansion by the central bank. As credit expands, investors have easier access to funds, which encourages speculation. Asset prices begin to be bid up, especially as the "greater fool theory" (Who cares if I overpay for an asset, as long as there is a bigger fool that I can sell it to?) begins to become an accepted investment strategy. Finally, in the midst of the bubble, a piece of bad news, either a real shock or a psychological shock, causes some investors to sell their assets and flee the market. As other investors observe this, they follow and begin to sell as well. Eventually, the selling reaches panic proportions and a market crash ensues.

In fundamentals-based models of asset bubbles, the process is similar to that envisioned by Kindleberger, but the emphasis is on real shocks that initiate or burst asset bubbles. Kaminsky and Reinhart (1999) and Higgins and Osler (1997) argue that asset bubbles adhere to the following script. First, broad and rapid financial liberalization takes place that frees banks to engage in riskier behavior and expand bank credit. Much of this credit is used to speculate in asset markets. Kaminsky and Reinhart calculate that real estate and stock markets rise by an average of 40 percent after financial liberalization. Eventually, some external shock takes place, such as a depreciation of the exchange rate, a change in monetary policy, or a slowdown in macroeconomic conditions, that causes investors to reevaluate their risk exposure. Market flight begins and prices collapse. As asset prices drop, net worths and collateral values fall, and bankruptcies dramatically increase because investors are so highly leveraged. As financial fundamentals deteriorate and default risk rises, credit tightens and the asset market crash spills over into the rest of the economy, slowing macroeconomic activity.

One of the important components of both belief-based and fundamentals-based explanations of asset bubbles is the fact that speculation is often financed with credit. This is not only a problem because it creates leverage and risk, but also because debt is always associated with moral hazard. Allen and Gale (2000) develop a simple model in which investors borrow to speculate in asset markets. The moral hazard created by this borrowing increases the attractiveness of risky assets (such as stocks) because they have higher returns. It also increases the attractiveness of assets with a limited supply (such as real estate and, in the short run, stocks) because their prices are the most likely to significantly appreciate, maximizing the benefits of financial leverage. As a result, prices on these risky, limited-supply assets get bid up over what can be justified based on fundamentals, leading to an asset bubble that is based upon the rational behavior of investors.

Because bank lending plays a crucial role in the build-up of bubbles, and because asset market crashes affect the financial fundamentals of banks, a close link can exist between asset bubbles and banking crises. An asset market crash can precipitate a banking crisis by increasing bankruptcies and reducing the net worths of banks. It is also possible that a banking crisis can precipitate an asset market crash by interrupting the flow of credit that is feeding a bubble. Or, there can exist simultaneous causation between the two that creates a feedback loop. Wilson, Sylla, and Jones (1990) investigate financial crises between 1830 and 1988. They report that banking crises and asset market crashes were consistently correlated in the era before the Federal Reserve and deposit insurance (1873–1914). Since then, there has been no correlation between the two in the U.S. For example, during the Great Depression the banking crisis followed the stock market crash by nearly 2 years, while during the 1987 stock market crash and other recent stock market crashes no banking crisis occurred at all. The authors find no empirical evidence that banking crises consistently cause market crashes or vice versa. That said, recent financial crises in Japan (discussed later in this chapter), East Asia (discussed in Chapter 9), and Argentina (discussed in Chapter 10) have each had simultaneous banking crises and asset market crashes. Thus, it appears that there may once again be a strong correlation between the two, although the causation remains unclear.

While they differ in their explanation of the causes of asset bubbles, belief-based and fundamentals-based explanations of bubbles come to similar policy conclusions regarding the best prescriptions for preventing market booms and busts. First, there is a solid rationale against indiscriminate financial deregulation, particularly in highly leveraged financial systems with a history of market volatility. This is not to say that financial deregulation is never justified—in many cases, it clearly enhances efficiency and can improve long-run growth. What is dangerous is a "cold shower" mentality among policy makers, where ambitious deregulation takes place over a short period of time without sufficient consideration of its short-term impact on financial stability. This is particularly true regarding regulations that affect the levels of debt-financed speculation that large financial institutions, particularly banks and investment funds, can engage in. (More on the specifics of what constitutes good financial regulation are discussed in Chapter 10.)

Second, there is a general presumption that a strong lender of last resort is a necessary evil. Bailout lending promotes moral hazard. However, without a lender of last resort, market volatility can spillover into the real economy through increased bankruptcies, diminished financial fundamentals, and reduced credit. A good example of how effective timely lending can be is the October 1987 stock market crash in the U.S., which is actually the largest single-day asset crash in U.S. history. The Fed prevented panic and widespread failure by providing prompt and significant increases in liquidity, giving the markets time to stabilize and avoiding any real impact on the macroeconomy. Once again, however, central banks need to be judicious in their use of this power in order to avoid encouraging moral hazard behavior.

CASE STUDY: Monetary Policy and Asset Bubbles

Economists have been grappling with a debate regarding the extent that stabilizing asset prices should be one of the goals of monetary policy. Lending booms precipitate asset bubbles, and the central bank can attempt to limit the size and the scope of these booms by tightening the money supply and credit when it sees asset prices beginning to take-off. (Of course, we know from New Institutional theories of finance that it is often difficult to discourage the expansion of credit if expectations are high enough.) This strategy, however, is not consistent with monetary policy as it has traditionally been handled, which places its emphasis on the aggregate price level. Asset prices, aside from the modest effect of real estate prices on the Consumer Price Index, are excluded from measures of the aggregate price level, so they have generally been excluded from consideration when determining monetary policy. This is beginning to change, however. The European Central Bank has clearly been considering asset prices more carefully when setting monetary policy, and there is some circumstantial evidence that the Federal Reserve has recently placed more weight on asset prices in their decision-making process than they have in the past (e.g., Alan Greenspan decried the "irrational exuberance" of stock market investors in a speech in 1996). However, no central bank has yet stated that asset prices are playing a primary role in shaping monetary policy.

If central bankers agree to include asset prices as an objective in monetary policy, then there remains a question as to how heavily they should be weighted in the decision-making process. In other words, how aggressively should policy respond to bubbles? Should asset prices be preemptively "pricked" before they become too large? Or should monetary policy only respond to bubbles after they pop in order to minimize their macroeconomic impact? Interestingly, we have the thoughts of Ben Bernanke (2002) on these issues before he became chairman of the Federal Reserve. In a speech given in to the National Association for Business Economics while he was a member of the Board of Governors, Bernanke laid out his view of what the appropriate response of monetary policy to asset bubbles should be.

In Bernanke's opinion, monetary policy is most effective at controlling macroeconomic variables such as inflation and output. It is not effective at controlling market activity at the microeconomic level, meaning asset prices. For that, financial regulation is a central bank's most effective tool because it works at the microeconomic level. By making sure that financial institutions are well capitalized, well diversified, and are transparent in their activities, central banks can limit the moral hazard lending and speculative finance that fuel asset bubbles. As a result, regulation, not monetary policy, is the most effective way of dealing with asset bubbles in their growth phase.

According to Bernanke, the problems with the "pricking hypothesis" (i.e., preemptively cutting the money supply and raising interest rates in order to drive down asset prices before a bubble begins in earnest) are twofold. First, there is no reason to think that a central bank should be any better at identifying asset bubbles than investors. As mentioned before, one of the characteristics of asset bubbles is that it is hard to contemporaneously determine whether appreciations are driven by a bubble or by underlying fundamentals. According to the rational expectations hypothesis, the only way that a central bank could do this is if they had better information than the public, which is unlikely for any sustained period of time. Any central banker that thinks that they are smarter than investors is at least as likely to make a mistake (i.e., contract monetary policy when a bubble is not taking place) as they are to preemptively end a bubble. In any case, if central banks think that an asset bubble is occurring, Bernanke believes it is better addressed through tightening lending restrictions than through changing monetary policy.

The second problem with the pricking hypothesis is that it may not be possible to safely pop a bubble. To stop an appreciation of asset prices, a central bank would have to increase interest rates to such an extent that it could slow the whole economy. In the words of Bernanke, using monetary policy to prevent a bubble is like trying "to perform brain surgery with a sledgehammer." It is too blunt an instrument to slowdown one sector of the economy without slowing down the whole economy. An example of this occurred during the Great Depression, when the Fed did increase interest rates in mid-1929 in an attempt to slowdown the growth of stock prices, but instead only ended up making the Depression worse than it could have been. Bernanke argues that the Fed would have been better served by tightening lending restrictions in 1929 in an effort to dampen speculation, then following this up by more effectively serving as a lender of last resort when the first banking failures took place.

To summarize, Bernanke suggests that monetary policy should be used to aggressively respond to asset bubbles only after they pop and only to the extent that lower asset prices affect aggregate output and employment. Central banks' power to tighten banking regulations and serve as a lender of last resort is a much more targeted and appropriate method to address asset bubbles when central bankers suspect that one is occurring. In these views, Bernanke seems to be expressing not only the view of the majority of central bankers but also of economists generally.

Empirical Evidence on Asset Bubbles

Once again, testing belief-based theories is difficult because beliefs are difficult to measure and impose no empirically testable hypotheses on measurable fundamentals. However, there have been a number of interesting studies that have examined the links between stock price volatility and changes in financial fundamentals. De Bondt and Thaler (1987) present evidence that stock prices overreact to new information, much more than would be predicted by the associated changes in fundamentals alone. Likewise, Schiller (1981) and French and Roll (1986) find evidence that stock prices fluctuate substantially more than financial fundamentals fluctuate. Figure 3.3 from Chapter 3 presents 1-year returns from stocks in the U.S. which illustrates just how volatile stock prices are—much more volatile than the macroeconomy as a whole. All of these results suggest that beliefs play a significant role in market instability.

Other researchers have investigated individual asset market crash episodes in the attempt to identify specific changes in financial fundamentals that triggered the collapse. Studies of the October 1987 crash, in which the stock market lost 20 percent in a single day, and the 2000 stock market crash, in which the NASDAQ stock index fell by 60 percent between March of 2000 and mid-2001, have failed to identify any plausible changes in financial fundamentals that could explain such large swings in prices. These studies also suggest that beliefs that are not associated with fundamentals play an important role in asset pricing.

Empirical studies have also been conducted attempting to identify the costs of asset crashes and whether crashes in some asset markets are more costly than in other markets. One study by Carroll, Otsuka, and Slacalek (2006) finds that a $100 reduction in housing wealth reduces consumption by $9, as opposed to only a $4 reduction in consumption from a $100 fall in equity wealth. Likewise,

Helbling and Terrones (2003) find that the declines in aggregate output associated with housing busts are twice as large as those associated with stock market crashes among a sample of rich countries.

Why would a housing market decline be more costly than a stock market crash? One reason a collapse in real estate prices is more costly is that most households have a larger fraction of their wealth in their homes than in equity or bonds. As a result, a drop or even a flattening of home prices significantly impacts consumption spending. Another reason why housing bubbles are potentially more costly than stock market bubbles is that real estate bubbles are more likely to be fueled by borrowing. Borrowing on real estate increases the likelihood of default, and when defaults occur, lenders are forced to reduce credit across the board, as described in New Institutional theories of finance. Some of the borrowing on homes that has taken place recently is in terms of first mortgages, but a great deal of it is through home equity loans, which have allowed homeowners to turn their home equity into cash. In fact, home equity withdrawals peaked at 10 percent of disposable income in the U.S. in 2005.

CASE STUDY: Is There a Bubble in the International Housing Market?

Figure 8.1 presents the dramatic increase in real housing prices in the U.S. between the mid-1970s and 2004. In the 10 years between 1995 and 2004, real home prices rose by nearly 40 percent. In some cities, real home prices rose by 75 percent over

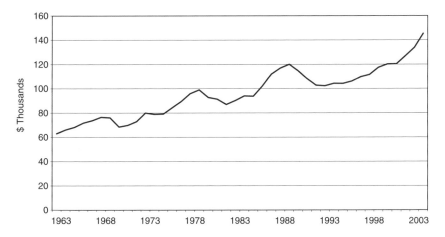

Figure 8.1
Average Real Home Prices in the U.S.
Source: U.S. Census Bureau.

this same period. Compare this to the two decades between 1975 and 1995 when real prices rose by a total of 10 percent.

The question is whether this housing boom was a bubble or whether these higher prices were justified based on economic fundamentals. Case and Schiller (2003) find evidence to support both hypotheses. Supporting the fundamentals hypothesis, Case and Schiller find that the ratio of housing prices to income was stable in 42 of 50 states. In fact, the ratio of mortgage payments to income actually fell in many of these states, meaning that, relative to income, homes were actually cheaper in 2004 than they were in the mid-1990s because of falling mortgage interest rates and fees. In the other eight states, however, fundamentals such as changes in income, population, and employment do not fully explain the increases in housing prices. In a similar study, Himmelberg, Mayer, and Sinai (2005) find that when accounting for lower financing costs, lower interest rates, income growth, taxes, population demographics, and other opportunity costs associated with purchasing a home as an investment asset, there is no general evidence of a nationwide home price bubble, even in high-appreciation cities. In fact, these authors find that the cost of housing was not significantly more expensive in 2004 than it was a decade earlier relative to incomes and rents. While these results do not mean that housing prices will not fall, they do suggest that any decline would be associated with a negative change in the fundamentals of the housing market.

On the other hand, there is also some evidence that beliefs played a role in generating real estate booms in certain markets. Case and Schiller conducted a survey of home buyers in three "glamour" cities of Boston, Los Angeles, and San Francisco and in one control city, Milwaukee. Their survey results indicate that an investment motive played a large role in many home purchases, meaning that many home buyers were purchasing homes as an investment based on the expectation that housing prices would appreciate significantly in the future. In fact, they report that home buyers in the three glamour cities expected prices of homes to appreciate by between 13 and 15 percent a year over the next 10 years (even in Milwaukee, prices were expected to appreciate by nearly 12 percent)! This seems like unreasonably high expectations, indicating that speculative mania and a bubble was taking place in certain areas of the U.S. housing market, at least in these three glamour cities and others like them. Additional evidence of a housing bubble comes from a study by the National Association of Realtors, who found that 25 percent of U.S. houses bought in 2004 were purchased as an investment, not for use as a primary residence.

A housing boom is not just taking place in the U.S., but internationally as well. Nominal housing prices rose by 119 percent in Australia, 165 percent in Spain, 231 percent in Ireland, 176 percent in Britain, and 115 percent in France between 1997 and 2006. On average, residential property has increase in value by 75 percent since 2000 in developed countries. These appreciations translate to an increase in wealth of $74 trillion, or roughly 100 percent of these countries' combined GDPs.

Not only are these real estate appreciations greater than in the U.S., but they are also much more precarious because, as discussed previously, most mortgages outside the U.S. are obtained at variable, not fixed, rates. Thus, an increase in mortgage rates directly leads to increases in the cost of owning a home, even for existing homeowners.

To many observers, these increases in international real estate prices appeared to be examples of Ponzi financing, as described by the Financial Instability Hypothesis model. Real estate is affordable as long as home prices continue to appreciate at 10 percent a year and owners can use home equity loans to cash out equity to make mortgage payments. Once that rate of appreciation begins to slow, however, owners find that they can no longer cover even the interest payments on their loans, leading to ballooning debt and, eventually, default.

CASE STUDY: The Credit Crunch of 2007

One important indication that an unraveling of Ponzi financing in the real estate market is beginning to occur in the U.S. and across the globe is the recent difficulties in the subprime mortgage market. The *subprime mortgage market* offers mortgage loans to high risk borrowers at low interest rates and down payments. Such credit was unavailable to high risk borrowers before the mortgage securitization boom. By early 2007, roughly 10 percent of all mortgage loans went to subprime borrowers. However, as interest rates rose in 2006 (many subprime loans are adjustable rate mortgages often offered at low initial, or "teaser", interest rates) and home price growth slowed, many subprime borrowers became unable to meet their obligations. Defaults in the subprime market rose by 42 percent in 2006. By March of 2007, 15 percent of all subprime borrowers were behind on their payments and more than 1.5 million households in the U.S. are expected to default by the end of the year. As a result, a number of smaller subprime lenders have declared bankruptcy or closed their doors, while many financial institutions have suffered significant losses and have been forced to markdown the value of many of their assets. This has significantly reduced credit and threatens to further reduce real estate prices and lead to massive financial instability.

The growth in the subprime mortgage market, like in the rest of the mortgage market, has been fueled by the securitization boom. The amount of securitized loans has risen to more than $3.2 trillion in 2006, nearly triple where it was at the beginning of the decade. As these types of financial arrangements have grown, many of the financial fundamentals that back them have become increasingly complicated—so much so that they are often not well understood, either by investors, credit rating agencies, or regulators. As securitized lending boomed, many loan originators may not have been sufficiently concerned with monitoring the credit risk of borrowers, confident that any loan that could be made could eventually be sold and securitized. Credit rating agencies, charged with providing the public with the most accurate information about the risk of assets backed with mortgages, were paid by the firms that were doing the securitization, creating a conflict of interest. Magnifying this conflict of interest is the fact that credit rating agencies cannot be held liable for any bad information they might have provided. Finally, regulators, particularly central banks, seemed unable to keep up with the increasing complexity of what was being sold and by whom.

The subprime mortgage market began to unravel beginning in August of 2007 when mortgage default rates spiked. As real estate prices tumble—they are expected to decline 10 percent to 30 percent by the end of 2008 relative to their 2007 highs—the number of mortgage borrowers that have been unable to meet their payments has continued to rise. When credit rating agencies began to down-grade billions of dollars of assets each week, for the first time many investors became aware of the true risk associated with their securitized assets and immedi-ately attempted to unload them. As the prices of securitized assets fell, the balance sheets of many financial institutions took large hits. Just as New Institutional theories of finance would predict, these declines in net worth forced financial institutions to restrict lending, leading to a credit crunch unseen in recent history. For example, one measure of the costs of credit intermediation, which is the risk spread between T-Bills and the Federal Funds rate, hit a 20-year high by Septem-ber of 2007. This credit crunch not only has constrained mortgage lending, but it also has affected consumer lending and even lending that is not securitized. New homebuilding in the U.S. is expected to fall by 30 percent in 2007, while retail sales are expected to slow significantly.

The credit crunch has not only affected U.S. financial markets, but financial markets across the globe. The European Union area held more than $500 billion in subprime mortgage securities in the U.S. at the beginning of 2007, leading to fears of large losses and a credit crunch there as well. The subprime col-lapse contributed to the bank run at Northern Rock in England (see the following case study). Assets worldwide—bonds, stocks, and real estate—have seen their price growth slow or even turn negative as investors realize that many of their assets are linked in complicated ways to U.S. financial markets. Many observers have begun to openly worry about the spread of financial panic and contagion (to be discussed in detail in Chapter 9), and almost all forecasters have signifi-cantly downgraded their economic growth forecasts for 2007 and 2008 across most countries.

The Federal Reserve and the European Central Bank have been aggressively dealing with this credit crunch by reducing interest rates and generously increasing the availability of loans to financial institutions. To critics, this response by central banks is simply compounding previous errors. First, in their roles as regulators, these central banks ignored the risk of securitized assets, leading to unchecked and unsustainable growth in these markets. Then, after the bubble burst, these same central banks are fueling moral hazard by bailing out financial institutions that carelessly assumed excessive risk.

More charitable observers would note that it is extremely difficult to accurately monitor financial institutions given the incredibly rapid pace of financial development, and while this crisis is unfortunate, the huge benefits that securitization have created cannot be ignored. The only way that this credit crunch could turn into something more than a small downturn is if central banks did not perform their role of lender of last resort and did not try to restore liquidity and confidence in the financial system. Regardless of which side of the debate one agrees with, it is very clear that financial innovation has created a new financial world that central banks will continue to struggle to understand and also to manage. While securitization and financial innovation played a large role in the Great Moderation across developed countries over the last 25 years, it might also be the greatest threat to its continuance.

CASE STUDY: The Northern Rock Bank Run

The bank run on England's Northern Rock bank in 2007 was the first run on a British bank in 140 years, surprising even the most well-connected financial observers. Northern Rock is England's fifth-largest mortgage provider. Northern Rock specializes in raising funds not through attracting deposits but through securitizing their mortgages. This strategy led to huge growth—Northern Rock had record profits in 2006—but at the cost of assuming significant balance sheet risk. As long as mortgage borrowers continued to pay on their mortgages, Northern Rock could continue to make the payments on the bonds they issued. But without deposits or other sources of funds to fall back upon in a time of crisis, Northern Rock was very susceptible to failure if default rates on the mortgages they owned began to rise. This is exactly what began to happen in 2007.

One of the factors that set the stage for the crisis at Northern Rock was the lack of strict regulation by British authorities. In a recent switch, banks like Northern Rock are no longer regulated by the Bank of England but by a new regulatory agency called the Financial Services Authority. This new agency appears to have been largely clueless about the true risk that Northern Rock has assumed in their securitized transactions. As default rates on mortgages began to rise and the price of securitized assets began to fall, Northern Rock found that they were unable to borrow funds from other banks and had to go to the Bank of England for help. Despite some internal reluctance, the Bank provided $26 billion in loans to Northern Rock out of fear that its failure would spark a general panic. Somewhat surprisingly, however, this loan only increased panic among depositors. This was in part because many depositors in Northern Rock were unaware that there was any trouble there until the loan was publicly announced. Even more importantly, depositor panic was sparked by the fact that deposits in England were not fully insured. Instead, depositors were only insured fully on the first £2,000 of deposits and insured only up to 90 percent on the next £33,000 of deposits. Facing a partial loss of their deposits if Northern Rock failed, a bank panic ensued with large numbers of depositors queuing outside all of Northern Rock's branches. This bank run was only quelled when the British government announced a change in policy to fully insure all deposits at banks across the country.

This surprising bank run illustrates the somewhat limited power of central bank lending to calm bank runs when panic is particularly acute, although the Bank of England's actions in this case did appear to prevent the spread of bank runs to other banks. It also illustrates the importance of full deposit insurance to preventing bank runs. Depositors are sure to flee banks when faced with the possibility of even relatively small losses.

CASE STUDY: The Japanese Banking and Financial Crises

Lasting 13 years, from 1991 to late 2003, the "Great Recession" in Japan was the longest below-average period of economic growth experienced by any developed country since World War II. While this recession was long lasting, however, the total contraction in output was not particularly large. Figure 8.2 presents output growth in Japan. Over this period, the worst 1-year growth rate was −2 percent (compared to −6 percent during the Great Depression) and growth averaged

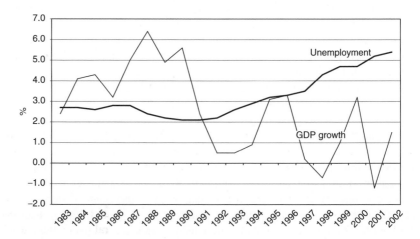

Figure 8.2
Output Growth and Unemployment in Japan.
Source: Bank of Japan.

0 percent over the entire time period. However, if the costs of this recession are measured in terms of potential output and not just growth, this recession was extremely costly. By 2004, Japan had fallen more than 25 percent behind the output level it would have achieved if the economy had grown at only 2 percent a year since 1991. To put this another way, even by conservative estimates this recession has cost Japan lost output that is roughly equivalent to the annual GDP of Italy. The social costs of this lingering recession have also been significant; crime has risen to historic highs and suicides rose by 50 percent between 1990 and 2003.

While Japanese macroeconomic performance has been bad, its financial conditions have been worse. This recession was associated with crashes in the real estate and stock markets, which at one time had fallen by more than 75 percent and in 2005 still remained more than 40 percent below their 1991 peaks. Even more importantly, one of the largest and longest banking crisis ever is still taking place in Japan. Japanese banks have bad loans of unprecedented proportions, and an extremely large government bailout would be needed to fully restore the solvency of the banking system. As the Japanese government struggles to develop a plan to conduct such a bailout, Japanese banks continue to tread water, limiting the amount of bank credit that is available to firms and households, which continues to hamper the recovery.

Three primary factors contributed to the banking crisis in Japan. The first is the structural inefficiencies and riskiness of the Japanese banking system. Like other Asian economies, the Japanese financial system relies much more heavily on bank lending than other developed countries, with bank finance being provided by a small number of very large banks. While Japanese bond and stock markets are relatively small, seven banks account for half of all private lending in the economy (Hoshi and Kashyap, 2004). This not only affects lending, but also affects savings. Japanese households hold more than 50 percent of their assets in currency and bank deposits (compare this to the U.S., where the number is 10 percent). This incredibly large pool of bank funds is the principal reason why Japan had eight of the ten largest banks in the world in the early 1990s.

The problem with such extreme bank concentration is that it does not promote the efficient provision of credit. Domestic competition is limited and Japanese banks are protected from international competition by trade and capital barriers imposed by their government. In addition, because there are no rules that separate banks from the corporations they lend to, most large Japanese banks and corporations have established formal working ties. These corporate/banking conglomerates are referred to as *Keiretsu*. While these Keiretsu were initially created to overcome asymmetric information problems between banks and firms in order to ease the flow of credit, in practice they have created an atmosphere of "crony capitalism" where loans are made on the basis of relationships and not profits. To illustrate just how unprofitable Japanese banking is, Hoshi and Kashyap (2004) find that the interest rate margin of Japanese banks (the difference between the interest rate received on assets and the interest rate paid on deposits) is only one-third of what it is in U.S. banks. Coupled with high default rates and little revenue from fees and nonlending activities, banks in Japan have not been profitable since the early 1990s.

Keiretsu conglomerates also create a great deal of moral hazard in the Japanese financial system because these conglomerates have determined, rightly it seems, that they are too big to fail and that the government will be forced to support them during bad times regardless of how they behave. Financial deregulation in Japan in the 1980s further magnified the problems associated with moral hazard; what few constraints banks had on their lending activities were weakened and the riskiness of lending behavior in Japanese banks immediately increased. By 1990, the financial fundamentals of Japanese banks were widely regarded by observers as being extremely fragile.

The second important factor in the banking crisis is the asset bubbles that took place in the stock and real estate markets during the 1980s. Hutchinson and McDill (1999) report econometric evidence that moral hazard and deregulation played a significant role in the bank lending boom of the 1980s that fueled these asset bubbles in Japan. As mentioned before, the booms and busts that took place in these markets were substantial, and there is no evidence that fundamentals alone can explain the size of the appreciations that took place. To provide just one example of how large the real estate bubble was, it is reported by Krugman (1999) that during the late 1980s the 1 square mile surrounding the Emperor's palace in the center of Tokyo was valued at more than all of the land in California. When the bubbles burst in 1990 (which was precipitated by an increase in interest rates by the Bank of Japan), not only were investors seriously hurt, but the banks that lent money to these investors were left holding large amounts of bad loans and less valuable collateral. This devastated the financial fundamentals of banks and precipitated the banking crisis. As banks collapsed, they restricted credit, which led to more panic selling and further declines in asset prices. Thus, a feedback loop existed between banks and asset markets, providing an excellent example of how asset bubbles and banking crises often interact.

The third and final factor in the banking crisis is deflation. Inflation fell during the beginning of the recession, and between 1995 and 2003 the price level fell during most years. One result of this was that nominal interest rates fell to, and even slightly below, zero. Kuttner and Posen (2001) investigate the causes of this deflation and largely blame the Bank of Japan (the central bank of Japan) and their reluctance to expand the money supply because of (unbelievably) fears of inflation. Panic sparked by the banking crisis also played a role by increasing currency and reserve holdings, which reduced the money multiplier and made it difficult for the Bank of Japan to increase the money supply when they belatedly attempted to do it in 2000. Deflation is costly to banks because it increases default rates in the banking system by increasing the real value of debt relative to assets. As first hypothesized in the Debt-Deflation theory, this occurs because debt contracts have fixed nominal values that do not adjust with the price level. As the financial position of firms and households deteriorate, bankruptcies and default rates increase. This leads to the panic selling of assets that further exacerbates the problems of default and bank insolvency.

Each of these three factors—structural inefficiencies, asset bubbles, and deflation—significantly weakened the financial fundamentals of Japanese banks. Kuttner and Posen (2001) find evidence, similar to that found by Ben Bernanke (1983) in the U.S. during the Great Depression, that the deterioration of financial fundamentals in the Japanese banking system led to increases in the cost of credit intermediation, credit rationing, and reductions in consumption and investment. In addition, declining fundamentals weakened the power of Japanese monetary policy. As discussed in Chapter 7, the weak position of Japanese banks reduced the power of traditional monetary tools and mechanisms to stabilize output in the midst of the recession. Also, given that deflation reduced nominal interest rates to close to zero, it is likely that Japan found itself in a liquidity trap, as hypothesized by Keynes. However, New Institutional theories point to tools other than open market operations and avenues outside of the traditional interest rate channel that central banks can use to stabilize output during contractions. Unfortunately, the Bank of Japan is very conservative and remains reluctant to this day to change its thinking or its operating procedures. As a result, it remains largely ineffective.

An important question regarding the banking crisis remains: What must be done to strengthen the financial fundamentals of Japanese banks and restore banking lending? Hoshi and Kashyap estimate that in 2004 the difference between the liabilities and viable assets of the entire Japanese banking system was approximately 40 trillion yen. In other words, to make Japanese banks solvent once again, an amount equivalent to 8 percent of Japan's annual income would have to be injected into the banking system, presumably by taxpayers. Such a bailout would only solidify the balance sheets of banks—it would do nothing about their structural inefficiencies that also pose a threat to the long-term viability of the banking system.

In addition, such a bailout only addresses the insolvency of the banking system. It does not address the financial weakness of Japan's insurance industry and government-run financial institutions, which suffer from many of the same problems that the banking system suffers from. Hoshi and Kashyap estimate that these two sectors would require an additional bailout that is larger than the bailout needed in the banking sector, bringing the total bailout package needed in 2004 to roughly 100 trillion yen, or 20 percent of Japan's GDP. The logistical problems (Who gets bailed-out first? What price should be paid for nonperforming loans?) and the political problems (Who pays and how?) that a bailout of this size creates explains why nothing even approaching a comprehensive bailout plan of this size and scope has been formulated. In the mean time, a large number of "zombie" banks continue to operate in Japan that are too weak to extend credit but have not been closed or bailed-out by the government.

Allen and Gale (1999) invoke an interesting comparison between the Norwegian government's response to its banking crisis in 1986 and the Japanese experience. In Norway, the government immediately bailed-out banks, costing them an amount equivalent to 0.9 percent of annual GDP. Immediately, credit intermediation resumed, banks became profitable, and Norway's recession ended relatively quickly. In Japan, the government did not engage in immediate bailouts, instead hoping economic growth would recover and that this would solidify the financial fundamentals of banks. When this did not occur, the recession lingered on. Since 2004, minimal economic growth in Japan has begun to gradually reduce the number of bad loans. But the cost of this passive approach has been additional years of lost time and output. In contrast, Allen and Gale argue that the Norwegian case illustrates the benefits of a "take-your-lumps" approach to bailouts. The sooner governments pay-up, the sooner financial systems stabilize and the economic recovery can begin. Until the Japanese government faces up to the large costs, both monetary and political, that it still must incur to end this crisis, the economic recovery is likely to remain fragile and liable to collapse at any time. Japan's growth rate in 2005 was only 2 percent, which is stronger than it has been but still meager for a country so far below its natural rate of output.

Conclusions

Recent financial crises across the globe illustrate many of the basic characteristics of modern banking crises and asset bubbles. First, banking crises and asset bubbles are very costly for similar reasons. They both reduce credit directly by increasing the risk associated with financial intermediation, and they also reduce credit indirectly by weakening the financial fundamentals of borrowers and lenders. The end result is a collapse of credit that lowers investment, lowers consumption, lowers productivity, and leads to an economic slowdown. For example, the prolonged banking crisis in Japan directly corresponded to the long recession in Japan in the 1990s. Many other banking crises and asset bubbles have also been directly correlated with recessions across countries. In the future, both empirical evidence and economic theory suggest that the current problems in the international housing market and the subprime mortgage markets do not bode well for growth in the near term across the globe.

Recent crises also illustrate that our modern macroeconomic theories of financial systems explain crises and bubbles quite well, with both beliefs and fundamentals playing an important role in creating these phenomena. While the destabilizing role of beliefs in modern banking crises has been limited by the provision of deposit insurance and stronger central banks, both of which reduce the likelihood of bank runs, beliefs appear to play a larger role in fueling the speculative manias that create asset bubbles. On the other hand, both the circumstantial and empirical evidence suggest that weak financial fundamentals play the predominant role in triggering banking crises. In modern banking crises, financial fundamentals have been weakened by financial deregulation that encourages moral hazard and debt-financed speculation in the banking system. This moral hazard and speculation have also helped fuel asset bubbles. Consistent with the words of Keynes (1936): "When the capital development of a country becomes a by-product of a casino, the job is likely to be ill done."

Another important aspect of modern crises has been the interaction between banking crises and asset bubbles. The same lack of regulation and moral hazard that weakens bank fundamentals also leads to excessive speculation and asset bubbles, creating a feedback loop in which asset market crashes leave banks holding large amounts of bad loans and less valuable collateral. This precipitates a banking crisis that restricts credit and leads to even more panic selling, further depressing asset prices. Thus, the presence of one magnifies the other, making the aggregate effect much worse than asset crashes or banking crises separately.

Finally, modern banking crises and asset bubbles have proved that good theory means little if policy makers do not use it. The dangers of injudicious financial deregulation have been long feared by many economists, but pressure continues to be exerted by investors, foreign governments, and international agencies to liberalize quickly. Liberalization has not only allowed lenders and borrowers to act without fully considering the risk that they are assuming, but it has also led to a failure to both regulate regulators and to increase the transparency of financial information, leading to corruption that has reduced bank efficiency and increased risk. Likewise, many governments have provided deposit insurance, central bank loans, and bailouts with a careful consideration of the incentives these actions create. These tools play an important role in stabilizing financial systems if used judiciously, but they also have potentially large costs both in fiscal terms as well as in terms of encouraging moral hazard. Too often, these costs and benefits have not been properly balanced: governments have provided too much security to investors that leads to excessive speculative behavior, or governments have been too slow to provide bailouts because of the financial and political costs involved, leading to prolonged recessions as in the case of Japan.

Our discussion of financial crises does not end here. Increasingly, financial panics have become globalized, with crises occurring not just in domestic banking and asset markets but in foreign exchange and international capital markets as well. The purpose of the following chapters is to discuss the nature and causes of these international financial crises.

PART IV

INTERNATIONAL FINANCE AND FINANCIAL CRISES

CHAPTER 9

Capital Flight and the Causes of International Financial Crises

Introduction

The last 25 years have seen an incredible expansion in the flow of capital and credit across countries. Part of this growth in capital flows has taken place between developed countries. But what makes this current era of globalization unique is that much of this explosion in capital flows has taken place between developed and less developed countries (LDCs). In the 1980s, private capital flows to LDCs amounted to only $174 billion, but grew to an incredible $1.3 trillion in the 1990s and more than $2 trillion a year today. China alone attracted more than $55 billion foreign capital inflows in 2004. Not only are there more international financial transactions, but these flows are also no longer only in the form of bonds issued by large industries, such as railroads, or by governments. Increasingly, foreign investment is flowing to a broader array of industries through a broader array of financial instruments. This international financial development has helped fuel a wide and unprecedented increase in world growth over the last 20 years.

Unfortunately, international financial transactions are subject to the same problems as domestic finance, but to an even greater extent. Asymmetric information is likely to be a larger problem in international lending because foreign investors may not have access to the same quality of information as domestic investors in many circumstances. In addition, the legal rights of foreign investors are often not as strong or as consistently enforced; for example, in many countries it is often difficult for foreign investors to enforce their rights to a share of the remaining assets when a domestic corporation goes bankrupt. Finally, governments are very involved in international financial transactions, whether through managing exchange rates or through more distortionary methods such as imposing taxes or limits on international financial transactions. Because foreign investors cannot vote or serve in the domestic government, politicians often have an incentive to

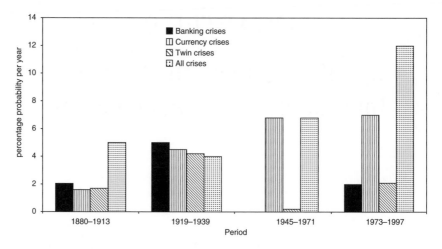

Figure 9.1
Frequency of Financial Crises.
Source: Bordo *et al.*, 2001.

use their power to exploit foreign investors in ways that benefit domestic interests. Together, these difficulties mean that international financial intermediation suffers from extensive market failure. The end result is that, as emphasized by New Institutional theories of finance, financial volatility is likely to be worse in economies that have opened their financial systems to international capital flows, making overall economic volatility greater as well.

In fact, higher levels of financial volatility are exactly what countries across the globe have experienced in this new era of globalized finance. Figure 9.1 presents the frequency of different types of crises as reported by Bordo *et al.* (2001). Financial crises have been twice as frequent in the most recent period (1973–1997) as they were before 1913; almost all of this increase was driven by an increase in the number of *currency crises*, or financial crashes within foreign exchange markets. These currency crises are precipitated by *capital flight*, or large and rapid withdrawals of funds by foreign and domestic investors anticipating either a depreciation of the exchange rate, a downturn in the economy, or both. Not only have currency crises become more frequent, but they have also changed in nature compared to previous eras. During the Bretton Woods period (1945–1971), currency crises were much more predictable and were associated with obviously bad macroeconomic policies such as high inflation rates and large current account deficits. However, since the mid-1980s, a number of crises have occurred in places like East Asia and Argentina that had recently been held up as model economies for the rest of the developing world to follow and in which macroeconomic policy appeared to be prudent.

When comparing the post-Bretton Woods period (1974–1979) to the Bretton Woods period (1945–1971), we see that the reason that financial crises have become more frequent is not because of an increase in the number of currency crises (in fact, they have occurred slightly less frequently). Instead, there has been a dramatic increase in the number of banking crises, and these banking crises have become increasingly associated with currency crises. Returning to Figure 9.1, banking crises in the modern period have become increasingly frequent, while during the Bretton Woods period they were nonexistent. As a result, there has been a large increase in the number of *twin crises*, or concurrent currency and banking crises. Twin crises are also commonly associated with a third crisis in domestic asset markets, so they might more appropriately be called triplet crises. Regardless, this twin crises phenomenon has been one of the distinctive features of recent economic crises in Argentina and in the East Asian crisis.

This change in both the frequency and the characteristics of international financial crises has surprised economists, causing them to reexamine their thinking regarding the macroeconomic impact of international finance. This chapter reviews some of this new research, with a focus on explaining the causes of capital flight, currency crises, and twin crises as well as examining how and why these types of financial crises have changed over time. In addition, the East Asian crisis, which is the largest international economic contraction since the Great Depression, is examined in detail and serves as an excellent case study of modern financial crises and how they can lead to macroeconomic volatility.

The Causes of Capital Flight and Currency Crises

Many governments fix their exchange rate or only allow their exchange rate to fluctuate within a narrow band relative to another currency, typically the dollar or the currency of a major trading partner. To maintain a fixed exchange rate, a country must stand ready to buy or sell their currency for *foreign reserves* (i.e., the foreign currencies of large industrialized countries, such as the dollar or the Euro, held by central banks) at the targeted rate, or the *peg*. The benefits of a fixed exchange rate system are that it reduces the exchange rate risk faced by exporters, importers, and foreign investors, which in turn encourages international trade and foreign investment. Of course, there are costs associated with fixed exchange rates as well, primarily that a country must give up control of its monetary and fiscal policy to support the peg. A fixed exchange rate means that a central bank must change the money supply in response to changes in the foreign exchange market (by purchasing or selling foreign reserves) instead of using monetary policy to stabilize domestic interest rates, the financial system, and aggregate output. A fixed exchange rate also means that the government must maintain fiscal discipline so that it can afford to maintain low money growth and also to provide resources to defend the peg if there is significant downward pressure on the exchange rate in the market. These costs are significant, but for poorer countries that rely heavily on international trade and that are desperate for foreign investment, the loss of monetary and fiscal control is often judged to be worth it.

Currency crises are precipitated by speculative attack and capital flight. Currency crises begin when foreign investors come to believe that the exchange rate is *overvalued*, meaning that the exchange rate peg is greater than the exchange rate that would exist if the government allowed the currency to be determined by supply and demand in the foreign exchange market (usually referred to as the *float exchange rate*). Investors respond by selling their domestic currency holdings (and their domestic assets as well) in exchange for foreign assets, forcing governments to sell their foreign reserves and buy their own currency in order to prevent it from depreciating. Eventually, investors and speculators observe that the government's foreign reserves are declining and recognize that it cannot defend its peg much longer. Even more panic selling takes place as investors attempt to leave as rapidly as possible before *devaluation*, or the reduction of the exchange rate peg, takes place. This increases the rate at which the government is losing foreign reserves until, eventually, the government runs out. At this point, the country is forced to abandon its peg and the exchange rate is devalued, typically by more than what would have been necessary if it had devalued in the early stages of the attack.

A devaluation has a large negative impact on any economy. Devaluation increases the real price of imports, which reduces aggregate supply when an economy heavily relies on imported inputs, such as oil. Devaluation also has a negative impact on aggregate demand when a country imports many necessities, such as food stuffs, because the higher prices of these necessities reduce the disposable income that is available to purchase other goods. Another and even more important cost of a large devaluation is that it can severely weaken financial systems by reducing the value of domestic assets relative to foreign-denominated debt. When banks and other domestic financial institutions purchase domestic assets that are financed with debt that needs to be repaid in a foreign currency, devaluation will greatly reduce net worth. This wreaks havoc on the financial fundamentals of lenders within a banking system, leading to credit and output contractions in a manner that is consistent with New Institutional theories of finance.

One question remains unanswered. What determines investors' evaluation that an exchange rate is overvalued? In other words, what triggers a speculative attack in the first place? There are two categories of theories regarding the factors that precipitate capital flight and currency crises: fundamentals-based theories and belief-based theories. Under fundamentals-based theories, such as the model proposed by Krugman (1979), currency crises occur when exchange rates become significantly misaligned with current macroeconomic conditions. For example, a government that stubbornly maintains a fixed exchange rate in the presence of high levels of inflation, high budget deficits, and low growth will eventually see speculative pressures build over time to the point when a currency crisis occurs. In fundamentals-based models of currency crises, the best indicator of whether an exchange rate is misaligned is a country's balance of payments. An overvalued exchange rate leads to a current account deficit because it makes imports cheaper relative to exports. As a result, the existence of a large current account deficit and a large capital account surplus (which indicates that the country is borrowing from abroad to pay for its current account deficits) is strong evidence that the exchange rate is overvalued and conditions are ripe for a currency crisis. One commonly used rule of thumb is that once a country's current account deficit reaches 5 percent of GDP, its exchange rate is overvalued enough to put it in immediate danger of a speculative attack and capital flight.

Fundamentals-based theories fit the features of currency crises that occurred during the 1970s and 1980s quite well. For example, the currency crises that struck throughout Latin America in the 1980s were all associated with large levels of international debt and large budget deficits. These deficits not only limited foreign reserve holdings, but they forced governments to finance their spending through increasing the money supply, leading to high rates of inflation (in some cases, such as Argentina, greater than 5,000 percent a year) and significant downward pressure on exchange rates. Another example of a crisis that followed this same general script was the Mexican Peso "Tequila crisis" in 1994.

In fundamentals-based theories, the best way to prevent future currency crises is to maintain prudent macroeconomic management. Specifically, governments should commit themselves to balanced budgets and low inflation. In addition, government regulation of the financial sector is needed to reduce moral hazard and ensure that foreign investment is used for productive and not just speculative and destabilizing purposes.

Critics of fundamentals-based theories argue that while the fundamentals of currency crisis countries are typically weak, they are also weak in many countries that never suffer a currency crisis. In other words, fundamentals alone are not sufficient to predict which countries will experience a crisis and when exactly these crises will occur. Instead, they argue that currency crises are often belief-based. These models are similar to the belief-based models of banking crises discussed in Chapter 8. For example, Obstfeld (1996) develops a model of rational expectations in which the return to currency speculators depends upon what each individual speculator believes about the behavior of other speculators. Because speculators realize that each government has a point at which the costs of maintaining a peg begin to outweigh its benefits, there is the possibility of multiple equilibriums and self-fulfilling currency crises depending upon the beliefs that are currently prevalent in the market. If speculators come to believe that other speculators believe that a currency crisis is going to take place, speculators withdraw their capital and a currency crisis takes place. If speculators do not believe that other speculators think that a crisis is going to take place, then no currency crisis takes place, regardless of the state of existing fundamentals.

The proponents of belief-based theories of currency crises point to the fact that it is often difficult to pinpoint a specific change in economic fundamentals that is large enough to justify most currency crises. For example, numerous crises in the 1990s such as in Russia (1998), Brazil (1998), and Argentina (2000) each started without a readily identifiable real shock that could explain the size of the currency crises that took place. Marshall (1998) argues that a model similar to the belief-based model of banking crises developed by Diamond and Dybvig is consistent with self-fulfilling currency crises that took place during the East Asian crisis in 1997–1999. Likewise, it is widely acknowledged that the capital flight experienced by Argentina in 2000 was in response to fears that Argentina would default on its sovereign debt (which, in fact, did happen after its currency crisis). However, it is difficult to identify exactly what sparked these fears.

Belief-based theories also provide an explanation for an interesting paradox of the 1990s: many of the countries that were most widely regarded as "good government" countries (East Asia, Argentina) suffered the worst currency crises. These models' explanation of this paradox is that the countries that were the most highly regarded were also the countries that attracted the most foreign investment, making them the most susceptible to investor panic and a self-fulfilling currency crisis.

The policy recommendations of belief-based theories are founded upon the idea that stabilizing expectations is the key to preventing and resolving currency crises. These theories argue for the imposition of short-term capital controls and market suspensions to limit capital flight during crisis, but more importantly for the need for an international lender of the last resort (a function that could be handled by a reformed and empowered International Monetary Fund [IMF]) to stabilize investors expectations and prevent panic in foreign exchange markets.

Contagion

One of the distinguishing features of currency crises and capital flight episodes that have occurred since the 1980s is that they have often been linked across countries. For example, during the 1980s, currency crises took place simultaneously throughout numerous countries in Latin America. During the 1990s, a currency crisis in Thailand spread to the rest of East Asia (1997), then to Russia (1998), Brazil (1999), Uruguay (1999), and Argentina (2000). This phenomenon is often referred to as *contagion*, which is more formally defined as a situation in which a currency crisis in one country increases the probability of a currency crisis in another country.

Once again, there are fundamentals-based theories of contagion and belief-based theories of contagion. Fundamentals-based theories focus on the role of real shocks that are correlated across countries. These shocks could be in the form of changes in the terms of trade (such as an increase in the price of raw materials such as oil), liquidity shocks (such as a contraction in the U.S. money supply that reduces world liquidity and increases interest rates), or macroeconomic shocks (such as a recession in the U.S. or Europe that reduces import demand and world aggregate demand).

Such shocks would be commonly felt by a large number of countries. However, these real shocks can also be spread through two additional channels. The first is through *trade linkages*. Here, a contraction in one country reduces that country's demand for imports, which in turn affects the aggregate demand of each of its trade partners. The other channel is through *financial linkages*. Many countries share similar institutional lenders, such as international portfolio funds or international banks. When a crisis occurs in one country, these lenders see the value of their assets and collateral fall. This forces these lenders to tighten credit constraints and to sell off assets across their international portfolio. In this way, capital flight occurs simultaneously across countries.

On the other hand, there are three alternative theories of contagion that are belief-based. The first is that contagion, like currency crises, is *self-fulfilling*. A crisis in one country leads investors to believe that investors are going to flee to other countries, regardless of their economic fundamentals. If this happens, investors across a broad range of countries begin to withdraw their funds and capital flight spreads.

The second belief-based channel of contagion is referred to as *herding*, which is also an important component of the Keynesian concept of animal spirits. When information is costly to investors, small investors have an incentive to "follow-the-leaders," meaning that they follow the actions of large investors with established reputations. The fact that many fund managers are paid based on how they perform relative to the market also increases the incentives for investor herding. As a result, if small investors see even one large investor broadly pull back based on a crisis in a single country (regardless of their reasons for doing so), enough investors could follow to trigger a speculative attack.

The third belief-based channel is referred to as a *wake-up call*. Here, a collapse in one country alerts investors to look for similar weaknesses in other countries that were previously ignored. For example, an investor might want to more closely scrutinize other countries that share similar macroeconomic policies with the crisis country. Or, a change in the structure of the international financial system, such as a change in banking regulations or the lending policies of the IMF, might cause investors to reevaluate their default risk exposure across countries, explaining why capital flight episodes are often correlated.

Once again, fundamentals-based and belief-based theories reach much different policy conclusions regarding the prevention of contagion. Fundamentals-based theories focus on prudent monetary and fiscal policies as well as on strict financial regulation to prevent moral hazard and maintain stable macroeconomic and financial fundamentals. Belief-based theories argue for stopgap measures, such as capital controls, as well as bailouts and emergency lending to countries experiencing, or in danger of experiencing, a currency crisis in order to help them defend their pegs and prevent the spread of contagion.

Empirical Evidence on Capital Flows, Currency Crises, and Contagion

Once again, it is difficult to directly test belief-based theories because beliefs and expectations are difficult to measure and because these theories do not predict a systematic relationship between things that are measurable, such as macroeconomic fundamentals, and currency crises. However, a number of empirical studies have attempted to identify the role that fundamentals play in currency crises and contagion and whether fundamentals provide a complete explanation of crises or if there remains a plausible role for beliefs.

The most comprehensive empirical study of currency crises was conducted by Eichengreen, Rose, and Wyplosz (2003a). They find that devaluations typically occur after periods of high money growth, high inflation, high unemployment, foreign reserve losses, and high credit growth—in other words, when macroeconomic fundamentals are weak. (Surprisingly, they did not find persuasive evidence to support the notion that budget deficits and fiscal policy play a role in currency crises.) However, the authors obtain other results that support the argument that beliefs also play a role in currency crises. The authors find that in most cases it is difficult to identify a specific event that initiates a crisis or to time exactly when a crisis began based on fundamentals data alone. In addition, they find that a few specific crisis episodes are difficult to explain based only on fundamentals. Finally, the authors find that countries that have experienced a currency crisis in the past are more likely to experience a crisis again, which could be an indication of the importance of a country's credibility and reputation in shaping investors' expectations.

A number of empirical studies have looked at the determinants of when and where contagion is most likely to occur. Eichengreen, Rose, and Wyplosz (2003b) find that crises elsewhere increase the probability of a crisis in another country by 8 percent on average. Using a model to forecast contagion, the authors find that the most significant determinant of the spread of contagion is the existence of trade links: speculative attacks are most likely to spread to countries that have higher levels of trade with the country that is in crisis. They also find empirical evidence that contagion is most likely to spread to countries with similar macroeconomic policies (fiscal and monetary policy) as the crisis country, which is evidence in support of the wake-up-call hypothesis.

In contrast, Kaminsky, Reinhart, and Vegh (2003) investigate five case studies of specific contagion episodes that have occurred since 1980 and find that trade linkages are not consistently associated with the spread of contagion. Instead, they find that the existence of leveraged common lenders played a large role in every single modern contagion. Specifically, when a crisis began in the first country, the authors find that highly leveraged institutional investors were forced to sell off assets across all the countries in their portfolio, spreading asset price declines and speculative pressure across a broad array of countries. Not surprisingly, these authors also find that contagion typically follows a boom in capital inflows followed by a rapid capital reversal, consistent with the assertion that hot money plays a role in the spread of contagion. Finally, the authors find that contagion episodes are typically initiated by surprise and unexpected announcements as measured by a sharp spike in bond yields, which could indicate that beliefs and expectations also play a role in the spread of contagion. Obtaining similar results, Kaminsky and Reinhardt (2000) provide econometric evidence that financial linkages play a larger role than trade linkages in the spread of contagion in modern crises. They also find that contagion is nonlinear in that as the number of countries experiencing crises increases, the probability of contagion spreading to new countries increases sharply.

One final empirical study that is relevant to the study of contagion is Rötheli (2000). The author investigates the lending behavior of three major Swiss Banks between 1987 and 1996 and finds evidence that changes in the lending behavior of one bank influenced the lending behavior of its competitors. This not only supports the existence of investor herding but also the role of financial linkages in spreading panic and capital flight.

Taken together, these empirical results support the existence of each of the causes of currency crises and contagion discussed earlier, both fundamentals-based and belief-based.

CASE STUDY: The Russian/LTCM Contagion Episode

A good example of how common lenders and financial linkages can spread contagion is the Russian currency crisis of 1998. In August of that year, Russia suffered a speculative attack and a fall in the ruble of 262 percent by January of 1999. In September of 1998, Long Term Capital Management (LTCM), a large and well-known hedge fund, surprisingly announced that they had gone bankrupt after speculating heavily in Russian bonds. (The buildup to the collapse of LTCM is discussed in more detail in Chapter 2.) Before this bankruptcy was announced, LTCM was forced to sell off billions of dollars of assets in both Russia and in other emerging markets in which it had holdings.

In the end, the panic selling of LTCM sparked panic selling by other investors, leading to significant falls in asset prices across most emerging countries and putting significant speculative pressure on their currencies. However, the countries that were the most severely affected were Hong Kong, Brazil, Mexico, and several of the former Soviet republics. Excluding the former Soviet Republics, there was almost no direct trade amongst these hardest-hit countries. Instead, what Hong Kong, Brazil, and Mexico had in common were some of the largest and most liquid financial markets among emerging economies and also the fact that these were the other countries that LTCM had invested most heavily in. In addition, the initial speculative episode in Russia came in the midst of the East Asian crisis. Many investors that had stakes in Russia also had stakes in East Asia, and the crisis there likely played a role in the size and the speed of the capital flight out of Russia. Thus, it appears that not only did financial linkages play a crucial role in this contagion episode, but that financial linkages are likely to play even larger roles in the spread of contagion in the future as financial markets develop and capital flows continue to expand across the globe, tying countries together like never before.

The Causes and Costs of Twin Crises

Between the end of World War II and the early 1980s, twin crises, or concurrent banking and currency crises, were extremely rare. However, over the last 20 years twin crises have become increasingly frequent. There are two reasons for the increased incidence of twin crises. The first reason is that, as discussed in Chapter 8, banking crises have become more frequent after the wave of financial deregulation that swept across the globe during the 1980s and 1990s. This financial liberalization has increased moral hazard, increased likelihood of asset bubbles and crashes, weakened financial fundamentals, and increased financial volatility. As a result, many emerging economies and even some developed countries (such as the Scandinavian countries and Japan) have suffered full-fledged banking crises, while other countries have suffered from banking problems severe enough to significantly disrupt financial intermediation (as in the U.S. during the Savings and Loan crisis).

The second reason that twin crises have become more frequent is that in this age of deregulated financial systems and massive capital flows across countries, currency crises are more costly to banking systems than ever before. As a result, currency crises are now more likely to lead to a banking crisis or to make an existing banking crisis worse. The biggest factor behind this is the increase in hot money, or foreign investment that is short term and denominated in foreign currencies. Many economies have accumulated large amounts of this hot money because of their confidence in their own economic stability, particularly in their ability to maintain and defend their fixed exchange rate. However, too often this confidence has been unfounded and countries have found themselves unable to fight-off a speculative attack. Eichengreen (2003c) reviews empirical research on the effects of financial liberalization, which has consistently found that currency crises are highly correlated with recent reductions in barriers to cross-country capital flows.

As previously discussed, when banks or other institutional lenders hold domestic-denominated assets and foreign-denominated debt, a large devaluation can significantly reduce net worth, increasing the financial costs of currency crises. For example, a 50-percent devaluation (which is not uncommon during a currency crisis) reduces the real value of domestic assets by half while doubling the value of foreign-denominated debt in terms of the domestic currency. The result is that insolvency often becomes endemic throughout a financial system following a currency crisis, leading to a collapse in credit intermediation. This financial collapse is only made worse if much of the debt that these lenders hold is short term because it increases the speed at which investors can withdraw funds from ailing banks, increasing the size of the currency crisis as well as the size of the devaluation. Even a relatively sound banking system with only modest amounts of hot money can quickly find itself on the verge of complete collapse after a currency crisis.

Kaminsky and Reinhart (1999) investigate specific twin crises episodes and find that the reason that twin crises have become more frequent in the 1990s and 2000s is because of the increasing deregulation of financial markets—in 18 of the 26 twin crisis episodes they examined, financial liberalization had taken place within the previous 5 years. The authors also find that twin crisis episodes follow a regular pattern. Financial liberalization precipitates dramatic increases in foreign investment, particularly hot money that fuels a domestic lending boom, asset bubbles in housing and stock markets, and large current account deficits. Eventually these asset bubbles burst, weakening financial fundamentals and often creating a banking crisis. As foreign investors observe this, they begin to flee the country, selling their domestic assets and domestic currency holdings as they go. This capital flight may start slowly, but picks up speed as speculators begin to participate. Speculative attacks lead to a currency crisis and a large devaluation that exacerbates the panic selling of assets and further weakens the financial fundamentals of banks. This magnifies the size of the banking crisis, which in turn magnifies the size of the currency crisis in a vicious cycle that leads to unusually large devaluations (during the East Asian crisis, Indonesia was forced to devalue by 75 percent), asset market crashes, severe banking crises, and unusually costly economic contractions. On the basis of these results, Kaminsky and Reinhart argue that twin crises are primarily caused by poor macroeconomic and financial fundamentals and are not self-fulfilling or belief-based. They find that those countries with the worst fundamentals were more likely to suffer from a twin crisis than a single crisis alone and also suffer the largest output losses during their twin crises episodes.

To make matters worse, not only do currency crises exacerbate banking crises, and vice versa, but policy makers find themselves in a Catch-22 in that they cannot act to make one crisis better without making the other crisis worse. The conventional prescription to end a currency crisis is to devalue in conjunction with tightening monetary and fiscal policy. The rationale behind these actions is to both send a signal to foreign investors that macroeconomic policy will be more responsible in the future, and also to increase domestic interest rates, making the country a more attractive place for investment. Unfortunately, these policies to moderate the currency crisis make the banking crisis worse. Devaluation reduces the net worth of banks, while tighter monetary and fiscal policies reduce aggregate output which increases default rates, doing further harm to banks. In addition, higher interest rates increase default risk by encouraging adverse selection, moral hazard, as well as increasing debt servicing payments. Of course, the opposite policy—to loosen monetary and fiscal policy in an attempt to reduce domestic interest rates, increase output, and stabilize financial fundamentals—only leads to more capital flight and further exacerbates the currency crisis.

A few studies have attempted to estimate exactly how costly twin crises are. Barro (2001) estimates the 5-year average cost of twin crises across a broad range of crises and finds that twin crises reduce growth by roughly 2.2 percent, 1.6 percent of which is attributable to the currency crisis and 0.6 percent of which is attributable to the banking crisis. However, Barro does not attempt to measure the interaction between the two crises and whether the existence of a currency crisis makes the costs of banking crises larger, and vice versa. Bordo et al. (2001) attempt to correct for this omission by trying to identify the interaction costs of twin crises. They find that the cumulative output cost of a twin crisis is 16 percent of GDP over and above the cost of an average recession—making twin crises very costly. Of this amount, 4.4 percent of the lost GDP is caused by the banking crisis and 8.7 percent is caused by the currency crisis, leaving the incremental lost GDP that is attributable to the interaction between the crises at approximately 3 percent of GDP. Using different econometric techniques and examining only emerging market economies, Hutchinson and Noy (2005) find that twin crises lead to additional reductions in output of between 13 and 18 percent of GDP, which is roughly equivalent to that found by Bordo et al. However, they fail to find any evidence that twin crises have costs that are greater than currency and banking crises separately. Hutchinson and Neuberger also differ from Bordo et al. in that they find that banking crises are more costly than currency crises; their results indicate that currency crises reduce GDP by between 5 and 8 percent over a 2–4-year period, while banking crises reduce GDP by between 8 and 10 percent of GDP. Thus, exactly whether currency crises or banking crises are the most costly and whether there are costly interactions between the two still remains a matter of some empirical uncertainty.

CASE STUDY: The East Asian Crisis

Between 1997 and 1999, international twin crises swept through East Asia unmatched in both size and scope save for the Great Depression. The East Asian crisis hit four of the largest economies in the region particularly hard: South Korea, Thailand, Indonesia, and Malaysia. These countries, and the rest of the region, had experienced unparalleled growth over the previous 35 years. Table 9.1 presents real output growth rates for East Asian economies between 1991 and 2000. During the 1970s and 1980s, growth rates across all of these countries commonly exceeded 10 percent, and between 1991 and 1996, with the exception of the Philippines, each of these countries averaged growth greater than 5 percent a year. While growth noticeably slowed in late 1996, growth still seemed to be fundamentally sound. In fact, in early 1997 the IMF published the following evaluation in its World Outlook: "(East Asia's) sound fundamentals bode well for sustained growth…(the IMF's endorsement) was rooted in the region's strong macroeconomic fundamentals; in (East Asia's) tradition of, and commitment to, efficient allocation of investment; and in the widespread belief that the external environment will continue to be supportive."

Just 8 months later, these East Asian economies were experiencing both banking and currency crises during which real wages fell by a third, unemployment tripled, and aggregate income fell by more than 10 percent. Hardest hit in these countries were the most vulnerable: the poor, the young, and women. One-fourth of the residents of the region, more than 22 million individuals, fell into poverty during the crisis.

How could a crisis of this size be such a surprise? This crisis was unanticipated by observers primarily because the East Asian crisis was not the result of bad monetary and fiscal policy, at least not in the form of higher inflation and large budget deficits. None of the East Asian countries was running large budget deficits (some were even running surpluses) and inflation throughout the region was low, in direct contrast with other currency crisis episodes.

The Currency and Banking Crises in East Asia

On closer inspection, many of the fundamentals of the economies in the region pointed to the possibility of both banking crises and currency crises occurring at some point. Regarding currency crises, most countries in East Asia were maintaining pegged (or floating within a small range) exchange rates with the U.S. dollar

Table 9.1 Percentage of GDP Growth in East Asia

	Thailand	Indonesia	Malaysia	Korea	Philippines	Singapore	Hong Kong	Taiwan	China
1991	8.2	7.0	8.5	9.1	−0.6	7.3	5.0	7.6	9.2
1992	8.1	6.5	7.8	5.1	0.3	6.3	6.2	6.8	14.2
1993	8.4	6.5	8.4	5.8	2.1	10.4	6.2	6.3	12.1
1994	8.9	15.9	9.2	8.6	4.4	10.1	5.5	6.5	12.7
1995	8.8	8.2	9.5	8.9	4.8	8.8	3.9	6.0	10.6
1996	5.5	8.0	8.6	7.1	5.8	7.3	5.0	5.7	9.5
1997	−0.4	4.6	7.8	5.4	9.6	8.4	5.0	6.8	8.8
1998	−10.4	−13.2	−7.5	−6.7	−0.5	0.4	−5.1	4.7	7.8
1999	4.2	0.2	5.4	10.7	3.2	5.4	2.9	5.5	7.1
2000	4.75	4.92	8.86	0.49	5.97	9.41	10.2	n.a.	8
2001	2.17	3.45	0.32	3.84	2.96	−2.37	0.46	n.a.	7.5
2002	5.33	3.69	4.15	6.97	4.43	3.29	1.89	n.a.	8.3
2003	6.87	4.1	5.31	3.07	4.52	1.09	3.22	n.a.	9.29

Source: International Financial Statistics of the IMF. Data for 1998 and 1999 are from the IMF's December 1997 World Economic Outlook.

Table 9.2   Current Account Balance as a Percentage of GDP

	1991	1992	1993	1994	1995	1996	1997
Thailand	−8.01	−6.23	−5.68	−6.38	−8.35	−8.51	−2.35
Indonesia	−4.40	−2.46	−0.82	−1.54	−4.27	−3.30	−3.62
Malaysia	−14.01	−3.39	−10.11	−6.60	−8.85	−3.73	−3.50
Korea	−3.16	−1.70	−0.16	−1.45	−1.91	−4.82	−1.90
Philippines	−2.46	−3.17	−6.69	−3.74	−5.06	−4.67	−6.07
Singapore	12.36	12.38	8.48	18.12	17.93	16.26	13.90
Hong Kong	6.58	5.26	8.14	1.98	−2.97	−2.43	−3.75
Taiwan	6.97	4.03	3.52	3.12	3.05	4.67	3.23
China	3.07	1.09	−2.19	1.16	0.03	0.52	3.61

Source: International Financial Statistics of the IMF.

before the crisis. Exchange rates were fixed to the dollar primarily in an effort to attract foreign investment. During the mid-1990s, however, the dollar appreciated significantly against the major currency in the region, the Japanese yen. In April of 1995, the dollar was trading at 100 yen, but rose to 150 yen per dollar by early 1997. This appreciation was due in large part to the strong U.S. economy and the weak Japanese economy (although it is difficult to justify the size of this appreciation based on fundamentals alone).

This large appreciation helped fuel already large current account deficits throughout East Asia (the weak demand for imports by Japan and Europe as well as a glut in the electronics market also contributed). Data on current accounts in the region can be seen in Table 9.2. Those countries that had the largest current account deficits—Thailand, Malaysia, and the Philippines—were also the countries that pegged most rigidly to the dollar. A common rule of thumb is that any country experiencing a current account deficit that is larger than 5 percent of GDP is in danger of suffering capital flight. By this measure, Korea, Indonesia, Malaysia, the Philippines, and Thailand were all in danger of suffering a currency crisis during 1995 and 1996. These large deficits were only sustainable as long as these countries continued to grow at high rates.

Another factor playing a role in the currency crises was the *carry trade*, a term which refers to the investment strategy of borrowing funds in low interest rate countries, then turning around and lending these funds in high interest rate countries. Throughout the 1990s, low interest rates in Japan and higher interest rates throughout the rest of Asia facilitated large capital inflows and current account deficits in many Asian countries outside of Japan. However, this carry trade is potentially risky for investors. Any change in perceived risk, exchange rates, or interest rates between countries can significantly alter returns to engaging in the carry trade and also swiftly reverse capital flows.

Thus, even though these countries had sound macroeconomic fundamentals in many respects, a naïve adherence throughout the region to fixed exchange rates and massive capital flows made them vulnerable to a currency crisis, particularly if economic growth slowed. However, no crisis appeared to be imminent to most observers until right before the first speculative attack, which occurred against Thailand in July of 1997.

The banking crises in the region were even more clearly driven by weak fundamentals. Asian economies rely more heavily on bank lending than elsewhere. For example, in Korea, 50 percent of corporate finance is done through banks, but banks also guaranteed 87 percent of corporate bonds as well. Only 7 percent of corporate financing in Korea is in equity. (Compare this to the U.S., where only one-third of corporate finance comes from banks.)

Beginning in the mid-1980s, countries throughout the region began to rapidly deregulate their financial systems, particularly banks. In response, domestic lending by banks grew by between 17 and 30 percent a year between 1991 and 1996, which fed real estate and stock market bubbles in many of these countries. These lending booms were fueled by a foreign borrowing boom; across East Asia, foreign investment grew at between 5 and 14 percent of GDP a year before the crisis (Corsetti, Pesenti, and Roubini, 1998). This foreign investment was largely dollar denominated. Table 9.3 presents the ratio of foreign liabilities to foreign assets in domestic banks. These remarkably high ratios mean that these countries were holding large amounts of domestic assets and foreign debt, exposing themselves to huge levels of exchange rate risk if devaluation occurred. To make things worse, much of this dollar-denominated debt was short term, or hot money. For example, in Korea 56 percent of their debt was foreign denominated, and 37 percent of this was short term. In total, roughly $50 billion of hot money was poised to leave Korea in the event of a speculative attack (Krueger, 2002).

Table 9.3   Ratio of Foreign Liabilities to Foreign Assets

	1993	1994	1995	1996	1997
Thailand	6.93	7.73	7.81	11.03	8.12
Indonesia	2.95	4.01	4.26	4.24	5.43
Malaysia	0.83	1.40	1.44	1.48	2.22
Korea	2.98	2.97	3.31	3.75	2.51
Philippines	1.14	0.97	1.10	1.72	1.71
Singapore	1.51	1.62	1.66	1.62	1.38
Hong Kong	1.42	1.43	1.56	1.65	1.59
Taiwan	n.a.	n.a.	0.61	0.61	0.62
China	0.99	0.94	1.17	1.20	1.36

Source: Bank of International Settlements (BIS) as reported by Corsetti, Pesenti, and Roubini (1998).

If all of this foreign investment had been put to productive uses, these banking systems would have been able to withstand a currency crisis. Unfortunately, this was not the case because of the poor quality and riskiness of the investment projects that the lending boom financed. The reason behind this financial fragility was moral hazard, which existed in three areas of Asian banking well before the crisis hit.

First, moral hazard was unchecked by regulation after the financial liberalization of the 1980s. Many bank managers found themselves facing few restrictions on the kind of loans they could make or the types of debt they could acquire. Because of low capital adequacy requirements, undercapitalized banks had little to lose by gambling on riskier and riskier assets, such as on stock and real estate markets experiencing bubbles.

Moral hazard also was encouraged by national and international bailouts. The widespread belief in many of these countries was that their government would bail banks out in the event of an economic downturn, which was not an unreasonable assumption given the extent of government intervention and subsidation in their banking systems. Even where explicit deposit insurance did not exist, implicit insurance did exist, as evidenced by the fact that not a single bank had ever failed in Korea, Thailand, Taiwan, and Malaysia before the crisis. In the event that things got exceptionally bad, these banks could also reasonably expect that they would be bailed-out indirectly by the IMF when their governments received a bailout.

Finally, the third source of moral hazard was the behavior of corporate borrowers. Corporations are highly subsidized and market power is much more concentrated in East Asian economies than in many other developed economies. Many outsiders have referred to the domination of most sectors of East Asian economies by a few large conglomerates as "crony capitalism." The result has been little competition in many markets and low returns on capital for these conglomerates. The best example of this is South Korea, a country with an exceptionally high degree of industrial concentration, primarily within 30 large conglomerates referred to as *Chaebols*. Before the crisis, as many as 7 of the 30 largest Chaebols were insolvent and the return on invested capital was less than the cost of capital in 20 of these Chaebols (Krueger, 2000). By 1998, 31 percent of Korean, 45 percent of Indonesian, and 18 percent of Malaysian and Filipino corporations were insolvent, up from their 1994 levels of 16 percent in Korea and 8 percent in Indonesia, Malaysia, and the Philippines (Pomerleano, 1998).

The end result of all of this moral hazard is that banks were holding large amounts of bad loans and had poor financial fundamentals even before the crisis began. Table 9.4 presents the amount of nonperforming loans as a percentage of total lending. With the exception of China, the countries with the highest percentage of nonperforming loans before the crisis in 1996 suffered the largest output losses. (To put these numbers in perspective, nonperforming loans in the U.S. are less than 1 percent of total loans.)

Table 9.4 Nonperforming Loans as a Percentage of Total Lending

	End of 1996 (%)	End of 1997 (%)
Thailand	13	36
Indonesia	13	15
Malaysia	10	15
Korea	8	30
Philippines	14	7
Singapore	4	4
Hong Kong	3	1
Taiwan	4	n.a.
China	14	n.a.

Sources: Column 1, Bank of International Settlements Annual Report, as reported by Corsetti, Pesenti, and Roubini (1998). Column 2, Peregrine (1997).

The interaction between the currency crises and the banking crises

How did these currency crises and banking crises interact to create a massive economic contraction throughout East Asia? Many countries, particularly Korea and Thailand, were on the verge of a banking crisis before the currency crisis began. Fears about Thailand's financial system and unsustainable asset bubbles sparked a speculative attack on the baht that began in July of 1997 and quickly spread to Indonesia and other smaller economies in the region. The crisis began in earnest in October, when Hong Kong and then Korea, the second largest economy in the region next to Japan (and the eleventh largest in the world), began to suffer a speculative attack. By December, most of these countries were in recession and their financial systems were quickly disintegrating.

The financial collapse took place quickly throughout the region because of the feedback between the currency crises and banking crises. As discussed earlier, this feedback is particularly strong when countries hold lots of hot money. As soon as the devaluations began, already weak Asian banks and corporations saw the real value of their domestic-denominated assets fall and their foreign-denominated assets rise. For example, in Indonesia the exchange rate depreciated by 75 percent, meaning that foreign-denominated debt quadrupled in value relative to domestic-denominated assets. As a result, many banks and corporations quickly became insolvent; in Thailand, 56 of the 58 largest banks in the country had closed within 3 months after the crisis started.

The effects of devaluation during the East Asian crisis are in many ways akin to the effects of deflation during the Great Depression. As explained in the Debt-Deflation theory, deflation increases the real value of debt relative to assets when nominal debt contracts are fixed. In East Asia, devaluation increased the real value of debt because much of it was foreign denominated. Thus, these crises have more in common than just their size.

All of the hot money attracted by East Asian economies exposed their financial systems to the possibility of massive capital flight. Capital outflows averaged 11 percent of GDP across Indonesia, Malaysia, Korea, the Philippines, and Thailand (before the crisis, inflows had been greater than 10 percent of GDP, meaning that the total reversal was exceptionally large). This further weakened the shaky fundamentals of East Asian banks. As banks found themselves too crippled to operate, credit disappeared, investment and consumption collapsed, output contracted, and the initial speculative attack that started this whole process was validated in the eyes of many foreign investors.

Korea, Thailand, Indonesia, and Malaysia were the countries that were the most severely hit by the crisis. Other countries in the region, such as Hong Kong, Singapore, Taiwan, and even the Philippines suffered recessions, but not as large as the four primary crisis countries. This variation can be explained by one observation: the countries with the most fragile banking systems were those that were the most severely affected by the currency crisis and suffered the largest contractions. Looking back at Table 9.4, the four crisis countries had the highest precrisis levels of nonperforming loans. On the other hand, the Philippines stand as a good example of the importance of financial stability. By almost every other macroeconomic measure, the Philippines had the worse fundamentals in the region. However, the Philippines actually began to reform their banking system before the crisis began and had been lowering their levels of nonperforming loans since the mid-1980s; as a result, they avoided the worse of the crisis. (The one exception to this relationship between banking stability and the size of the crisis is China, which did not have a convertible currency and has strict controls on capital inflows. These factors limited the amounts and kinds of foreign investment that entered and could leave the country, sheltering it from the crisis.)

One final factor that played a role in the East Asian crisis was the involvement of the IMF. Unlike previous currency crisis episodes in which the granting of a bailout by the IMF signaled the end of the crisis, the IMF's bailouts throughout the fall of 1997 worsened the crises in each of these countries as well as sparked the spread of the crisis across the region. Chapter 10 looks at the IMF's actions during this crisis in more detail and attempts to explain this anomaly.

The role of speculation and contagion in the crisis

The East Asian crisis is also a case study of contagion. How did a crisis in a single country, Thailand, spread throughout an entire region within a matter of months and across the globe within a matter of 18 months? The initial blame of many observers fell on large institutional investors, who were accused of intentionally precipitating a crisis in order to profit from it. After his country was forced to devalue in the face of a speculative attack, Malaysian Prime Minister Mahathir Mohamad immediately blamed the crisis on foreign financiers such as George Soros (the fact that he also blamed the crisis on Jewish speculators and claimed that IMF policies were part of a Western conspiracy to recolonize Asia did not lend his claims any credibility). Large international hedge funds, like the Quantum Fund managed by Soros, became easily identifiable symbols of what many claim is wrong with the financial liberalization and globalization that has taken place within world financial markets since the 1980s.

However, capital flight does not necessarily mean that foreign investors caused the crisis. Since the mid-1980s, Argentina, Venezuela, South Africa, and Sri Lanka were all closed to short-term foreign investment at the time they suffered economic crises. Foreign investors who left East Asia were in large part properly responding to poor fundamentals in these economies, particularly in regard to overvalued exchange rates and unstable banking systems. In support of this conclusion, Froot, O'Connell, and Seasholes (2001) present empirical evidence that foreign investors did not begin to pull out significant amounts of capital before the crisis occurred (in other words, trying to "manufacture" a crisis), only during and after the crisis.

Besides the weak banking fundamentals and overvalued exchange rates in the region, fundamentals also played a role in the spread of contagion through trade linkages and financial linkages. Not only did these East Asian economies trade with each other, but more importantly, they traded heavily with Japan, which was going through its own protracted recession and banking crisis throughout the 1990s. This eliminated a major export destination for many of these countries and worsened their current account deficits. In addition, Japan was the major source of foreign investment for many of these countries, both directly through lending by its banks and indirectly through the carry trade, where many investors borrowed in Japan and lent in the rest of Asia. Kaminsky and Reinhardt (2000) argue that both credit-constrained institutional investors in Japan and the collapse of the carry trade played a large role in fueling capital flight and contagion throughout the East Asian region.

However, it is difficult to completely rule out the importance of beliefs in the spread of contagion during the East Asian crisis. Eichengreen, Rose, and Wyplosz (2003b) and Hutchinson and Neuberger (2005) present empirical evidence that fundamentals alone are insufficient to explain the full extent and particularly the timing of the crisis. Both Williamson (2004) and Eichengreen (2003b) argue that while the crisis in Thailand was clearly based on fundamentals, belief-based contagion was the primary factor in the spread of the crisis after that. The facts that fundamentals across the region differed significantly and that the crisis spread so widely (eventually even to Russia and Latin America) suggests that belief-based panic played some role in the East Asian crisis.

However, the channel by which beliefs spread contagion remains unclear. In support of the herding hypothesis, Froot, O'Connell, and Seasholes (2001) find that the correlation drawn between what different foreign investors do is now higher than ever before because of the better dissemination of information. This creates a herding mentality among fund managers that increases the chances of panic and capital flight. Others, such as Goldstein (1998), favor the wake-up-call hypothesis, arguing that the similarity of macroeconomic policies across the region raised questions in investors' minds about the soundness of the "Asian Miracle," causing them to treat what is true about one country as true about the entire region. Still others argue that these panics were simply self-fulfilling and could occur at any time and at any place once investors become worried about other investors fleeing.

Regardless of the source of the contagion in East Asia, it is clear that the loss of foreign investors' confidence has had long-lasting effects on growth in the region. The Asian Development Bank reports that growth in Indonesia, Malaysia, the Philippines, South Korea, and Thailand was 2.5 percent lower in the postcrisis period (2000–2006) than it was in the precrisis period (1990–1996). The Asian Development Bank finds that most of this decline can be explained by lower investment rates across these countries that have not returned to their precrisis levels. This is despite the fact that these countries have made an attempt to reform their institutions to create a more attractive environment for foreign investors. This suggests that the consequences and costs of contagions can be much larger than previously appreciated.

Conclusions

International financial crises have become more common, first after World War II with the proliferation of currency crises under the Bretton Woods system in response to unsustainable macroeconomic policies, and more recently as banking crises have become more frequent after the financial liberalization of the 1980s. One disastrous result of this has been more twin crises, in which weak banks quicken the pace of capital flight and the size of currency crises, while more capital flight and large devaluations further weaken fragile banking systems in a vicious cycle. In the case of the East Asian crisis, the result was an international economic contraction unmatched by any economic crisis except the Great Depression.

Fundamentals definitely play an important role in creating the conditions under which international financial crises occur. Macroeconomic imbalances such as high inflation, budget deficits, and current account deficits are clearly associated with currency crises and capital flight. Trade linkages have been important in the spread of contagion in the past. In recent crises, financial linkages between countries are increasingly creating contagion by spreading capital flight through things such as the carry trade. Most importantly, indiscriminate financial deregulation, moral hazard lending, and currency mismatches between domestic-denominated assets and foreign-denominated debt lead to fragile banking systems that cannot withstand even a modest shock to the financial system.

But poor fundamentals alone are only necessary for a crisis, they are not sufficient to guarantee a crisis. Crises are too idiosyncratic to be explained by fundamentals alone; countries with poor macroeconomic and financial fundamentals do not necessarily experience a crisis, and often the timing and the events that trigger a crisis or the spread of contagion are not easily identifiable. Beliefs and expectations also appear to be important, particularly in explaining the spread of capital flight and contagion once a single crisis has taken place, either through the wake-up-call effect, through the herding behavior of investors, or because investors' returns are so intertwined that crises are self-fulfilling.

The primary lesson of recent international financial crises is that establishing and maintaining strong and stable banking systems is of utmost importance. Here, an interesting comparison can be made between the East Asian crisis and the financial impact of the 9/11 attacks in the U.S. While only a minimal amount of capital flight took place after 9/11, over a trillion dollars worth of wealth in the U.S. disappeared as financial markets crashed following the attack. The economy slowed, investors remained skittish, and banks reduced the supply of credit; however, the banking and financial system remained overall sound. The reliance on equity and not just bank borrowing, the preponderance of long-term debt and not just short-term debt, the existence of well-diversified portfolios, a proactive lender of last resort, and regulations restricting moral hazard and risky lending and borrowing behaviors each played an important role in creating the remarkably resilient financial system that the U.S. and many other developed countries enjoy today. New Institutional theories of finance help us understand these differences by explaining exactly how differences in microlevel fundamentals lead to differences in macroeconomic performance.

With this in mind, the East Asian financial crisis begins to look very much like the Great Depression. During the Great Depression in the U.S., a fragile banking system with large amounts of fixed nominal debt could not withstand the high bankruptcy rates and reductions in net worth that were caused by deflation. In East Asia, it was fragile banking systems with large amounts of foreign-denominated debt that could not withstand the high bankruptcy rates and reductions in net worth that were the result of devaluation.

Given this analogy between the Great Depression and the East Asian crisis, why did not more economic observers foresee the East Asian crisis coming? Clearly, the role of beliefs in shaping the timing and the size of the crisis cannot be discounted. But at a deeper level, it is important to remember that the modern era of globalization really began with the fall of the Berlin Wall in 1989, less than 10 years before the East Asian crisis. Many of the repercussions of globalization had not been, and still are not, fully understood. This is particularly true in regard to policies, both domestic and international, that can be adopted to steady international capital flows and prevent or minimize future international financial crises. Such policies are the focus of Chapter 10.

CHAPTER 10

International Financial Crises: Policies and Prevention

Introduction

Over the last 20 years, a sustained movement has taken place across developed, emerging, and less developed economies to remove barriers to the movement of financial assets across countries. This wave of financial liberalization has led to more highly developed international and domestic financial markets that have dramatically increased the levels of foreign investment flowing into all regions of the world, both rich and poor. Many "growth miracle" countries, such as in East Asia, were able to maintain historic rates of growth over more than 40 years; such growth rates would have previously been impossible but now are possible because of the astonishing increase in foreign capital that is now available to be used to fund domestic investment.

What we have learned during our discussions of banking and currency crises, however, is that while financial liberalization improves the flow of funds to regions of the world that need them the most, it also, in the words of former Chairman of the Federal Reserve Alan Greenspan, improves "the transmission of financial disturbances far more effectively than ever before" (Greenspan 1998). In other words, while it is easier for capital to flow in, it is also easier for capital to flow out. This is exactly what happened during the East Asian crisis, with devastating results.

The questions, then, are these: Is financial liberalization worth it? And are there ways to increase the stability of capital flows and financial systems without abandoning the efficiency and growth-enhancing aspects of financial deregulation and development? This chapter discusses possible reforms of the current international financial system and potential policies that could be adopted to prevent and/or moderate future international financial crises. It begins by reviewing empirical studies of the costs and the benefits of financial liberalization. Next, the emerging consensus regarding the appropriate role that governments should play in regulating domestic financial systems is examined, including a look at the debate over whether capital controls are an effective way to reduce the chances of capital flight. Also, the need for international financial regulations, and the need for international regulators, is investigated.

Another important objective of this chapter is to evaluate the International Monetary Fund (IMF) and its role in managing economic crises. Is the IMF to be blamed (as many critics charge) for recent economic contractions like those in Argentina or East Asia, through its own stupidity, through its role as a proponent for globalization and the interests of the rich, or through its role in funding moral hazard? This chapter investigates the IMF's actions during recent crises, its track record in resolving economic crises, and potential reforms of both its polices and its structure that could enhance its effectiveness in dealing with future international financial crises.

The Benefits and Costs of Financial Liberalization

Beginning in the mid-1980s, many countries throughout the world began a process of rapid financial liberalization and deregulation. In one survey, Williamson and Mahar (1998) report that 24 of 34 poor and rich countries examined in 1973 were classified as having repressed international capital flows while only two had open capital markets. By 1996, zero countries were classified as having repressed financial flows while 18 were classified as having open financial markets. This financial liberalization includes (1) eliminating controls on lending and asset holdings, (2) removing limits on deposit expansion and debt holdings, (3) reducing restrictions on bank capital requirements, (4) abolishing interest rates controls, (5) allowing for the private ownership of banks, (6) permitting foreign banks to operate domestically, (7) eliminating multiple exchange rates, and (8) allowing the free movement of funds across international borders.

As we have discussed over the last two chapters, there is both theoretical and empirical support for the argument that financial liberalization, particularly rapid and indiscriminate deregulation, has led to increases in financial instability and output volatility. Studies show that over the last 20 years, financial liberalization has precipitated asset and lending bubbles, banking crises, currency crises, and twin crises. The primary cause of this higher volatility is injudicious deregulation that encourages moral hazard and riskier behavior by borrowers and lenders in financial systems.

However, there are also sound theoretical reasons to believe that financial liberalization increases financial efficiency and growth, particularly in the long run. As discussed in Chapter 1, financial development has a number of growth enhancing effects for an economy. Financial liberalization is likely to lead to financial deepening, or increases in the size and scope of financial intermediation. Financial development increases the quality and quantity of information, which minimizes market failure and increases financial efficiency. Financial development fosters higher levels of savings and investment that can be used to fund increases in capital, education, and technology, which in turn increases aggregate supply. Financial development also reduces the costs of production by reducing the uncertainty associated with borrowing and investment, which increases aggregate supply by encouraging both competition and specialization. All of these factors, working in isolation and together, increase financial efficiency and economic growth.

In addition to these direct benefits, Eswar Prasad (2006) has reviewed the impact of our current era of globalization. He finds that emerging economies not only directly benefit from globalization in the ways described above, but also indirectly benefits in three ways. First, financial liberalization creates foreign competition for domestic lenders, which increases their efficiency. Second, this competition also forces domestic lenders and their governments to adopt higher regulatory standards in terms of loan safety rules, accounting standards, and corruption prevention. Finally, foreign capital increases the threat of capital flight and the cost of irresponsible macropolicy, forcing governments to follow better macroeconomic policy in terms of lower deficits and lower inflation.

Empirical evidence supports the argument that financial liberalization increases efficiency and growth, but with some significant caveats. Galindo, Micco, and Ordoñez (2002) find that financial liberalization increases growth by 1.3 percent on average, with larger growth effects in sectors that are more reliant on external finance. The growth effects of liberalization are larger when good institutions are in place, particularly laws that protect the property rights of lenders (such as bankruptcy laws and contract enforcement mechanisms). Their results indicate that liberalization increases growth through increasing both the size and the overall efficiency of financial systems. In another study, Tornell, Westermann, and Martinez (2003) find that in countries with highly regulated financial markets, financial liberalization increased growth by a remarkable 2.4 percent a year on average. Figure 10.1 presents growth rates before and after financial liberalization episodes between 1980 and 1999. Clearly, liberalization has had a dramatic positive impact on most of these countries' growth rates in the short run, in many cases changing large negative growth rates into significantly positive growth rates. The authors find that most of this growth is attributable to large increases in the supply of credit and investment. Unsurprisingly, however, the authors also find that financial liberalization significantly increases credit risk and the probability of experiencing a recession or depression, which raises questions about just how sustainable these dramatic turnarounds are.

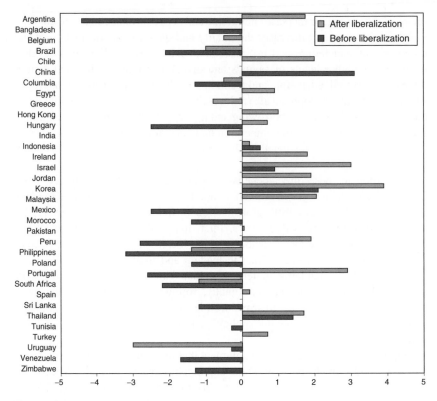

Figure 10.1
Growth Before and After Financial Liberalization.
Source: Tornell, Westermann, and Martinez, 2003.

Raising another cautionary note, Eichengreen (2003c) finds that opening an economy to foreign investment increases growth, but only when the economy is already generally efficient and open to international trade. This indicates that liberalizing foreign investment is only beneficial when it takes place within stable economies that have liberalized other aspects of their economy first. Similarly, Edwards (2001) finds that financial liberalization increases growth in rich countries but reduces growth in poorer countries. Edwards attributes this to the weaker institutions, regulations, and financial fundamentals within less-developed countries that increase the probability that liberalization weakens financial fundamentals, increases financial volatility, and leads to economic crises.

Thus, as an empirical issue, the benefits of financial liberalization are not clearcut, but instead are dependent upon the circumstances within each country. There is good reason to believe that financial liberalization does significantly increase growth, but only in economies that have already established sound fundamentals, solid institutions, and efficient markets.

Guidelines for Domestic Financial Regulation

The last two decades have taught us that when it comes to financial deregulation, it is possible to have too much of a good thing too quickly. Financial deregulation has often taken place indiscriminately without proper consideration of the risks associated with the unfettered actions of borrowers and lenders. In many countries, deregulation has meant no regulation. In these countries, moral hazard ran rampant throughout financial systems, creating a fragile house of cards that tumbled after the slightest economic tremor.

Financial markets are not perfectly competitive, primarily because of the problems associated with imperfect and asymmetric information. Market failure provides a rationale for governments to regulate the microeconomic behavior of lenders in order to reduce the riskiness and fragility of financial systems, particularly banks. Unfortunately, while even the most fervent free-trade economists recognize the importance of government regulation in ensuring well-functioning financial systems, too often governments across the world have closed their eyes to the risks of financial liberalization—often in the face of pressure from business interests exerted through developed governments and the IMF—with devastating consequences.

As a result, all economies, but particularly less developed and emerging economies, need to rethink their approaches to financial regulation and liberalization. This does not mean constructing impregnable barriers to foreign investment—that would be throwing the baby out with the bath water. Instead, it means being smarter about the controls and incentives that are put into place, which can encourage borrowers and lenders to better balance risk versus return when engaging in financial transactions. Of course, there is not complete agreement as to how best to do this. However, a consensus is gradually emerging among economists, which appears to be based on new finance theory, empirical studies, and the history of recent financial crises. This consensus focuses on five broad guidelines that governments should follow when constructing their regulatory policies in the future.

Governments should more closely regulate the financial fundamentals of banks in order to reduce default risk
This means that government regulators should more directly monitor the assets, liabilities, and capital holdings of banks. In particular, this requires restricting the connected lending that banks can make to any particular borrower as well as enforcing the Basel agreement and the capital requirements it places on banks. Such tighter restrictions are aimed at reducing the levels of moral hazard in

banking systems, helping to ensure that only projects with merit receive funding. Maybe even more importantly, governments should focus on limiting the levels of foreign-denominated debt that banks can hold in order to reduce exchange-rate risk exposure and prevent the massive losses in net worth that accompany devaluations (such as what occurred during the East Asian crisis).

Another important aspect of establishing stronger bank fundamentals is developing ways to encourage (or require) banks to hold more long-term debt. Long-term debt not only is less susceptible to capital flight, but it also helps to transfer risk (and higher returns) from borrowers to lenders. This requirement, however, is very difficult to achieve given the limited development of bond and equity markets throughout much of the world. Providing tax and other incentives to corporations that directly finance their operations through debt and equity markets is one way to foster financial-market growth in the long run. In the short run, one way around this lack of domestic financial markets would be to allow more foreign banks to directly operate within countries. Foreign banks have better access to foreign bond and stock markets. They are also typically subject to more extensive regulation from international authorities as well as regulators in their home country. However, provisions must me made to guarantee that these foreign banks engage in domestic lending and do not just serve as a conduit for channeling domestic savings to hot money destinations around the world.

Finally, governments need to make sure that they regulate the regulators. Barth, Caprio, and Levine (2006) find that stronger bank regulation is actually associated with lower efficiency and a higher likelihood of a financial crisis in countries without strong legal and political institutions. Regulation can also be a means by which bureaucrats can gain leverage to engage in corruption. Good governments need to supervise themselves as well as banks in order to make sure that this does not happen.

Governments should improve the quantity and quality of financial information
One of the reasons that crises such as the East Asian crisis come as such a surprise to many observers is a general lack of *transparency*, meaning the poor quality of the financial information that is provided by governments and financial institutions. This is particularly true regarding activities that have little impact on bank balance sheets but are still associated with a great deal of risk, such as the trading of currencies, futures, and options. Without accurate information, financial institutions and government cannot be held accountable by shareholders, bondholders, creditors, and taxpayers.

Part of the problem in getting good information in many countries is that many financial institutions are insulated by the fact that they are owned by a small number of individuals or by the government. One way to improve financial transparency is to privatize more financial institutions and force them to issue stock and bonds that are publicly held. The more widely that stock and bonds are distributed, the more quality information investors will demand from corporations and their governments. In addition, the reporting and accounting standards in many are minimal and need to be strengthened. The study just cited by Barth, Caprio, and Levine (2006), which found that strict regulation can increase volatility when good legal and political institutions are not first in place, also found that the availability of quality financial information is consistently correlated with bank efficiency across countries.

Governments should abandon fixing exchange rates to a single currency
This point deals more with macroeconomic policy than with financial regulation, in particular. When a country pegs to a single currency, there is always a danger that this currency will become out-of-line with the currencies of its competitors and create trade imbalances that can lead to currency crises. This is exactly what happened in East Asia during the mid-1990s with exchange rates that were pegged to the dollar. Even if it costs a country some foreign investment, governments cannot afford to fix exchange rates and simply hope that financial institutions are not exposing themselves to too much exchange rate risk. Instead, governments should move toward floating exchange rates or fixing exchange rates to a broad bundle of global and regional currencies, forcing markets to incorporate potential exchange-rate risk into their decision making. This is exactly what many emerging countries are, in fact, doing. For example, China abandoned their fixed dollar peg for a policy of targeting the Yuan to a weighted average of currencies from a range of countries.

Governments should limit bailouts and let bad banks fail
By continually bailing-out irresponsible banks, governments have implicitly told managers that there is no downside risk to their actions. The result has often been rampant moral hazard and risky bank portfolios in many economies. Instead of letting insolvent "zombie" banks continue to limp along with the government's financial help, governments should close bad banks as quickly as possible and pay off depositors as necessary. This will often mean incurring large up-front costs, both in terms of the money that must be spent to reimburse depositors and also in terms of the temporary disruptions in credit that accompany bank closings. However, without these tough measures, experience shows us that banking crises will linger and moral hazard will continue to exist, increasing the probability of future economic crises.

Some governments also need to stop bailing-out bad corporations. One way to do this is to establish better bankruptcy laws under which corporations can restructure their debts in a systematic manner while protecting the interests of creditors. However, it is important not to impose a "one-size-fits-all" approach to bankruptcy and financial law reform. Beck and Levine (2005) find that countries with legal systems based on common law, which respects informal institutions and legal arrangements already in place, perform much better than countries with a history of top-down, federally imposed laws.

Governments should take a more slow and measured approach to future financial liberalization

On the basis of an extensive review of recent financial liberalization episodes, Eichengreen, Arteta, and Wypolsz (2003) argue that successful liberalization should follow a staged approach implemented over a period of time, not a "cold-shower" approach in which liberalization takes place all at once. They emphasize four points. First, capital flows should be deregulated after domestic goods markets have been opened to international trade. More international competition increases the efficiency of domestic markets and improves the likelihood that foreign investment will be used productively. Second, stock and bond markets should be deregulated before banks. This will encourage more long-term financing and discourage an over-reliance on short-term debt and hot money. Third, countries should abandon fixed exchange rates before they liberalize their banking systems because pegging encourages banks to ignore exchange-rate risk. Fourth, in order to minimize exchange rate fluctuations that occur under floating exchange rates, governments need to establish fiscal and monetary credibility with markets. In the end, this measured approach means that financial liberalization in highly regulated economies should take place over years or decades, not months.

Likewise, Eswar Prasad (2006) argues that in order to receive the direct and indirect benefits of foreign capital flows, governments first must have (1) efficient financial systems, (2) open and competitive product markets, and (3) reasonable macroeconomic policy. In other words, financial liberalization can only strengthen growth when the fundamentals for solid growth are already in place. Thus, his research indicates that financial liberalization should not be the first stage in a program for development, but rather a reform that can increase growth in a country once growth is already established.

To achieve this, both domestic governments and particularly the world community need the patience to be satisfied with slow but positive progress and not be solely focused on large and immediate payoffs. One role of the IMF in the future should be to help encourage this patience by providing short-term financing to countries that are attempting such thoughtful liberalization, not just providing IMF bailouts only after a crisis has occurred.

The Pros and Cons of Capital Controls

Many of the policy guidelines just discussed, such as constraints on the amounts of short-term and foreign-denominated debt, involve imposing explicit limits or taxes aimed at reducing the flows of capital into and out of a country. The efficacy of such capital controls has been a matter of intense debate among economists. Some have argued that capital controls are necessary, particularly if imposed as a short-term measure during an emergency in order to stem the tide of contagion and limit the size of crises. These economists point to the East Asian crisis as an example of the potential effectiveness of capital controls. China had strict controls on capital outflows and inflows in place before the crisis and, as a result, only experienced a mild slowdown even though across almost every measure of financial fundamentals Chinese banks were the poorest in the region. Malaysia also imposed capital controls on outflows of short-term capital in late 1998 in an effort to avoid an IMF bailout. Kaplan and Rodrik (2001) argue that even though the capital outflow controls were imposed late in the crisis, Malaysia actually outperformed Korea and Thailand in the period following their IMF bailouts.

Other countries have imposed controls on capital inflows in order to limit capital outflows. Between 1991 and 1998, Chile imposed a 30 percent reserve deposit that had to be held against all foreign investment inflows for 1 year. After funds had been in the country for 1 year, the reserve deposit requirement expired. This reserve deposit served as a tax on capital inflows during their first year in the country, encouraging longer-term foreign investment and discouraging hot money inflows.

While capital controls have the obvious advantage of limiting or delaying capital outflows in the event of a crisis, there are some significant costs associated with them. First, capital that cannot flow out may never flow in if the controls are anticipated or impose costs on foreign investors. Edwards (1998) argues that the Chilean reserve deposits did have some minor benefits, such as reducing stock market volatility, but increased the cost of capital by roughly 20 percent and reduced foreign capital inflows. Second, controls tend to encourage corruption by government officials who monitor these capital flows. Third, capital controls on outflows are relatively easy to avoid in practice through legal ploys such as offshore or dummy corporations. Referring back to the Chilean case, Edwards reports that because of the costs associated with reserve deposits, a great deal of avoidance took place. However, there is also good reason to think that because the Chilean controls were market-based, they were more efficient and suffered from less avoidance and corruption than controls that simply impose quantity limits.

Because of these problems, many economists argue that encouraging more foreign ownership of banks and encouraging firms to rely more heavily on equity as opposed to debt are superior ways of reducing the riskiness of financial systems. However, for most countries it will take years before such changes would begin to have a significant impact on the economy. In the mean time, given the risk associated with hot money, targeted controls on short-term and foreign-denominated capital flows might represent the best choice from imperfect policy alternatives and a reasonable method of minimizing lending booms and busts.

International Financial Regulation

As banks and financial systems become increasingly globalized, many have begun to question whether regulators and the regulations they enforce should not be internationalized as well. Currently, there are a small number of international organizations that establish regulatory principles and standards for stocks, bonds, insurance companies, and banks. However, each of these organizations is advisory in nature and has no real enforcement power other than through their powers of persuasion and peer pressure on domestic governments.

The most influential of these international organizations is the Basel committee, which is composed of representatives from the world's central banks. The Basel committee works to establish international guidelines for the regulation of banking systems. The Basel accord was described in Chapter 6, the key feature of which establishes capital adequacy standards for banks. Under the Basel accord, all bank assets are classified into four risk categories, with the riskiest categories requiring higher capital requirements than the less risky categories. Unfortunately, there are a number of problems with this approach. Because there are only four risk categories, banks have incentives to engage in the riskiest activities within each of these categories because they provide the highest return relative to their cost of capital. For example, all mortgages and bonds are treated alike, regardless of the risk of the individual borrower. Another problem with the accord is that some assets are classified as being less risky than other assets when they are not. The most egregious example is the fact that short-term interbank lending, a form of hot money that is very risky, is actually classified in the second lowest risk category. Because of all of these problems, there is often little relationship between a bank's capital requirements and its true risk exposure.

To deal with these issues, a Basel 2 accord has been negotiated and is due to become effective in January 2008 (although as of the time of writing this book it will not take effect until January of 2009 in the U.S.) Under Basel 2, short-term bank lending would be weighted more heavily; capital requirements would be more closely tied to the credit ratings of individual borrowers, securitized assets would be included in calculating capital requirements, and banks would have to provide some measure of their interest rate risk and adjust their capital holdings accordingly (though, somewhat worryingly, banks can use their own private models to measure their risk exposure). Despite these reforms, however, the predominant problem with the Basel accord remains: there still is no reliable international enforcement mechanism. Instead, each individual country that agrees to the Basel accord has to enforce it on its own. Enforcement is often difficult for regulators in many countries given political realities and the financial costs associated with getting tough with large financial institutions. For example, U.S. regulators have declared that only 26 internationally active U.S. banks will be subject to this new accord. As a result, adherence to the Basel accord will continue to be inconsistent at best. This will not change until a real international regulator with teeth is created that can enforce consistent international standards. This is unlikely to happen in the foreseeable future.

Thinking about bank regulation more creatively, there may be ways to harness market forces to discipline banks. Calomiris and Litan (2000) have argued that instead of imposing capital requirements on banks, Basel 2 should require banks to finance a certain portion of their assets by regularly issuing long-term bonds. This plan would have three advantages. First, it would reduce risk by reducing the short-term borrowing of banks. Second, it would increase the reporting and information requirements on banks because bond holders would require full financial disclosure before buying bonds. It would also mean that the bonds that banks issue would be evaluated by credit-rating agencies. While credit ratings are not perfect, they do provide a reasonable evaluation of the overall risk of corporations on average. Finally, issuing long-term debt is more costly for banks that have been evaluated as being more risky. The lower the credit rating, the higher the interest rates that must be paid on these bonds, giving banks a financial incentive to reduce the risk of their operations. This proposal, and other market-based mechanisms like it, can be used in place of direct regulation and are worth careful consideration, both because of their potential effectiveness and because they can reduce banking system risk with the smallest impact on efficiency.

The IMF, Its Policies, and Its Critics

A brief overview

After World War II, an international system of fixed exchange rates known as the Bretton Woods agreement was established. The IMF was given the responsibility of evaluating and approving applications for devaluation by member countries that were experiencing unsustainable imbalances in their balance of payment accounts. This process of evaluation was implemented to prevent "beggar thy neighbor" policies. These policies, which were widely adopted to the detriment of the world economy during the Great Depression (see Chapter 5), prescribed competitive devaluations by countries in an attempt to make their exports cheaper and run sustained trade surpluses. The IMF was also given the responsibility of strengthening and liberalizing world trading institutions, which had suffered a complete breakdown during World War II. In order to facilitate this process, the IMF provided temporary financing to countries experiencing short-term economic instability in return for promises of reform. The IMF has a set amount of resources for use ($220 billion in 2006), contributed by member countries, to make these loans.

After the collapse of the Bretton Woods system in the early 1970s, the IMF no longer had a worldwide system of fixed exchange rates to maintain, but the rest of its mission remained largely unchanged. Many countries, particularly poorer countries, continued to maintain fixed exchange rates on their own. In many of these cases, poor macroeconomic policy, such as high inflation or large budget deficits, led to overvalued exchange rates. An overvalued exchange rate helped to attract foreign investment and reduce the price of imports. But when investors and speculators observed that the foreign reserves of a country were declining, capital flight began and a currency crisis occurred until (1) the country devalued and/or (2) the country received a loan from the IMF that was large enough to restore market confidence that no future devaluation would occur.

IMF lending comes attached with requirements for economic reform. These reforms consist of *structural adjustment conditions*, or microeconomic-level market reforms aimed at increasing efficiency and productivity. This would include reforms of the legal system, the elimination of price and quantity regulations in goods markets, the removal of barriers to international trade, and the liberalization of the financial system. They also involve *austerity conditions*, or the imposition of macrolevel reforms such as government spending cuts, tax increases, and reductions in money growth aimed at restoring the sustainability of the government's fiscal situation and reducing future pressures to increase the money supply and inflation.

Paul Krugman (1999) has referred to the rationale for imposing austerity and structural adjustment conditions in response to a crisis as "the confidence game." In order to reduce capital flight, the IMF tries to restore the confidence of foreign investors by pushing for reforms that make the economy more efficient and attractive for investment. Most importantly, contractionary monetary and fiscal policy drive up real interest rates, making the country more profitable for foreign investors. Historically, it has generally been the case that after accepting these bailout conditions and adopting reforms, the tide of economic crisis was stemmed. Intervention by the IMF usually signaled the trough of the crisis and a reduction in capital flight (if not a resumption of inflows), although it often took years for these countries to return to their natural rates of output.

The critics: hawks and doves

The crisis resolution policies and operating procedures adopted by the IMF have recently come under heavy criticism, particularly after the East Asian crisis. Interestingly, this criticism has come from many different sources across the political and ideological spectrum. Jean Tirole (2002) has classified these critics into two camps: hawks and doves. Hawks place their primary focus on implementing policies that enhance economic efficiency, attract foreign investment, and encourage long-term economic growth. Doves place their primary focus on crisis resolution and policies that stabilize the economy in the short term.

Criticisms of the IMF and the arguments that take place between hawks and doves primarily boil down to four key questions.

Should the IMF provide bailouts?

Hawks are very critical of IMF bailout lending, primarily because they believe that it actually leads to more crises by encouraging moral hazard and risky behavior by governments, financial systems, and foreign investors. In order for markets to act efficiently, individuals must consider all the costs and the benefits associated with their funding decisions. Far too often, lenders have ignored much of the downside risk of their lending because of the belief that they would be bailed-out by their governments if economic conditions deteriorated in the future. On the basis of the history of many of these governments, this is a reasonable belief. Much of this bailout money often comes from the IMF, meaning that the IMF is essentially providing lenders with free insurance. By ending these bailouts, lenders would be forced to incur more of the costs associated with their risky actions.

One example of how IMF loans often do not work the way they are supposed to is the fact that once a country has gotten one loan, it is likely to come back to the IMF for repeated loans over long periods of time. Easterly (2006) defines a country as a "prolonged user" if it has been borrowing under an IMF program for 7 years of any 10-year period. Using this definition, 44 countries were prolonged users between 1971 and 2000, accounting for nearly half of all IMF lending. Many countries need these repeated bailouts because these loans often do not create real incentives for change. It is very difficult for the IMF to cut lending nations off and admit mistakes, which allows some countries to get "hooked" on IMF loans without ever really dealing with their fundamental problems.

Hawks also believe too much lending and aid encourages corruption. Knack (2004) finds that increases in aid reduce the quality of bureaucracy and increases corruption, primarily because bailout funds are easily diverted by corrupt leaders. Easterly (2006) looks at data on corruption and ranks countries into deciles. He reports that while the lowest decile of corrupt countries do receive less funding from the IMF, the second lowest decile of countries in the corruption data receive no less help from the IMF than the average country.

Doves, on the other hand, agree that the IMF should not be providing loans to crisis countries, but instead believe the IMF should be providing grants to crisis countries that do not have to be repaid. Many doves lament the fact that many poorer countries are left with huge amounts of foreign debt that must be serviced and repaid following a crisis. This debt hangover limits these countries' ability to deal with many of the other social and economic issues that they face.

To correct this, many doves have been working with developed governments to provide debt-relief packages to those countries that are highly indebted to the IMF and World Bank. Of course, hawks would argue that such debt-relief programs only encourage more moral hazard by reducing the penalties governments pay for making bad policy decisions.

Doves also argue that transitioning from providing loans to providing grants would actually free the IMF to provide more resources to the countries that deserve it most. Currently, the IMF has been stuck in a defensive lending pattern with many highly indebted countries and has been forced to lend them an ever-increasing share of their funds in an effort to stave off their default. The result is that fewer resources are available for other countries in need. By writing-off a large fraction of these loans, the IMF could then devote all future resources to more worthy governments. Of course, if past loans are forgiven, IMF resources would be much more limited in the future unless developed countries become much more generous. Moving away from debt and towards grants would mean that the IMF would have to rely on developed countries to continually provide new resources for grants, making their financing stream even more contingent on political forces than it currently is.

One potential solution to the bailout problem has been suggested by Anne Krueger (2002), deputy managing director of the IMF. She has proposed an international bankruptcy system that would be administered by the IMF. Under this system, when a country is on the precipice of a debt or currency crisis, it could apply to the IMF for the right to suspend debt payments and block capital outflows. Creditors as a group would then be asked to negotiate a restructuring of the timing and amount of payments they would receive in the future. In return for concessions, creditors would receive the help of the IMF in facilitating a mutually beneficial agreement. There are many difficulties that need to be addressed before such a plan could be implemented, not the least of which is the difficulty of enforcing such negotiated agreements across a large group of foreign investors in a large number of countries with much different legal standards. The potential lack of protection for investors under such a plan, and the chilling effect such a plan could have on foreign investment, is a big source of concern for many hawks.

Should the IMF impose conditions on their bailouts?
One way to reduce the moral hazard incentives created by bailouts is to ensure that these bailouts have costs associated with them. One reason hawks support the imposition of structural adjustment and austerity conditions is that they impose significant costs, both economic and political, on borrowing countries. However, these conditions are not strictly punitive in nature. Hawks believe that conditionality imposes reforms that increase efficiency and growth. Krueger (1998) and Edwards (1998) report empirical evidence that structural adjustment conditions improve economic growth. Faster growth is good by itself, but it also increases the chance that the country will repay their loan, and without repayment future

IMF lending cannot take place (unless the IMF receives additional resources from member countries). In addition, Hawks argue that the IMF does not have the power to act preemptively within a country. A bailout is the IMF's one chance to create leverage that can be used to press for economic reform within countries that need it.

Doves have been very critical of both the kinds and the number of conditions attached to IMF lending. Many doves are concerned about the ways that imposing external reform infringes on the rights of sovereign nations. The protestors who regularly disrupt World Bank/IMF annual meetings have many grievances, but one of the most universal complaints is that these institutions take advantage of crisis situations to force capitalism, globalization, and liberalization down the throats of the poor at the behest of the rich. While many of these complaints are overly simplistic, there are serious reasons to be concerned about the structural adjustment and austerity programs the IMF has recently imposed.

Let us begin by discussing structural adjustment conditions. In the mid-1980s, fewer than three structural adjustment conditions were attached to an average IMF loan. In the 1990s, this average had jumped to 12 conditions. Looking at some recent cases, however, the problem becomes even worse. In the Indonesian bailout, 140 structural adjustment conditions were imposed. Many of these reforms were widely recognized as being badly needed, such as stricter bank lending standards. Also included, however, were requirements to deregulate Indonesian gas and plywood markets. In Korea, regulations restricting layoffs were eliminated and barriers protecting the automobile market from international competition were removed. While these reforms might enhance efficiency, it is clear that problems in the plywood and automobile markets played little role in creating the crisis, and deregulating these markets will not prevent future crises. As a result, many East Asians felt like rich nations were taking advantage of the crisis to impose reforms on them not because they were absolutely necessary for recovery but because they would benefit foreigners. In the end, these "laundry list" mandates create lingering resentment that makes the IMF, not irresponsible governments, the bad guys. This perception increases the difficulty of the IMF's mission.

Even within the IMF there is a realization that it is suffering from "mission creep" and that the IMF has been asking for reforms that are beyond its mission and areas of expertise, which is primarily in macroeconomic, monetary, and financial policy. Goldstein (2001) conducted a survey of IMF staffers who reported that they believed that only 30–40 percent of structural adjustment conditions typically imposed during a crisis were "critical to a recovery." One troubling implication of this is that as the number of conditions has gone up, compliance with these conditions has gone down. Part of this is that countries legitimately have a hard time implementing such a large number of requirements, but just as important is the fact that countries feel freer to pick and choose what reforms they will work to implement when there are so many of them they are told to adopt.

Why is mission creep occurring if even those that work within the IMF are worried about it? The primary reason is that particular structural adjustment conditions are often pushed at the behest of the IMF's large member countries, primarily G-7 countries such as the United States. Developed countries often push for bailouts where they have important economic interests (e.g., the U.S. pushed for a bailout of Mexico in 1994) and where they have important political interests (e.g., the U.S. pushed for bailouts in Turkey and Pakistan in 2001). Doves argue that by placing their own interests first, these developed countries weaken the ability of the IMF to freely choose and enforce economic policies that are critical for success. Just as importantly, they weaken the political commitment to reform within crisis countries by too easily allowing opponents of reform to scapegoat the IMF as a tool of the rich.

Should IMF policies focus on restoring capital flows or stabilizing output?
The austerity conditions imposed by the IMF have been just as controversial. Hawks believe that tough austerity conditions are needed because they are costly and prevent countries from obtaining loans too easily from the IMF, encouraging moral hazard. In addition, Hawks believe that restoring capital inflows is the key to restoring economic growth. By taking tough actions such as cutting money growth and budget deficits, governments can increase interest rates and help to reestablish the confidence of foreign investors in the governments' commitment to reform. This is the basis of what we referred to earlier as "the confidence game." In fact, the main criticism made by Hawks of austerity conditions is that they are often not tough enough. Governments often implement these austerity policies only while they are being closely watched by the IMF. Once the crisis is past and the IMF is less vigilant, restraint is often abandoned.

Austerity conditions have come under withering criticism from many Doves. By asking countries to cut money growth, cut government spending, and raise taxes, the IMF is asking governments to drive down aggregate demand and drive up interest rates. These policies run counter to traditional Keynesian stabilization policy and are likely to hurt domestic macroeconomic performance in the short run. Doves do not agree that the best way to build the confidence of investors is to drive the country deeper into recession; to Doves, austerity conditions seem akin to the discredited practice of bleeding the sick to make them healthier.

The confidence game approach of austerity has worked in the past, but only when the real source of the problem was bad macroeconomic policy, such as in the Latin American crises of the 1980s. In these cases, macroeconomic reform was crucial because bad macroeconomic policies were the primary cause of the problem. However, when the problem is more microeconomic in nature, such as risky banking systems and inefficient product markets, austerity conditions only make the situation worse by reducing aggregate demand and weakening financial fundamentals, which together serve to further reduce credit and amplify the contraction in output. By continuing to press for austerity conditions in their lending, Doves argue that the IMF creates the impression that it worries more about the psyche of foreign investors than it does about the economic condition of those on the ground who are really suffering from the crisis. Once again, this poisons the political climate surrounding IMF interventions and actually increases the risk of social and political turmoil within these countries, which is obviously not conducive to a resumption in growth.

Should the IMF allow countries to impose capital controls?
Referring to our previous discussion on capital controls, Hawks believe that allowing the possibility of implementing capital controls will significantly reduce foreign investment and harm growth. In fact, many Hawks argue that the IMF should remove existing capital controls by demanding that more aggressive financial liberalization be a part of every loan the IMF provides. On the other hand, Doves argue that emergency situations often require imperfect solutions and that the imposition of capital controls is one way to prevent contagion and the spread of panic that can turn a single recession into an international depression. In addition, Doves typically argue that permanent controls on some forms of foreign investment, particularly hot money, are often necessary to keep financial fundamentals strong and reduce credit risk and economic volatility.

CASE STUDY: The IMF in East Asia and Argentina

The crises in East Asia and Argentina have become the focal point of reference for critics of the IMF. These crises have many things in common. First, both Argentina and East Asia were held to be model economies by the IMF before the crises occurred. Second, the depressions that took place were twin crises. In each case, currency crises were driven by exchange rates that were fixed to the dollar. When the dollar appreciated significantly in the mid-1990s, these countries' currencies became overvalued relative to regional trading partners. The banking crises were fueled by rapid and indiscriminate financial liberalization that took place during the early 1990s, which led to large capital inflows of hot money, risky lending driven by moral hazard, and fragile financial fundamentals. As a result, when currency crises struck and devaluation occurred, the value of foreign-denominated debt ballooned relative to the falling value of domestic assets, leading to a collapse in net worths and in financial intermediation. The final important similarity between these crises is that in each case, economic conditions actually deteriorated after the IMF became involved. After these countries devalued and the IMF provided bailouts, the output contractions became larger and the crisis began to spread to other countries in the region. For example, Argentina received a bailout in 1999. By 2002, unemployment had risen to 25 percent and 56 percent of Argentines had seen their incomes fall below the poverty line.

In East Asia and Argentina, the IMF imposed programs of structural adjustment and austerity. The structural adjustment conditions, as mentioned earlier, were numerous and ranged well beyond previous conditionality. Austerity conditions requiring tighter monetary and fiscal policy were imposed despite the fact that macroeconomic policy in these countries, particularly in East Asia, was prudent. For example, even though Korea had inflation of less than 5 percent and a budget surplus, the IMF asked them to reduce inflation and government spending in an effort to increase interest rates. These austerity conditions pushed interest rates in Korea from 9 percent to over 40 percent. This had a devastating impact on investment and consumption. In addition, as emphasized by New Institutional theories of finance, these higher interest rates significantly increased bankruptcy risk, both by increasing debt burdens and also by reducing the quality of loan applicants because of moral hazard and adverse selection. The end result was that financial intermediation collapsed and acute banking crises took place across the region.

In an effort to deal with the currency crises, the IMF's austerity conditions made the banking crises and recessions worse, which in turn made the currency crises worse. It is not clear whether the IMF really understood that there were twin crises going on in any of these countries. For example, in addition to the austerity and structural adjustment conditions that the IMF imposed, crisis countries were often asked by the IMF to immediately impose bank holidays, spooking depositors and worsening both the banking crises and capital flight. The IMF appears to have acted almost reflexively—imposing austerity in the belief that it had worked in the past, so it would work again—without any real consideration of the country-specific factors or the financial fundamentals that existed on the ground.

In East Asia, the IMF realized the extent of both the problem and its mistakes and attempted to reverse itself, backing off from many of the austerity and structural adjustment conditions it initially imposed as the crisis began to spread. In Argentina, however, the IMF's actions after the crisis have only compounded existing problems. In 2001, more than $10 billion of the IMF's original $40 billion loan was frozen because of the IMF's dissatisfaction with the pace of Argentina's reforms, particularly with Argentina's inability to reduce government spending and its deficit. In 2002, Argentina defaulted on a World Bank loan. In 2003, the IMF and the World Bank restructured Argentina's debt payments, then it was forced to do so again under another threat of default in 2005. At the time of writing this book, Argentina had still not followed the conditions of its borrowing, but the IMF has continued to lend and delay repayments because of political pressures and because Argentina now owes the IMF so much money (more than $32 billion, or 15 percent of total IMF lending) that the IMF cannot afford to let it fail. Not only has the IMF lost a great deal of credibility—which encourages moral hazard and inhibits the IMF's ability to enforce future lending agreements—but Argentina's recovery has been stunted by the uncertainty surrounding this constant threat of default, leaving it unable to regain the confidence of foreign investors.

Reforming the IMF

The criticism of the IMF as a reactive organization with little creativity or insight in its thinking is one that has been repeatedly made by some of the world's most influential economists. These critics argue that both the culture and the policy approach of the IMF needs to be reformed. Nobel laureate Joseph Stiglitz (2002), former chief economist and vice president of the World Bank between 1997 and 2000, and noted development specialist Jeffrey Sachs (1997, 2005) have been harsh in their criticism of the IMF's decision-making processes. They have argued that the IMF is autocratic and decisions are often imposed from above by IMF's leaders without debate and with little country-specific knowledge of the details of each individual crisis. Rarely does the IMF ask for outside advice from those with particular expertise in a country or on a specific issue, but instead almost reflexively imposes policy measures adopted during the last crisis. As a result, the IMF appears to be consistently fighting the last crisis, refusing to think creatively about solving problems but instead applying similar programs across time and across countries even when the fundamentals are quite different.

Another criticism that these economists have made is that the IMF is more sensitive to the demands of developed countries than the needs of those countries that are suffering from a crisis. This should not be surprising given that the IMF is a political institution and that large donors, which are the largest economies, have the most political influence. These developed countries often push for rapid financial liberalization before the proper market reforms and regulatory infrastructure is in place. Pressure from developed countries also prevents the IMF from making reasonable accommodations to the domestic political circumstances in crisis countries. As things stand now, in the opinion of Paul Volker, former chairman of the Federal Reserve: "When the Fund consults with a poor and weak country, the country gets in line. When it consults with a big and strong country, the Fund gets in line. When the big countries are in conflict, the Fund gets out of the line of fire" (Volker and Gyohten, 1992). For the IMF to work properly, the officials at the IMF have to be granted more independence by member countries to do their jobs, then be held accountable by these same countries if they fail to be effective.

The IMF does appear to be listening to its critics and trying to learn from its past mistakes in East Asia and Argentina. It has begun to move toward a more informal structure that encourages debate, inviting more diversity of opinion and information into the decision-making process. To this end, negotiations have been taking place aimed at giving more voting power to emerging market economies relative to developed countries. It has also moved toward rethinking its policy responses, pushing for more gradual liberalization and emphasizing legal and regulatory reform before liberalization and crises take place. The IMF is also pledging to be more sensitive to building domestic political support for its policies. Finally, the IMF is attempting to develop new "early warning" techniques to help identify potential crises as well as construct an international bankruptcy system to deal with crises before the crisis-bailout-crisis cycle begins. However, it will take more than lip service to deal with these significant problems. This is in part because the potential hurdles in implementing these reforms are high, but also because the world's confidence in the IMF's ability to provide effective leadership has been badly shaken.

Conclusions

There is an old adage that the most expensive words in finance are "this time it's different." This also applies to international financial crises. Over the last 20 years, countries that have liberalized their financial systems have been able to attract remarkable levels of foreign investment which has fueled growth rates that would have previously been unthinkable. However, too often this financial liberalization has taken place indiscriminately, ignoring the importance of maintaining sustainable levels of foreign investment and sound financial fundamentals. The result has been more frequent and more costly financial crises.

In the future, countries must ensure that liberalization is implemented more responsibly through the appropriate, but limited, regulation of financial systems. In regards to domestic regulation, the general consensus among economists is that this means the following: Governments that liberalize should more closely monitor the financial fundamentals of banks (particularly lending financed with hot money); regulators should attempt to reduce moral hazard by limiting bailouts and imposing stricter capital requirements; central banks should move away from exchange rates fixed to a single currency so that financial systems are forced to hedge against exchange rate risk; and, finally, governments should consider imposing both long-term capital controls to limit hot money inflows and short-term capital controls in the event of sudden capital flight. However, because financial institutions are becoming more international, domestic regulation alone will not prevent all crises. In the future, countries also must develop international regulatory institutions and provide these institutions with more enforcement power. The Basel agreement is only the beginning of what should be a more comprehensive process.

The IMF has a large role to play if these domestic and international reforms are ever to take place. Too often, the IMF has shot itself in the foot by imposing conditions on its lending that are not absolutely necessary, ignoring domestic political considerations and encouraging resentment. On the other hand, the IMF has been too lenient by providing bailouts too easily. In fact, in an effort to prevent default, the IMF often has provided additional lending even when the country fails to comply with the conditions of previous loans (for instance, in Argentina). Coupled with the IMF's mistakes of imposing austerity conditions on countries in which bad macroeconomic policy was not the cause of the crisis, the IMF has lost the confidence of much of the world and, as a result, much of its power.

One possible alternative is to disband the IMF, but the vast majority of economists and policy makers do not believe that this would solve anything. The IMF did not cause any of the crises we have talked about, although they could often be blamed for not helping enough to prevent or moderate them. One emerging consensus among economists is that the better solution is to reinvent the IMF along two lines. First, the IMF should actually be given more independence and power, particularly the power to say no to bailouts of badly governed countries that have fallen into the bailout-crisis-bailout trap or that fail to live up to the conditions of their previous loans; the power to say no to governments that indiscriminately bailout poorly run financial institutions and finance moral hazard lending; and finally, the power to say no to developed countries that try to pressure bailouts or attach additional conditions to bailouts in order to further their own economic or geopolitical interests.

The second line of reform is that the IMF should largely reinvent itself and change from being a closed, reactive, crisis-management institution to being an open, proactive, reform-management institution. The IMF has an incredible wealth of resources that could be made available to countries before crises hit. For example, there is a needed role for the IMF to provide loans and advice to countries that are implementing the gradual, sequenced financial liberalization programs that have been successful in the past. The same is true for needed reforms of legal systems, regulatory agencies, stock and bond markets, monetary and exchange rate management, and banking systems. This kind of consistent engagement before crises occur will also help when crises strike because the IMF will be better able to build the domestic political support it needs for its programs to be successful, as well as obtain the on-the-ground information it needs to craft appropriate policy responses.

Any reform of the IMF and of domestic regulation will not be easy to implement given the complicated political calculations involved. Without them, however, many countries will never be able to enjoy the full benefits of financial development and globalization. Instead, they will suffer from economic volatility that not only undermines globalization's payoffs, but many countries' commitment to free markets and capitalism itself.

PART V

CONCLUSIONS

CHAPTER 11

What We Have Learned, What We Still Need to Learn about Financial Macroeconomics

A Brief Review

Finance has long been underrepresented in the study of macroeconomics. While the growth of financial intermediation has outpaced the growth of income across most developing, emerging, and less developed countries, the importance of finance in macroeconomic theory has diminished in the postwar era until recently. This is despite the facts that financial volatility has long been associated with macroeconomic volatility and that one of the principal objectives of macroeconomic research has been to understand business cycles. All of the major economic crises of the 20th century have been associated with financial crises, so it would seemingly be obvious that finance would be at the forefront of macroeconomic research. However, even while financial variables have played an important role in economic forecasting—for example, many of the variables that compose the Index of Leading Economic Indicators are financial variables—the most crucial debates among economists during the postwar era have taken place over other issues such as monetary policy and the role of expectations.

Early macroeconomic theories, including the Debt-Deflation theory, did place a great deal of emphasis on financial systems, particularly on the role of expectations, financial speculation, and the money supply. Because of the obvious role that financial collapse played in the Great Depression, Keynes placed financial volatility at the forefront of his General Theory. In Keynes' theory, financial systems nurture animal spirit speculation, which creates investment and aggregate demand volatility that drives business cycles. In his words: "the tendency to transform doing well into a speculative investment boom is the basic instability in a capitalist system."

However, the study of the macroeconomic implications of finance gradually fell out of favor beginning in the 1960s. First, Keynesians superseded post-Keynesian models, such as Minsky's Financial Instability Hypothesis model, as the dominant heirs to Keynes' legacy and as the mainstream interpreters of his work. Keynesians discounted finance by focusing on equilibrium models that emphasize consumption volatility and minimized the impact of financial volatility. After them came the Monetarists, who focused exclusively on external shocks to the money supply. Next came Neoclassical models such as the Rational Expectations model and Real Business Cycle models, which focused on unanticipated demand shocks and real shocks to aggregate supply, respectively, completely ignoring heterogeneity and market failure in the financial sector. While monetary policy continued to receive attention from Monetarists and Neoclassicals, money was not viewed as a financial asset. This left the microeconomic operations of financial markets as a minor consideration at most. In each of these models, financial instability is only a symptom of macroeconomic volatility and not vice versa, making the study of financial systems largely uninteresting and of minor consequence.

One of the big problems in macroeconomics is that these same models that discount the importance of finance are the same ones that are taught to most students of macroeconomics. Just take a look at any popular intermediate macroeconomics textbook: there is very little detailed discussion of financial topics such as the causes and effects of credit rationing, banking crises, asset bubbles, twin crises, and contagion. The result has been generations of economics students who think that the study of finance is about following the stock market. This lack of careful thinking about the macroeconomic implications of finance has hindered economists' ability to understand macroeconomic volatility as well as their ability to design policies to minimize it.

Thankfully, things are changing. New Institutional theories of finance have placed their primary focus squarely on the macroeconomic effects of imperfect competition and market failure in financial systems. These theories have shown how even small changes in the financial fundamentals of borrowers and lenders (such as changes in their net worth, cash flows, future profitability, etc.) can lead to large changes in perceived default risk. Changes in perceived risk in turn lead to large changes in the supply of credit that can amplify even small negative shocks into large economic contractions. New Institutional theories of finance have done very well in explaining recent crises that have been largely driven by financial crisis, such as in East Asia and Japan. History has shown us that the existence of banking crises, asset crashes, and currency crises appear to be the primary factors that separate an average recession from a severe depression; depressions differ from recessions primarily to the extent that the financial sector collapses, bringing down financial intermediation, investment, consumption, and output. Because of this focus on financial market failure, New Institutional theories provide quite persuasive explanations of major economic contractions from the Great Depression to the Argentinean financial crisis.

The ultimate goal of economic research is not just to understand macroeconomic volatility, but to develop policies that can help prevent future financial and economic crises so that all countries can enjoy the full benefits of financial development. This appears to be possible; in the U.S. and other developed countries, there is a good argument to be made that financial development has significantly increased economic stability from the 1980s onwards. In order to develop the appropriate policies, however, we first have to make sure what we know and what we do not know. It has been said once in this book, but it is worth repeating, that the most expensive words in finance are "this time it's different." Only by understanding where we have been can we see where we need to go to get to where we want to be. The alternative is to continue to make the same mistakes that have been made in the past, falling into the same traps time and time again.

What We Have Learned about Financial Macroeconomics

There are three principal lessons that economists have learned about the role that financial systems play in macroeconomics.

Financial intermediation is about information
Financial intermediation involves the trading of money across time. The future always involves uncertainty, not only because our knowledge of the future is imperfect, but also because of asymmetric information and the fact that borrowers have better information regarding their own likelihood of repaying than lenders. These information problems complicate the provision of credit because they lead to adverse selection before a loan takes place and moral hazard behavior after a loan is made. As a result, lenders face much higher default risk on their asset portfolios than they would if financial markets were perfectly competitive. This leads to borrowers receiving much less credit than is socially optimal.

Because financial intermediation does not take place if lenders face too much uncertainty about getting their money back, one of the primary responsibilities of borrowers is to prove that they can meet the conditions of the financial transactions they want to engage in. The only way to alleviate these concerns is for borrowers to provide specific, quality, and persuasive information about their ability to meet their financial commitments to lenders. Thus, information becomes the biggest input into financial intermediation. If lenders do not have the proper information and cannot be reasonably assured that they will be repaid, then credit will not be provided regardless of the level of the money supply in the financial system or the interest rates borrowers are willing to pay. By ignoring heterogeneity and imperfect information in financial markets, Classical and Neoclassical theories assumed that total liquidity and the money supply were good measures of the amount of financial intermediation that was taking place within an economy.

However, this is not necessarily the case in markets with imperfect and asymmetric information.

The link between liquidity and credit is most likely to break down when perceived default risk is at its highest. The question is then: how do financial agents form their expectations of the default risk associated with a financial transaction? The Rational Expectations model asserts that rational choice governs the formation of expectations, which means that expectations are entirely based on economic fundamentals and only unanticipated shocks affect macroeconomic behavior. Keynesians believe that beliefs are largely irrational, self-fulfilling, based upon speculation, subject to herding, and inherently volatile. Classical and Real Business Cycle proponents ignore this question.

New Institutional theories of finance take many of the aspects of these previous theories and combine them to form a more coherent picture of how individuals form their risk perceptions. Like the Rational Expectations model, New Institutional theories believe that expectations are rational and based upon fundamentals. In particular, these theories focus on how changes in the financial fundamentals of borrowers and lenders affect the potential risk associated with financial intermediation. Unlike the Rational Expectations model, however, New Institutional theories identify reasons why financial markets are not perfectly competitive—particularly how moral hazard and adverse selection lead to persistent excess demand for credit. Like Keynesians, New Institutional theories show how cyclical movements in the financial fundamentals of borrowers and lenders lead to cyclical movements in expectations and confidence that create financial volatility, which in turns amplifies business cycles. By focusing on financial fundamentals and financial volatility, New Institutional theories have provided important insights into crises from the Great Depression to the East Asian crises, to the recent collapse of the subprime mortgage market.

Information and expectations not only affect financial intermediation, but they also affect monetary policy. During periods in which fundamentals are weak and risk perceptions are high, increases in the money supply might not lead to any expansion in credit, or a "pessimism trap." In addition, because monetary policy is most likely to affect those lenders and borrowers with the weakest fundamentals and credit histories, namely smaller and newer banks and firms, monetary policy does not affect all individuals equally, complicating the impact of policy decisions.

One final implication of the importance of imperfect information is that the market failure it creates provides a role for government in facilitating credit, specifically in three ways: (1) assuring the quality and transparency of information; (2) providing deposit insurance to prevent speculative panic that can create destabilizing bank runs; and (3) creating legal systems that protects the rights of lenders in the event of a default while also preventing the exploitation of borrowers who fail to meet their commitments.

Financial development increases standards of living and growth, but it also increases macroeconomic volatility in the absence of careful regulation and sound infrastructure

Financial development has changed the very nature of macroeconomics, generally for the better. Consider the effects of just one aspect of financial development: the securitization of home mortgages. Securitization has significantly reduced the costs of obtaining home loans at the same time that it has expanded the pool of mortgage funds, leading to dramatic increases in homeownership even amongst those with very poor credit histories. In addition, by allowing previous homeowners to refinance their mortgages easily at lower interest rates, securitization has increased disposable income and served to stabilize output growth in many countries over the last few turbulent years. Recent financial innovations such as securitization have been primarily driven by two factors. First, information and communications technology has improved the quality of information, which is the most important input into financial transactions. Information technology has also significantly reduced the computational costs associated with these complicated financial transactions. Second, deregulation has created an environment that encourages experimentation, which is exactly what financial entrepreneurs have done.

A large number of studies cited in this book indicate that larger and more efficient financial markets can increase growth by 1–2 percent a year, which if sustained over a period of years can lead to dramatic increases in standards of living. Most excitingly, these growth benefits are not only enjoyed by rich countries, but can be enjoyed by emerging and even poor countries as well.

Economic theory gives us a number of reasons why financial development increases economic growth in the long run. Financial development improves the quality and quantity of information, which is crucial to efficient and sufficient financial intermediation. Financial development leads to financial deepening, or an increase in both the size and the number of financial transactions, which reduces costs, encourages specialization, and increases productivity. Financial development allows for better pooling, transferring, and diversification of risk. Financial development encourages savings, which increases the pool of loanable funds available for investment. Finally, financial development allows lenders to better identify entrepreneurs who are worthy of financing and who will eventually develop new products that increase productivity.

Unfortunately, however, the benefits of financial development are often not all that they could be. Because of the uncertainty associated with financial intermediation, financial systems are inherently volatile. As financial systems play a larger role in an economy, there is a greater chance that they will create macroeconomic volatility. Once again, consider the securitization boom. While it has greatly increased homeownership and wealth, excessive lending spurred by inaccurate risk assessments has led to a collapse in the subprime lending market in 2007 that threatens to interrupt all financial intermediation in the near future. To pick one empirical study investigating the relationship between finance and business cycles, Easterly, Islam, and Stiglitz (2001) find that among less developed countries, financial development significantly increases macroeconomic volatility once credit expands beyond a certain percentage of GDP. Many macroeconomic theories have no explanation for such findings. In this book we have discussed a number of reasons why financial systems are unstable and why an increased reliance on finance might increase macroeconomic volatility. The most persuasive explanations come from New Institutional theories of finance, which show how even small changes in the financial fundamentals of borrowers and lenders can significantly change the perceived risks associated with lending, leading to large swings in credit which in turn create volatility in investment, consumption, and production. These financial cycles hit the smallest, the newest, and the weakest firms and households the hardest.

When is the potential for financial instability the greatest? We have examined a number of empirical studies in this book which indicate that indiscriminate financial deregulation creates lending booms not linked to economic fundamentals but fueled by moral hazard and adverse selection. These lending booms feed asset bubbles that gradually weaken the financial fundamentals of borrowers and lenders. Eventually, a negative shock occurs and asset bubbles pop, financial positions deteriorate, default rates increase, and lenders are forced to significantly restrict credit either by increasing its price or imposing credit limits. Tighter credit reduces aggregate demand and aggregate supply, magnifying the effects of the negative shock. If severe enough, these conditions can also lead to banking crises, where banks fail or come so close to failing that bank intermediation comes to a complete halt. This collapse in credit significantly reduces consumption and investment and leads to further reductions in aggregate demand and aggregate supply. Empirical results suggest that past banking crisis episodes that have followed deregulation can be exceptionally costly in terms of lost output—upwards of 300 percent of precrisis GDP.

To make sure that financial development does not mean greater economic insecurity, domestic financial regulation has to be refocused around policies that solidify the fundamentals of the financial system without restricting the ability of individuals to engage in financial innovation. Policies that would help to provide a better balance between the benefits of financial development and its potential risk begin with adopting and enforcing the Basel 2 agreement's capital requirements, restricting connected lending, reducing foreign-denominated debt levels, opening markets to more foreign banks, and encouraging more long-term lending (particularly through nurturing stronger bond and stock markets). Regulatory supervision also has to apply to regulators themselves in an effort to prevent them from becoming a source, not the solution, to corruption in banking systems. This involves better monitoring of regulators from both domestic and international observers (another important part of Basel 2).

In addition, governments need to stop encouraging moral hazard by bailing-out bad banks and corporations. Instead, governments should repay depositors and act promptly to close bad banks. At the same time, governments must allow poorly run corporations to go bankrupt. While the short-run costs of such a tough policy can be significant, historical evidence suggests that the total costs of bailouts, in terms of both the direct costs in government spending and in terms of lost output, grow significantly if ignored and left to fester.

Finally, and most importantly, according to the most extensive empirical research on bank regulation to date, regulation is needed to improve financial transparency. This means that lenders, borrowers, and the regulators themselves have to be governed by stricter reporting and accountancy standards that are consistent across countries. Rating agencies and other information intermediaries also have to be held to stricter standards (their lack of scrutiny of securitized assets was one contributing factors to the subprime mortgage crisis). Without quality information, it is impossible for markets to effectively discipline borrowers and lenders. With greater transparency, more resources will flow to the most efficient markets that will use them in the most productive ways. Likewise, those countries that restrict or provide corrupted information will find themselves at a disadvantage in attracting foreign investment, creating incentives to improve their accounting and reporting standards.

International capital flows increase standards of living and growth, but also increase macroeconomic volatility in the absence of careful regulation and sound infrastructure
Like financial development itself, opening an economy to foreign investment has large potential benefits, but it is also associated with a great deal of risk—more risk than developing through domestic finance alone. Foreign investment is associated with the same problems of imperfect information and asymmetric information, only worse. However, during our recent globalization boom, advances in information technology, expanding world GDP, and pro-trade policies have allowed investors to overcome many of these information problems, with the result being a dramatic expansion in international capital flows. This capital has not just been flowing to a few industries in rich countries, but to a wide variety of sectors in economies across the globe, both rich and poor.

Once again, the empirical evidence indicates that opening borders to foreign investment can increase growth significantly by between 1 and 2 percent a year, not only through increasing the amount of credit but also the efficiency of intermediation. Foreign capital has all of the other advantages of financial development, but comes without the cost of having to increase domestic savings in order to increase the supply of loanable funds. Using foreign investment, countries today can enjoy benefits of financial deepening, improved efficiency, and higher investment and productivity without having to reduce their consumption.

Hedge funds are an example both of what is right and also what is potentially wrong in our modern era of globalization. Hedge funds have attracted levels of foreign investment that were never before thought possible, and much of this money has flown into less developed countries. Of course, the downside of capital flows is that what comes in can go out. In the case of hedge funds, their objective of making large, quick profits can lead to the kinds of speculative behavior that fuels panic in a fashion similar to that envisioned by Keynes.

Over the last 30 years, there has been a significant increase in the occurrence of international financial crises. Currency crises, capital flight, and contagion appear to have both belief-based and fundamentals-based causes. On the fundamentals-based side of the ledger, poor macroeconomic policies, common shocks, trade linkages, and financial linkages (which appear to be increasingly important in modern crises) all play a role in fostering and spreading financial crises. However, risky fundamentals are only necessary, not sufficient for a crisis to occur. Picking where and when crises occur is impossible if the choice is based on fundamentals alone. It also seems that beliefs play an important role in capital flight and contagion, either because beliefs are self-fulfilling, because of herding effects among speculators, or because crises serve as wake-up calls to investors.

Under what circumstances are capital flight, contagion, currency crises, and twin crises most likely to occur? Here, the evidence is unequivocal. Large international financial crises are typically associated with rapid and injudicious liberalization of international capital flows. Rapid liberalization sparks large capital inflows, domestic lending booms, and asset bubbles driven by moral hazard. Much of this money is often hot money, meaning it is short term and dominated in a foreign currency such as dollar. Over time, the financial fundamentals of borrowers and lenders become increasingly fragile and exchange rates become overvalued. At some point, a shock occurs that pricks asset bubbles and precipitates the first wave of capital flight, made easy by the prevalence of hot money. As capital begins to leave, downward pressure is placed on the exchange rate. If the government is unable to defend its peg, a currency crisis occurs and a large devaluation takes place. When this happens, banks see their financial positions deteriorate significantly as capital leaves and as devaluation reduces the real value of their domestic-denominated assets relative to their foreign-denominated liabilities. Banks are then forced to sell their assets and tighten credit.

In the end, a series of viscous cycles can set in. In one cycle, capital flight and falling asset prices lead to tighter credit and more panic selling, increasing the pace of capital flight and falling asset prices. In another cycle, devaluation reduces the stability of the banking system, and a less stable banking system worsens capital flight and makes the devaluation even larger. Eventually, economic fundamentals can deteriorate to such an extent that an economy is left with twin currency and banking crises, during which financial intermediation completely stops and economic activity is severely limited. In the end, the costs of the currency and banking crises together are significantly greater than their costs if one or both had occurred in isolation. This is exactly what happened during the East Asian crisis.

The best way to end capital flight and twin crises is to prevent them before they ever occur. To do this, it is necessary to attract the right kind of foreign investment in the first place. Too often, financial deregulation has meant no regulation as countries have been attracted by the allure of easy capital and hot money without proper consideration of the risks involved. Specifically, empirical research indicates that financial liberalization is likely to increase macroeconomic volatility in the absence of strong institutions (such as legal systems and bankruptcy laws), efficient financial systems (such as open and competitive bond and stock markets), and goods markets that are open to international trade. This suggests a staged process of reform, where other aspects of the economy are opened and deregulated first. Once the foundation for stable growth is established, the last stage in this process should be the opening of financial markets and banking systems to international capital flows. Unfortunately, because of both internal politics and outside pressure from foreign investors and governments, financial liberalization has often come before everything else, leading to growth that is built upon a foundation of sand and liable to be washed away during the first storm.

Recent experience also suggests other avenues for reducing the volatility of foreign investment. The financial fundamentals of financial institutions deserve more scrutiny, and governments should enact regulation aimed at increasing the soundness of financial fundamentals and also the transparency of financial information. In addition, there is growing consensus that governments must act to abandon rigid exchange rate pegs to a single currency, which encourages foreign investors and banks to ignore exchange rate risk, setting the stage for future currency crises. Finally, many economists are now adopting the view that governments should impose capital controls before crises occur by placing permanent limits on the amount of hot money or other deposits that banks can attract, as well as by standing ready to impose temporary capital controls over a broader variety of assets if a crisis begins. While these controls are costly, they may well be preferable to the alternative, which is financial collapse.

What We Do Not Know

Given these advances in economic theory, it is safe to say that despite bumps in the road, we are better for the journey. Economists now have a deeper understanding of the role of financial systems in macroeconomics than we would have if we had started where we are right now. Still, challenges remain. Economists have not come to an agreement on a single, unified model which can sufficiently explain all aspects of modern macroeconomics and which would provide clear policy guidelines that would allow us to minimize financial volatility and maximize growth. Before this ultimate goal can be attained, however, there are at least four questions that need to be addressed.

Is price rationing or quantity rationing the most important mechanism in creating persistent excess demand for credit and fluctuations in the level of credit?
There are two primary New Institutional theories of finance. In the Financial Accelerator model, changes in the cost of credit intermediation drive changes the quantity demanded of credit. In models of credit rationing, lenders impose quantity limits on borrowers, and changes in these limits change the supply of credit.

Both these models share many similar predictions, particularly the fact that changes in the financial fundamentals of lenders and borrowers lead to changes in perceived default risk. In the Financial Accelerator model, higher default risk increases the costs of credit intermediation. In models of credit rationing, changes in default risk lead to changes in credit limits. In either case, changes in risk lead to procyclical movements in credit that amplify business cycles, both through changing aggregate demand and also through influencing the risk of production, which changes aggregate supply. Both these models also predict that finance plays an asymmetric and nonlinear role over the business cycle, primarily affecting credit during contractions when borrowers are most sensitive to changes in the costs of credit intermediation and are most likely to be up against their credit limits. Finally, these models predict that business cycles have asymmetric effects on individuals and are most likely to affect smaller, newer, and weaker borrowers and lenders.

Much of the empirical evidence supporting New Institutional theories of finance are consistent with both price rationing and credit rationing. This includes results such as the fact that financial fundamentals are closely linked to aggregate economic activity and that the output of small, finance-dependent firms is much more volatile than the output of large firms.

However, while many of the two models' implications are the same, there are also important differences between the Financial Accelerator model and models of credit rationing. These differences have important macroeconomic consequences that make it imperative that we attempt to evaluate and distinguish between the two models. First, the existence of credit rationing implies that the provision of credit is discontinuous. Once a borrower reaches the credit limit, intermediation abruptly stops. This raises the potential importance of credit links, in which suppliers are linked to producers and producers linked to final customers in financing chains. If one firm in the chain reaches its credit limit, the chain is broken and credit can disappear throughout the system. Such sharp cutoffs do not take place in the Financial Accelerator model.

Second, interest rates are an important component of the cost of credit intermediation. As a result, changes in interest rates are a reflection (though not a perfect indicator) of changes in credit conditions in the Financial Accelerator model. However, in a model of credit rationing, interest rates have little empirical relation to changes in credit limits. In fact, credit limits are imposed in the first place because lenders are reluctant to change interest rates in the face of moral hazard and adverse selection. Thus, if economists are to understand movements in interest rates and their macroeconomic implications, it is important to know whether credit is rationed through changes in price or through changes in quantity limits.

Third, the distinction between credit rationing and price rationing has a number of important implications for monetary policy. In models of credit rationing, where interest rates do not necessarily reflect conditions in the credit market, the interest rate channel of monetary policy does not exist, requiring economists to consider alternative channels of monetary transmission. In models of credit rationing, the possibility of credit links imply that monetary policy can have much more significant welfare effects on small firms and households than in the Financial Accelerator model. Finally, in the Financial Accelerator model, capital adequacy requirements imposed by central banks are effective ways of reducing risk and the costs of credit intermediation. However, in models of credit rationing, capital adequacy regulations can tighten credit limits that make movements in credit even more procyclical than they would otherwise be.

Fourth, the existence of credit rationing also implies the possibility of equity rationing. In fact, important interactions can take place between the two in which competition between banks and equity investors for the highest quality borrowers leads to the imposition of tighter limits on borrowing in order to keep interest rates low and the prices of stocks high. In other words, more competitive financial systems could actually create more market failure and lead to less financial intermediation. This is a surprising implication of credit rationing that does not exist in the Financial Accelerator model and raises important questions for future research, which need to be more fully explored.

At this point, economic research does not clearly point to the importance of one form of market failure over another. Empirical evidence that interest rate spreads are countercyclical supports the Financial Accelerator model. However, the fact that empirical studies indicate that investment is inelastic to changes in price and that nonprice commitments, such as collateral, play an important role in determining credit support models of credit rationing. There is also some empirical evidence provided by Friedman and Kuttner (1993) that both changes in the price and changes in the quantity of credit together play a role in predicting macroeconomic behavior. Taken as a whole, the fact is that we simply cannot say which of these mechanisms are most important. In addition, there has been little research investigating whether there are interactions between price and quantity rationing. This is a potentially fertile area of inquiry and deserves much greater attention in the future as the New Institutional research agenda moves forward.

What fraction of macroeconomic volatility can be explained by financial volatility?
Another way to phrase this question is "if financial volatility disappeared, would
business cycles disappear?" While economists have learned that financial volatility
plays a prominent role in the amplification and possibly the creation of macroeconomic volatility, we still do not have a clear idea of how to quantify exactly how
important it is.

The primary factor that complicates this question is that financial systems have
the potential to both magnify and moderate economic volatility. The securitization
boom perfectly illustrates this: it has led to both mortgage refinancing that has moderated recessions, and has also led to the subprime mortgage crisis that threatens
to spark an economic contraction.

We have talked about the ways that financial systems can amplify shocks through
market failure as described in New Institutional theories of finance by fueling
boom/bust cycles. We also know that after the financial deregulation movement of
the 1980s, banking crises have become more common and extremely persistent.
In addition, currency crises have become more common and costly in this era
of globalization where banks heavily rely on hot money. Finally, asset bubbles
continue to take place and are more costly when they occur in conjunction with
banking crises and currency crises. As a result, according to a study by Bordo
et al. (2001), recessions that involve twin financial crises are 16 percent larger in
terms of lost GDP than average recessions, indicating that financial systems bear
considerable responsibility in creating macroeconomic volatility. In fact, the most
severe depressions in economic history, from the Great Depression to the East
Asian crisis, have been associated with financial crises.

On the other hand, we also know that financial development reduces risk and
allows households to better smooth their consumption and firms to sustain investment. Financial innovations such as securitization have allowed households to
better stabilize their disposable income, a factor which clearly moderated the
2001 recession in the U.S. Not only has financial development played some role
in minimizing swings in business cycles, but it has also played a role in duration
stabilization, or the fact that recessions in developed countries have become less
frequent during the postwar era, particularly over the last 25 years.

Another factor that complicates this question is that financial development also
changes the workings of monetary policy and has an impact on economic volatility
through that avenue as well. More on that topic is discussed below.

In the end, we are not completely sure what share of macroeconomic volatility
can be laid at the feet of financial systems. More empirical and theoretical work
needs to be done before we can accurately quantify the culpability of finance.
However, what we can say with assurance is that financial systems have the potential to both undermine and enhance stability. In countries with sound regulation,
developed institutions, competitive goods markets, and efficient financial systems,
there is reason to believe that financial development actually reduces economic

instability. However, in the absence of these factors, more finance is likely to be associated with more economic instability. As a result, the answer to this question is likely to differ significantly across countries, necessitating a great deal of cross-country empirical work in the future.

How does monetary policy work and can it be used effectively to stabilize financial systems and aggregate output?
During the postwar era, recessions in the U.S. have become slightly smaller but significantly less frequent. Empirical studies such as Romer and Romer (1994) indicate that more effective monetary policy has been largely responsible for this stabilization. However, the benefits have not been as large as they could have been because of mistakes made by policy makers who have occasionally overused monetary policy, leading to excessive inflation. This has then forced central banks to reverse course to reduce inflation, creating policy-driven business cycles.

The empirical research suggesting that stabilization policy has been beneficial overall does not, however, put an end to the long-standing debate between those who argue for the active use of monetary policy (Keynesians) and those who argue for policy rules (Monetarists and neoclassicals). In many ways, the debate has moved into three new areas. The first deals with the monetary transmission mechanism. New Institutional theories of finance, particularly models of credit rationing, raise questions about traditional interest rate channels of monetary policy. Instead, they emphasize balance sheet channels of monetary transmission, where changes in the money supply affect the financial fundamentals of borrowers and lenders, leading to fluctuations in credit and economic activity.

In some ways these balance sheet channels suggest that monetary policy is more powerful than previously thought because it can work through both aggregate demand and aggregate supply (by affecting the risk of production). However, balance sheet channels also significantly complicate the conduct of monetary policy. Balance sheet channels imply that the power of monetary policy is nonlinear and fluctuates as fundamentals and risk perceptions change. For example, during periods of weak fundamentals and high-risk perceptions, traditional open market operations could be completely ineffective. Under such circumstances, monetary policy might require the use of different tools, such as discount lending to small banks that are the most credit constrained. Finally, balance sheet channels primarily work through the weakest borrowers and lenders, creating complex distributional considerations for policy makers. These issues, and more like them, are not yet fully understood, raising important questions in many minds about whether monetary policy should be actively used in such ignorance.

The second area of debate in monetary policy deals with whether monetary policy will continue to be as powerful in the future, or whether financial innovation reduces its effectiveness. As financial innovation continues to take place, the monetary transmission mechanism continues to change as well. For example, the increasing globalization of financial markets and the decreasing importance of banks in financial intermediation have the potential to reduce the control that central banks have over their domestic money supplies and interest rates, weakening their power. The 2001 recession in the U.S. is an example of how monetary policy can have unpredictable effects. During this recession, lower interest rates did little to spur investment and consumption directly, but the refinancing boom made possible by financial innovation significantly stabilized disposable incomes and aggregate demand. Because of this complexity, it has been difficult for economists to directly measure the power of monetary policy. Not the least of the difficulties in measuring the power of monetary policy is the fact that when the money supply fluctuates as output remains stable, it may not mean that monetary policy has become less powerful, just more effective.

The final area of debate is the role of monetary policy in preventing banking crises, asset bubbles, and currency crises. The easiest, and least controversial, of crises to prevent are currency crises. The solution is to avoid rigidly fixing exchange rates to a single currency, despite their appeal in attracting foreign investment. In general, a consensus is emerging that the benefits of increased foreign investment are outweighed by the potential economic and social costs of currency crises.

Preventing asset bubbles is more controversial. Traditionally, stabilizing asset prices has not been a high priority for central banks in setting monetary policy. However, as financial systems increase in size and as households have more of their wealth saved in volatile assets such as stocks and real estate, central banks have to decide how much more they should weigh asset price inflation relative to aggregate inflation. Should central banks try to "prick" bubbles in their early stages before growth endangers economic stability? This is a crucial question for many central banks to answer as soon as possible given the current global housing boom and the fact that many stock markets still appear to be overvalued, even after the bear markets of the early 2000s. There is some movement among central banks toward weighing asset prices more heavily in setting monetary policy than has been done in the past, but there is also a general opinion, shared by Fed chairman Ben Bernanke among others, that monetary policy is too blunt a tool to effectively end bubbles without also ending macroeconomic growth.

The policy prescriptions regarding banking crises are also controversial and depend upon whether you believe these crises are primarily caused by fundamentals or beliefs. Fundamentals-based theories argue that central banks should play a limited role as a lender of last resort because easy lending encourages moral hazard behavior; instead, central banks should focus on regulation to ensure sound financial fundamentals. On the other hand, belief-based theories argue that preventing panic is of the utmost importance and both central bank lending and deposit insurance play important roles in stabilizing expectations. Thus, a debate continues over how active central banks should be in their lending before crises take place. However, once a crisis has occurred, both fundamentals- and belief-based theories agree that the best remedy for minimizing the costs of a crisis is to take your lumps and immediately bailout insolvent banks in order to restart financial intermediation as soon as possible.

In the end, the complexity, the number of the problems and the potential benefits that policy makers must consider ensures that monetary policy will continue to be a controversial and intense area of research for the foreseeable future.

Can the International Monetary Fund (IMF) serve as a world lender of last resort and stabilize international finance?
Economists are gradually coming to a consensus regarding the objectives that the IMF should seek to achieve. The IMF should encourage more flexible exchange rate systems to prevent moral hazard, encourage gradual and staged liberalization with the help of loans before crises take place, abandon the reflexive imposition of structural adjustment and austerity conditions during a crisis, say no to bailing-out poorly run banks and corporations, say no to bailing-out poorly run governments that do not live up to the terms of their loans, and increase the openness and transparency of the IMF's own decision making.

There are two primary areas of continued disagreement, however. The first is whether the IMF should play the "confidence game" and continue to ask governments in the midst of a crisis to contract monetary and fiscal policy in an effort to increase interest rates and reattract capital flows. Proponents of this policy insist that the immediate restoration of capital flows is a necessary precondition to a resumption in growth. However, this prescription goes against Keynesian stabilization policy. Keynesians question how contractionary policy that pushes an economy deeper into depression can ever serve to entice back foreign investors.

The second source of disagreement is in regard to the effects of imposing capital controls aimed at limiting capital outflows, both before and particularly after a crisis has begun. Some argue that such controls are only prudent to minimize the size of capital flight and prevent contagion. Others argue that capital controls are ineffective and only discourage investment and growth in the long run.

The primary problem the IMF faces, however, is not about what the IMF should do, but about what it can do. The IMF's principal problem is not theoretical, but political. In the past, it has been the IMF's large donors that have pushed for many bailouts, excessive conditionality in lending, and "cold shower" liberalization without proper consideration of the facts on the ground. The question then is whether large donor nations will ever let the IMF do its job according to economic knowledge, or if the IMF will be just a tool that developed countries use to achieve their own economic and foreign policy objectives. While the IMF is attempting some internal reforms, at this point it appears unlikely that the IMF will ever be granted the independence it needs to do its job properly.

Concluding Conclusions

Finance is important, not just because it stimulates growth, but also because it has the potential to stabilize standards of living and even entire societies. Remarkable increases in financial development and innovation over the last generation have shown us both the extraordinary possibilities and the potential pitfalls associated with the financialization of modern macroeconomics. Financial systems are often the engine that powers economic growth, but it can also be the wobbly wheel that derails the whole train.

The good news is that we are learning. Remember, this era of globalization and the financial development that accompanied it began in 1989 with the fall of the Berlin Wall. This new era is not yet middle-aged. There are good indications that our understanding of the implications of financialization is maturing. We are developing theories that explain important pieces of this puzzle, although at this point we still lack a unified theory that provides a comprehensive explanation of the macroeconomic effects of finance within open economies. In addition, we are gradually developing policies that may yet prove to prevent future financial crises and allow countries to experience the full benefits of globalized financial systems. Unfortunately, developing such a unified theory and implementing the needed policy reforms will not be simple. As you undoubtedly know by now, however, if it was simple, it would not be economics.

Bibliography

Adams, John, 1819 [2003], *The Letters of John and Abigail Adams*, Abigail Adams, ed., John Adams, and Frank Suffleton, Penguin Books: New York, NY.

Aghion, Phillipe, George-Marios Angeletos, Abhijit V. Banerjee, and Kalina B. Manova, 2005, "Volatility and Growth: The Role of Financial Development," Harvard University mimeo.

——, Peter Howitt, and David Mayer-Foulkes, 2005, "The Effect of Financial Development on Convergence: Theory and Evidence," *The Quarterly Journal of Economics* vol. 120, 173–222.

Alesina, Alberto and Lawrence H. Summers, 1993, "Central Bank Independence and Macroeconomic Performance: Some Comparative Evidence," *Journal of Money, Credit, and Banking* vol. 25, 151–162.

Allen, Franklin and Douglas Gale, 1998, "Optimal Financial Crises," *Journal of Finance* vol. 52, 1245–1284.

—— and ——, 1999, "Bubbles, Crises, and Policy," *Oxford Review of Economic Policy* vol. 15, 9–18.

—— and ——, 2000, "Bubbles and Crises," *The Economic Journal*, vol. 53, 236–255.

Artis, Michael J., Zenon F. Kontolemis, and Denise R. Osborn, 1997, "Business Cycles for G7 and European Countries," *Journal of Business* vol. 70, 249–279.

Asea, Patrick K. and Brock Blomberg, 1998, "Lending Cycles," *Journal of Econometrics* vol. 83, 89–128.

Bagehot, Walter, 1873 [1991], *Lombard Street: A Description of the Money Market*, Orion Editions: Philadelphia, PA.

Barro, Robert, 2001, "Economic Growth in East Asia Before and After the Financial Crisis," NBER Working Paper No. 8330.

Barth, James R., Gerard Caprio Jr., and Ross Levine, 2006, *Rethinking Bank Regulation: Till Angels*, Govern Cambridge University Press: Cambridge, UK.

Barth, Marvin III and Valarie A. Ramey, 2001, "The Cost Channel of Monetary Transmission," *NBER Macroeconomics Annual* vol. 16, 199–240.

Beck, Thorsten, Asli Demirgüç-Kunt, Luc Laeven, and Ross Levine, 2004, "Finance, Firm Size, and Growth," World Bank mimeo.

—— and Ross Levine, 2005, "Legal Institutions and Financial Development" in C. Menard and M. Shirley, eds., *Handbook of New Institutions Economics*, Kluwer Academic Publishers: Norwell, MA.

Bernanke, Ben S., 1983, "Nonmonetary Effects of the Financial Crisis in the Propagation of the Great Depression," *American Economic Review* vol. 73, 257–276.

——, 1995, "The Macroeconomics of the Great Depression: A Comparative Approach," *Journal of Money, Credit, and Banking* vol. 27, 1–28.

——, 2002, "Asset Price 'Bubbles' and Monetary Policy," Remarks before the New York chapter of the National Association for Business Economics, New York, New York, October 15.

—— and Cara S. Lown, 1991, "The Credit Crunch," *Brookings Papers on Economic Activity* vol. 2, 205–239.

—— and Harold James, 1991, "The Gold Standard, Deflation, and Financial Crises in the Great Depression: An International Comparison," in G. Hubbard, ed., *Financial Markets and Financial Crises*, University of Chicago Press: Chicago, IL.

—— and Mark Gertler, 1987, "Banking and Macroeconomic Equilibrium," in William A Barnett and Kenneth J. Singleton, eds., *New Approaches to Monetary Economics*, Cambridge University Press: Cambridge, MA.

—— and ——, 1989, "Agency Costs, Net Worth, and Business Fluctuations," *American Economic Review* vol. 79, 14–31.

—— and ——, 1990, "Financial Fragility and Economic Performance," *Quarterly Journal of Economics* vol. 105, 87–114.

—— and ——, 1995, "Inside the Black Box, The Credit Channel of Monetary Policy," *Journal of Economic Perspectives* vol. 9, 27–48.

——, ——, and Simon Gilchrist, 1996, "The Financial Accelerator and the Flight to Quality," *The Review of Economics and Statistics* vol. 78, 1–15.

——, ——, and ——, 1998, "The Financial Accelerator in a Quantitative Business Cycle Framework," in J.B. Taylor and M. Woodford, eds., *Handbook of Macroeconomics* Elsevier: Amsterdam, Netherlands.

Bernstein, Jared, Heather Boushey, and Lawrence Mishel, 2003, *The State of Working America*, Cornell University Press: Ithaca, NY.

Blanchard, Oliver and John Simon, 2001, "The Long and Large Decline in U.S. Output Volatility," *Brookings Papers on Economic Activity* vol. 1, 135–174.

Boivin, Jean and Marc Giannoni, 2006, "Has Monetary Policy Become More Effective?" *Journal of Economics and Statistics* vol. 88, 445–463.

Bordo, Michael, Barry Eichengreen, Daniela Kingebiel, and Maria Soledad Martinez, 2001, "Is the Crisis Problem Growing More Severe?" *Economic Policy* vol. 24, 51–82.

Boyd, John C., Sungkyu Kwak, and Bruce Smith, 2005, "Real Output Losses Associated with Modern Banking Crises," *Journal of Money, Credit, and Banking* vol. 37, 977–999.

Calomiris, Charles W., 1993, "Financial Factors in the Great Depression," *Journal of Economic Perspectives* vol. 7, 61–85.

—— and Robert E. Litan, 2000, "Financial Regulation in a Global Marketplace," *Brookings-Wharton Papers on Financial Services* vol. 2000, 283–323.

Caprio, Gerard and Daniela Klingbiel 2003, "Episodes of Systematic and Borderline Financial Crises," mimeo, World Bank Database.

Carroll, Christopher, Misuzu Otsuka, and Jirka Slacalek, 2006, "How Large is the Housing Wealth Effect? A New Approach," mimeo, Johns Hopkins University.

Case, Karl E. and Robert J. Schiller, 2003, "Is there a Bubble in the Housing Market?" *Brookings Papers on Economic Activity* vol. 2, 299–342.

Cecchetti, Stephen C., 2006, *Money, Banking, and Financial Markets*, McGraw-Hill: New York, NY.

Chirinko, Robert, 1993, "Business Fixed Investment Spending: A Critical Survey of Modeling Strategies, Empirical Results, and Policy Implications," *Journal of Economic Literature* vol. 31, 1875–1911.

Corsetti, Giancarlo, Paolo Pesenti, and Nouriel Roubini, 1998, "What Caused the Asian Currency and Financial Crisis?: Parts I and II," National Bureau of Economic Research Working Paper No. 6833 and 6834.

De Bondt, Werner and Richard Thaler, 1987, "Further Evidence on Investor Overreaction and Stock Market Seasonality," *Journal of Finance* vol. 62, 558–580.

De Meza, David and David C. Webb, 1987, "Too Much Investment: A Problem of Asymmetric Information," *Quarterly Journal of Economics* vol. 102, 281–292.

Dell'Ariccia, Giovanni, Enrica Detragiache, and Raghuram Rajan, 2005, "The Real Effect of Banking Crises," IMF Working Paper 05/63.

Demirgüç-Kunt, Asli and Enrica Detragiache, 1998, "The Determinants of Banking Crises in Developing and Developed Countries," IMF Staff Papers No. 45, 81–109.

——, ——, and Poonam Gupta, 2000, "Inside the Crisis: An Empirical Analysis of Banking Systems in Distress," IMF Working Papers 00/156.

—— and Ross Levine, 1996, "Stock Market Development and Financial Intermediaries: Stylized Facts," *The World Bank Economic Review* vol. 10, 291–321.

—— and Vojislav Maksimovic, 1996, "Stock Market Development and Financing Choices of Firms," *The World Bank Economic Review* vol. 10, 341–369.

Diamond, Douglas W. and Philip H. Dybvig, 1983, "Bank Runs, Deposit Insurance, and Liquidity," *The Journal of Political Economy* vol. 91, 401–419.

Diebold, Francis X. and Glenn D. Rudebusch, 1999, *Business Cycles: Durations, Dynamics, and Forecasting*, Princeton University Press: Princeton.

Dornbusch, Rudiger, 1997, "How Real is U.S. Prosperity?" Column reprinted in World Economic Laboratory Columns, MIT.

Easterly, William, 2006, *The White Man's Burden: Why the West's Efforts to Aid the Rest Have Done So Much Ill and So Little Good*, Penguin Press: New York, NY.

——, Roumeen Islam, and Joseph E. Stiglitz, 2001, "Volatility and Macroeconomic Paradigms for Rich and Poor Countries," in Jacques Dreze, ed., *Advances in Macroeconomic Theory*, Palgrave: New York, NY.

Edwards, Sebastian, 1998, "Capital Flows, Real Exchange Rates, and Capital Controls: Some Latin American Examples," NBER Working Paper #6800.

——, 2001, "Capital Flows and Economic Performance: Are Emerging Economies Different?" NBER Working Paper # 8076.

Eichengreen, Barry, 2003a, "A Century of Capital Flows," in Barry Eichengreen, ed., *Capital Flows and Crisis*, The MIT Press: Cambridge, MA, 155–185.

——, 2003b, "Understanding Asia's Crisis," in Barry Eichengreen, ed., *Capital Flows and Crisis*, The MIT Press: Cambridge, MA, 251–276.

——, 2003c, "Capital Account Liberalization: What Do the Cross-Country Studies Tell Us?" in Barry Eichengreen, ed., *Capital Flows and Crisis*, The MIT Press: Cambridge, MA, 49–69.

——, Andrew Rose, and Charles Wyplosz, 2003a, "Exchange Market Mayhem: The Antecedents and Aftermath of Speculative Attacks," in Barry Eichengreen, ed., *Capital Flows and Crisis*, The MIT Press: Cambridge, MA, 99–153.

——, ——, and ——, 2003b, "Contagious Currency Crises," in Barry Eichengreen, ed., *Capital Flows and Crisis*, The MIT Press: Cambridge, MA, 155–185.

—— and Carlos Arteta, 2000, "Banking Crises in Emerging Markets: Presumptions and Evidence," Working Paper, in M. Blejer and M. Skreb, eds., *Financial Policies in Emerging Markets*, The MIT Press: Cambridge, MA.

——, ——, and Charles Wyplosz, 2003, "When Does Capital Account Liberalization Help More than It Hurts?" in Barry Eichengreen, ed., *Capital Flows and Crisis*, The MIT Press: Cambridge, MA, 71–96.

Fazzari, Steven M., R. Glenn Hubbard, and Bruce C. Peterson, 1988, "Financing Constraints and Corporate Investment," *Brookings Papers on Economic Activity* vol. 1, 141–195.

——, 1992, "Keynesian Theories of Investment and Finance: Neo, Post, and New," in Steven M. Fazzari and Dimitri B. Papadim, eds., *Financial Conditions and Macroeconomic Performance*, M.E. Sharpe, Inc.: Armonk, NY.

Fisher, Irving, 1933, "The Debt-Deflation Theory of Great Depressions," *Econometrica* vol. 1, 337–357.

Friedman, Benjamin M., 2005, *The Moral Consequences of Economic Growth*, Knopf: New York, NY.

—— and Kenneth N. Kuttner, 1993, "Economic Activity and the Short-term Credit Markets: An Analysis of Prices and Quantities," *Brookings Papers on Economic Activity* vol. 2, 193–283.

Friedman, Milton, 1968, "The Role of Monetary Policy," *American Economic Review* vol. 58, 1–17.

—— and Anna Schwartz, 1963, *A Monetary History of the United States, 1867–1960* Princeton University Press: Princeton, NJ.

French, Kenneth R. and Richard Roll, 1986, "Stock Return Variances: The Arrival of Information and the Reaction of Traders," *Journal of Financial Economics* vol. 17, 5–26.

Froot, Kenneth A., Paul G. J. O'Connell, and Mark. S. Seasholes, 2001, "The Portfolio Flows of International Investors," *Journal of Financial Economics* vol. 69, 151–193.

Galindo, Arturo J., Alejandro Micco, and Guillermo Ordoñez, 2002, "Financial Liberalization: Does it Pay to join the Party?" *Economia* vol. 3, 231–261.

Gertler, Mark and Simon Gilchrist, 1993, "The Role of Credit Market Imperfections in the Monetary Transmission Mechanism: Arguments and Evidence," *Scandinavian Journal of Economics* vol. 95, 43–64.

Gilchrist, Simon and Charles P. Himmelberg, 1995, "Evidence on the Role of Cash Flow for Investment," *Journal of Monetary Economics* vol. 36, 541–572.

Goldstein, Morris, 1998, *The Asian Financial Crisis: Causes, Cures, and Systematic Implications*, Institute of International Economics: Washington, DC.

——, 2001, "IMF Structural Conditionality: How Much is Too Much?" Institute for International Economics Working Paper 01-4.

Gorton, Gary, 1988, "Banking Panics and Business Cycles," *Oxford Economic Papers* vol. 40, 751–781.

Green, Richard K. and Susan M. Wachter, 2005, "The American Mortgage in Historical and International Context," *Journal of Economic Perspectives* vol. 19, 93–114.

Greenspan, Alan, 1998, Testimony Before the Subcommittee on Foreign Operations of the Committee on Appropriations, U.S. Senate, March 3.

Hamilton, Alexander, 1781 [1979], *Papers of Alexander Hamilton*, Harold C. Syrett, ed., Columbia University Press: New York, NY, pp. 606.

Hawtrey, Ralph George, 1913, *Good and Bad Trade*, Constable & Co.: London.

Heisenberg, W., 1971, *Physics and Beyond*, George Allen & Unwin Ltd: London.

Helbling, Thomas and Marco Terrones, 2003, "When Bubbles Burst," in *World Economy Outlook*, Chapter 2, IMF: Washington, DC, 61–94.

Hellmann, Thomas and Joseph E. Stiglitz, 2000, "Credit and Equity Rationing in Markets with Adverse Selection," *European Economic Review* vol. 44, 281–304.

Hicks, John R., 1937, "Mr. Keynes and the 'Classics'; a Suggested Interpretation," *Econometrica* vol. 5, 147–159.

——, 1969, *A Theory of Economic History*, Clarendon Press: Oxford, UK.

Higgins, Matthew and Carol Osler, 1997, "Asset Market Hangovers and Economic Growth: The OECD During 1984-93," *Oxford Review of Economic Policy* vol. 13, 110–134.

Himmelberg, Charles, Christopher Mayer, and Todd Sinai, 2005, "Assessing High House Prices: Bubbles, Fundamentals and Misperceptions," *Journal of Economic Perspectives* vol. 19, 67–92.

Hoshi, Takeo and Anil K. Kashyap, 2004, "Japan's Financial Crisis and Economic Stagnation," *Journal of Economic Perspectives* vol. 18, 3–26.

Hutchinson, Michael M. and Ilan Noy, 2005, "How Bad Are Twins? Output Costs of Currency and Banking Crises," *Journal of Money, Credit, and Banking*, vol. 37, 699–724.

—— and Kathleen McDill, 1999, "Are All Banking Crises Alike? The Japanese Experience in International Comparison," in C. Freeman, ed., *Why Did Japan Stumble? Causes and Cures*, Edward: England.

Iacoviello, Matteo, 2005, "House Prices, Borrowing Constraints, and Monetary Policy," *American Economic Review* vol. 95, 739–764.

Jefferson, Thomas, 1861, *The Writings of Thomas Jefferson*, H.A. Washington, ed., H.W. Derby: New York, NY.

Jevons, William Stanley, 1884, *Investigations in Currency and Finance*, Macmillan: London.

Kaminsky, Graciela L. and Carmen M. Reinhart, 1999, "The Twin Crises: The Causes of Banking and Balance-of-Payments Problems," *American Economic Review* vol. 89, 473–500.

—— and ——, 2000, "On Crises, Contagion, and Confusion," *Journal of International Economics* vol. 51, 145–168.

——, ——, and Carlos A. Vegh, 2003, "The Unholy Trinity of Financial Contagion," *Journal of Economic Perspectives* vol. 17, 51–74.

Kaplan, Ethan and Dani Rodrik, 2001, "Did the Malaysian Capital Controls Work?" NBER Working Paper #8142.

Kayshap, Anil and Jeremy C. Stein, 2000, "What Do a Million Observations on Banks Say About the Transmission of Monetary Policy?" *American Economic Review* vol. 90, 407–428.

——, ——, and David Wilcox, 1993, "Monetary Policy and Credit Conditions: Evidence from the Composition of External Finance," *American Economic Review* vol. 83, 78–98.

Keynes, John Maynard, 1936 [1964], *The General Theory of Employment, Interest, and Money*, Macmillian: London.

——, 1937, "The General Theory," *Quarterly Journal of Economics* vol. 51, 209–223.

Kindleberger, Charles, 1978, *Manias, Panics, and Crashes: A History of Financial Crises*, Basic Books, Inc.: New York, NY.

King, Robert G. and Ross Levine, 1993, "Finance and Growth: Schumpeter Might be Right," *Quarterly Journal of Economics* vol. 108, 716–737.

Kiyotaki, Nobuhiro and John Moore, 1995, "Credit Cycles," *Journal of Political Economy* vol. 105, 211–248.

Knack, Stephen, 2004, "Aid Dependence and the Quality of Governance: Cross-Country Empirical Tests," *Southern Economic Journal* vol. 68, 310–329.

Knoop, Todd A., 2004, *Recessions and Depressions: Understanding Business Cycles* Praeger Publishers: Westport, CT.

Kuttner, Kenneth N. and Adam S. Posen, 2001, "The Great Recession: Lessons for Macroeconomic Policy from Japan," *Brookings Papers on Economic Activity* vol. 2, 93–160.

—— and Patricia C. Mosser, 2002, "The Monetary Transmission Mechanism: Some Answers and Further Questions," *Federal Reserve Board of New York Policy Review* May, 15–26.

Krueger, Anne O., 1998, "Whither the World Bank and the IMF?" *Journal of Economic Literature* vol. 36, 1983–2020.

——, 2001, "International Financial Architecture for 2002: A New Approach to Sovereign Debt Restructuring," Address Given at the National Economists' Club Annual Members' Dinner American Enterprise Institute, Washington DC.

——, 2002, "IMF Stabilization Programs," in M. Feldstein, ed., *Economic and Financial Crises in Emerging Market Economies*, University of Chicago Press: Chicago, IL.

Krugman, Paul, 1979, "A Model of Balance-of-Payments Crises," *Journal of Money, Credit, and Banking* vol. 11, 311–325.

Krugman, Paul, 1994, *The age of Diminished Expectations*, The MIT Press: Cambridge, MA.

——, 1999, *The Return of Depression Economics*, W.W. Norton: New York, NY.

Kydland, Finn E. and Edward C. Prescott, 1982, "Time to Build and Aggregate Fluctuations," *Econometrica* vol. 50, 1345–1370.

Lang, William and Leonard Nakamura, 1995, "'Flight to Quality' in Bank Lending and Economic Activity," *Journal of Monetary Economics* vol. 36, 145–164.

Levenson, Alec and Kristen Willard, 2000, "Do Firms Get the Financing They Want? Measuring Credit Rationing Experienced by Small Businesses in the U.S.," *Small Business Economics* vol. 27, 83–94.

Levine, Ross, 1997, "Financial Development and Economic Growth: Views and Agenda," *Journal of Economic Literature* vol. 35, 688–726.

——, Norman Loayza, and Thorsten Beck, 2000, "Financial Intermediation and Growth: Causality and Causes," *Journal of Monetary Economics* vol. 46, 31–77.

—— and Sara Zervos, 1998, "Stock Markets, Banks, and Economic Growth," *American Economic Review* vol. 88, 537–558.

Long, John B. Jr., and Charles I. Plosser, 1983, "Real Business Cycles," *Journal of Political Economy* vol. 91, 39–69.

Lucas, Robert E., 1972, "Expectations and the Neutrality of Money," *Journal of Economic Theory* vol. 4, 103–124.

Mankiw, N. Gregory, 1986, "The Allocation of Credit and Financial Collapse," *Quarterly Journal of Economics* vol. 101, 455–470.

Marshall, David, 1998, "Understanding the Asian Crisis: Systematic Risk as Coordination Failure," *Economic Perspectives* vol. 22, 13–28.

Matsuyama, Kiminori, 2007, "Credit Traps and Credit Cycles," *American Economic Review* vol. 97, 503–516.

Mayer, Martin, 2001, *The Inside Story of How the World's Most Powerful Financial Institution Drives the Markets*, Free Press: New York, NY.

Mitchell, Wesley C., 1941, *Business Cycles and Their Causes*, University of California Press: Berkley, CA.

Minsky, Hyman P., 1982, *Can 'It' Hapen Again? Essays on Instability and Finance*, M.E. Sharpe, Armonk, NY.

Modigliani, Franco and Merton H. Miller, 1958, "The Cost of Capital, Corporation Finance and the Theory of Investment," *American Economic Review* vol. 48, 261–297.

Mojon, Benoit, Frank Smets, and Philip Vermeulen, 2002, "Investment and Monetary Policy in the Euro Area," *Journal of Banking and Finance* vol. 26, 2111–2129.

Muth, John, 1961, "Rational Expectations and the Theory of Price Movements," *Econometrica* vol. 29, 315–335.

Nilsen, Jeffrey H., 2002, "Trade Credit and the Bank Lending Channel," *Journal of Money, Credit, and Banking* vol. 34, 226–253.

Obstfeld, Maurice, 1996, "Models of Currency Crises with Self-fulfilling Features," *European Economic Review* vol. 40, 1037–1047.

Peek, Joe and James A. Wilcox, 2006, "Housing, Credit Constraints, and Macro Stability: The Secondary Mortgage Market and Reduced Cyclicality of Residential Investment," *American Economic Review* vol. 96, 135–140.

Peregrine, 1997, "Peregrine Sees Asian Ex-Japanese Bad Debts at $500B," NY: Bloomberg, L.P. November 11–12.

Perez, Stephen J., 1998, "Testing for Credit Rationing: An Application of Disequilibrium Econometrics," *Journal of Macroeconomics* vol. 20, 721–739.

Phillips, Arthur W., 1958, "The Relation between Unemployment and the Rate of Change in Money Wage Rates in the United Kingdom, 1862–1957," *Economica* vol. 25, 283–299.

Phillips, Kevin, 2000, *Wealth and Democracy*, Random House: New York, NY.

Pomerleano, Michael, 1998, "The East Asian Crisis and Corporate Finances: The Untold Micro Story," World Bank Policy Research Working Paper #1990.

Prasad, Eswar, 2006, "Financial Globalization: A Reappraisal," IMF Working Paper WP/06/89.

Rajan, Raghuram G. and Luigi Zingales, 1998, "Financial Dependence and Growth," *American Economic Review* vol. 99, 559–586.

Ramey, Garey and Valerie A. Ramey, 1995, "Cross-Country Evidence on the Link Between Volatility and Growth," *American Economic Review* vol. 85, 1138–1151.

Ranciere, Romain, Aaron Tornell, and Frank Westermann, 2003, "Crises and Growth: A Re-evaluation," NBER Working Paper #10073.

Romer, Christina D., 1999, "Changes in Business Cycles: Evidence and Explanations," *Journal of Economic Perspectives* vol. 13, 23–44.

——, and David H. Romer, 1994, "What Ends Recessions?" *NBER Macroeconomics Annual* vol. 9, 13–57.

Romer, David, 2001, *Advanced Macroeconomics*, McGraw Hill: Boston.

Rötheli, Tobias F., 2000, "Competition, Herd Behavior, and Credit Cycles: Evidence from Major Swiss Banks," *Journal of Economics and Business* vol. 53, 585–592.

Sachs, Jeffrey, 1997, "The IMF is a Power Unto Itself," *The Financial Times* December 11.

——, 2005, *The End of Poverty: Economic Possibilities for our Time*, The Penguin Press: New York, NY.

Schiller, Robert, 1981, "Do Stock Prices Move Too Much to Be Justified by Subsequent Changes in Dividends?" *American Economic Review* vol. 71, 421–436.

Schmidt, Reinhard H., 2001, "Differences Between Financial Systems in European Countries: Consequences for EMU," in Deutsche Bank, ed., *The Monetary Transmission Process: Recent Developments and Lessons for Europe*, Palgrave Publishers: Hampshire, UK.

Schumpeter, Joseph A., 1911, *The Theory of Economic Development*, Harvard University Press: Cambridge, MA.

Smith, Adam, 1776 [1981], *An Inquiry into the Nature and the Causes of the Wealth of Nations*, Liberty Press: Indianapolis.

Stanca, Luca Matteo, 2002, *The Role of Financial Markets in Generating Business Cycles*, The Edwin Mellen Press: Lewiston, NY.

Stiglitz, Joseph E., 1990, "Symposium on Bubbles," *Journal of Economic Perspectives* vol. 4, 13–18.

——, 2002, *Globalization and its Discontents*, W.W. Norton: New York.

—— and Andrew Weiss, 1981, "Credit Rationing in Markets with Imperfect Information," *American Economic Review* vol. 71, 333–421.

——, and Bruce Greenwald, 2003, *Towards a New Paradigm in Monetary Economics*,
Cambridge University Press: Cambridge, UK.

Stock, James H. and Mark W. Watson, 2002, "Has the Business Cycle Changed and
Why?" in Mark Gertler and Ken Rogoff, eds., *NBER Macroeconomics Annual 2002*,
MIT Press: Cambridge, MA, 159–218.

Summers, Peter M., 2005, "What Caused the Great Moderation? Some Cross-Country
Evidence," *Economic Review* vol. 90, 5–32.

Tirole, Jean, 2002, *Financial Crises, Liquidity, and the International Monetary System*,
Princeton University Press: Princeton, NJ.

Tornell, Aaron, Frank Westermann, and Lorenza Martinez, 2003, "Liberalization,
Growth and Financial Crises: Lessons from Mexico and the Developing World,"
Brookings Papers on Economic Activity vol. 2, 1–88.

Volker, Paul A. and Toyoo Gyohten, 1992, *Changing Fortunes: The World's Money and
the Threat to American Leadership*, Times Books: New York, NY.

Wicksell, Knut, 1936, *Interest and Prices: A Study of the Causes Regulating the Value
of Money*, Macmillian: London.

Williamson, John, 2004, "The Years of Emerging Market Crises: A Review of Feldstein,"
Journal of Economic Literature vol. 42, 822–837.

—— and Molly Mahar, 1998, "A Survey of Financial Liberalization," Princeton Essays
in International Finance no. 211.

Wilson, Jack W., Richard E. Sylla and Charles P. Jones, 1990, "Financial Market Panics
and Volatility in the Long Run, 1830–1988" in E. White, ed., *Crashes and Panics*,
Dow-Jones Irwin: Chicago, IL, 85–125.

Wojnilower, Albert M., 1980, "The Central Role of Credit Crunches in Recent Financial
History," *Brookings Papers on Economic Activity* vol. 2, 277–326.

Index